T0330251

Geographies of the Super-Rich

Geographies of the Super-Rich

Edited by

Iain Hay

Flinders University, South Australia

Edward Elgar
Cheltenham, UK • Northampton, MA, USA

Published by
Edward Elgar Publishing Limited
The Lypiatts
15 Lansdown Road
Cheltenham
Glos GL50 2JA
UK

Edward Elgar Publishing, Inc.
William Pratt House
9 Dewey Court
Northampton
Massachusetts 01060
USA

A catalogue record for this book
is available from the British Library

Library of Congress Control Number: 2012946680

This book is available electronically in the ElgarOnline.com
Social and Political Science Subject Collection, E-ISBN 978 0 85793 569 4

ISBN 978 0 85793 568 7 (cased)

Typeset by Servis Filmsetting Ltd, Stockport, Cheshire
Printed and bound by MPG Books Group, UK

Contents

Figures

Tables

Contributors

Jonathan V. Beaverstock is Professor of Economic Geography at the University of Nottingham, UK. He completed his PhD at the University of Bristol and BA at the University of Wales, St David's University College, Lampeter. He is the author of over 100 journal articles, book chapters, published conference papers and proceedings, including three books (authored and edited), the latest being: *The Globalization of Advertising* (Routledge 2011). He has given considerable public service to the UK research councils and charities, and sits on the editorial boards of *Geoforum* and *Global Networks*. In 2006 he was bestowed an Honorary Professorship at the University of Otago, New Zealand, and has recently been appointed Visiting Professor at the University of Ghent, Belgium. Jonathan Beaverstock is currently one of the leading researchers on the subject of the global super rich.

Sébastien Chauvin is an Assistant Professor of Sociology at the University of Amsterdam, the Netherlands, a researcher at the Amsterdam Institute for Social Science Research (AISSR), the Netherlands, and an Associate Researcher with the *Institut de Recherche Interdisciplinaire sur les Enjeux Sociaux* (IRIS), France. He has published books and articles on the sociology of work and employment (*Les agences de la précarité. Journaliers à Chicago*, Paris: Le Seuil 2010), social capital and the upper class, migration and ethnic studies, and the sociology of gender and sexuality (*Introduction aux gender studies. Manuel des études sur le genre*, Brussels: De Boeck, with L. Bereni, A. Jaunait and A. Revillard).

Bruno Cousin is an Assistant Professor of Sociology at the University of Lille 1, France, a researcher at the *Centre Lillois d'Études et de Recherches Sociologiques et Économiques* (Lille 1/CNRS), France, and an affiliate with the *Groupe de Sociologie Politique et Morale* at EHESS, France. He is the author of peer-reviewed articles and book chapters on urban segregation, social capital, upper-classes sociability, the refusal of social or ethnic mix, and the sociology of intellectuals. Currently, he is also Vice President of the French Sociological Association, in charge of international relations.

Melanie Fasche is a geographer based in Berlin and affiliated as external PhD candidate in Urban and Regional Economic Studies at HafenCity

University Hamburg, Germany. She has worked in Berlin as a freelance consultant in public policy projects with a focus on creative industries and arts and has been Visiting Lecturer in Urban Studies at Free University Berlin, Germany. Previously she has held fellowships at Columbia University, US, Technical University Berlin, Germany, Institute of Regional and Structural Planning (IRS), Erkner/Berlin, Germany, and University of New South Wales, Australia. Her diploma thesis 'Glocalization, gentrification and creative business services: a case study of Newtown, Sydney' was honoured with the Young Researchers Award by the German-speaking Association for Australian Studies (*Gesellschaft für Australienstudien e. V.*). Fasche is currently finishing her dissertation on the value-making process of contemporary visual art.

Sarah J.E. Hall is an Associate Professor in Economic Geography at the University of Nottingham, UK. She completed her PhD at the University of Bristol, UK, and BA at Cambridge University, UK. She is the author of over 30 journal articles, book chapters and practitioner orientated research reports. Her research interests centre on financial elites with particular interests in: their reproduction through business education; global elite labour markets and working practices; and their consumption of financial services through wealth management. Her research has been funded by the Economic and Social Research Council, The Nuffield Foundation and The British Academy. She serves on the ESRC Peer Review College and has acted as editor for several special issues of social science journals.

Iain Hay is Matthew Flinders Distinguished Professor of Human Geography at Flinders University, Australia. He completed his PhD at the University of Washington, US, as a Fulbright Scholar and more recently received a LittD from the University of Canterbury, NZ, for 20-plus years of post-doctoral work on geographies of domination and oppression. He is author or editor of ten books including *Money, Medicine and Malpractice in American Society* (Praeger 1992) and *Qualitative Research Methods in Human Geography* (3rd edn Oxford 2010); is General Editor of Springer's 'International Handbooks of Human Geography' series; and has had editorial roles with journals that include *Applied Geography*, *Ethics, Place and Environment* and *Social and Cultural Geography*. In 2006, Hay received the Prime Minister's Award for Australian University Teacher of the Year. He is immediate past President of the Institute of Australian Geographers.

Pauline McGuirk is Professor of Human Geography and Director of the Centre for Urban and Regional Studies at the University of Newcastle, Australia. She completed her PhD at Trinity College Dublin, Ireland. Her research interests are in urban political geography and she has published widely on urban governance, its geographies and its changing forms. Her recent work has involved critical investigations of transformations in Sydney's governance as it has emerged as a global city-region, and on new forms of governance associated with the emergence of residential master-planned estates. McGuirk has been a Visiting Fellow at the University of Glasgow, UK, Durham University, UK, Bristol University, UK, University of British Columbia, Canada and Trinity College Dublin. She serves on the editorial boards of *Progress in Human Geography*, *Irish Geography*, *Geography Compass* and *Geographical Research*. She is a Fellow of the Institute of Australian Geographers and of the Geographical Society of New South Wales.

Phil McManus is an Associate Professor in the School of Geosciences, The University of Sydney, Australia. After completing qualifications in urban planning at Curtin University, Australia, and environmental studies at York University, Canada, he completed his PhD in geography at the University of Bristol, UK. He is author or editor of four books, notably *Vortex Cities to Sustainable Cities* (UNSW 2005) and, with John Connell, *Rural Revival?* (Ashgate 2011). He has published numerous refereed journal articles on a range of urban, environmental and animal related issues. His co-authored book *The Global Horseracing Industry: Social, Economic, Environmental and Ethical Perspectives* (Routledge) is due for release in early 2013. McManus is President of the Institute of Australian Geographers.

Laurence Murphy is Professor of Property at the University of Auckland, New Zealand. He completed his PhD in geography at Trinity College Dublin, Ireland. He has published on homeownership, mortgage securitization, commercial property development, entrepreneurial urban governance and gentrification. He is on the editorial boards of the *International Journal of Housing Markets and Analysis* and the *Pacific Rim Property Research Journal*. In 2009 he was a Visiting Professor at Trinity College Dublin and in 2010 he was appointed a Fellow of the Royal Institution of Chartered Surveyors.

Chris Paris is Emeritus Professor at the University of Ulster, UK and was Professor of Housing Studies at the University of Ulster from 1992 to 2008. He has held visiting professorships at Royal Melbourne Institute of Technology, Australia, and Hong Kong University, in Hong Kong, and visiting fellowships in many other universities including Cambridge and Oxford in the UK, and the Australian National University, La Trobe, Flinders and Queensland University of Technology in Australia. Paris has wide international experience of scholarly research as well as applied research for government, statutory agencies and the private sector. His current research includes multiple homeownership in affluent societies and housing issues of ageing populations. Paris is author/co-author/editor of over 30 books, monographs and research reports on housing, planning and urban policy and over 100 journal publications. His most recent book, *Affluence, Mobility and Second Home Ownership*, was published in 2011 in the Routledge Housing and Society series.

Choon-Piew Pow is an Associate Professor in the Department of Geography at the National University of Singapore, in Singapore. His research focuses on the critical geographies of the urban built environment and interrogating the complex inter-relationship between urban forms and the social-spatial reproduction of urban life in Asian cities. His ongoing research project examines the planning discourses and practices revolving around the contested notions of 'urban sustainability' and the construction of 'eco-cities' in China. He is the author of the book *Gated Communities in China: Class, Privilege and the Moral Politics of the Good Life* published by Routledge in 2009.

Susan M. Roberts is Professor of Geography at the University of Kentucky, US. She is also a member of the Committee on Social Theory at the University of Kentucky. Her PhD is from Syracuse University, US. She has interests in political and economic geography, and in the political economy of inequality and development. She has published on global finance, the geopolitics of globalization, and the politics of non-governmental organizations in Mexico. She is co-author of *Economic Geography: Places, Networks, Flows*, with Andrew Wood (Routledge 2010). In 2006 she was awarded the Sturgill Prize for contributions to graduate education at the University of Kentucky. More recently she was named as the 2012–13 Fulbright University of Turku (Finland) Scholar.

Richard H. Schein is Professor of Geography at the University of Kentucky, US, where he also has affiliated appointments in American Studies, Historic Preservation, and the Committee on Social Theory. He writes about American cultural landscapes, with special attention to their historical development and imbrications with questions of race, cultural and social (re)production, democratic process and social justice. In 2011 he was named Distinguished Historical Geographer by the Association of American Geographers and *Historical Geography* and in 2012–13 he held the Fulbright Bicentennial Chair in American Studies at the University of Helsinki, Finland.

John Rennie Short is Professor of Public Policy at the University of Maryland Baltimore County (UMBC), US, and prior to this was Professor of Geography at Syracuse University, US. From 1978 to 1990 he was Lecturer at the University of Reading, UK. He has held visiting appointments as Senior Research Fellow at the Australian National University, Australia, as the Erasmus Professor at Groningen University, the Netherlands, and as the Leverhulme Visiting Professor at Loughborough University, UK. Among his research fellowships are the Vietor Fellowship at Yale University, US, the Dibner Fellowship at the Smithsonian Institution, US, the Kono Fellowship at the Huntington Library, US, and the Andrew Mellon Fellowship at the American Philosophical Library, US.

His main research interests are in urban issues, environmental concerns and cartographic representation. Recent books include *Korea: A Cartographic History* (2012), *Globalization, Modernity and The City* (2012), *Cities and Suburbs* (2010), and *Cartographic Encounters* (2009). He is a founding co-editor of the journal *Society and Space*, founding editor of the book series *Space, Place and Society*, and founding co-editor of the *Critical Introduction to Urbanism* book series.

Thomas Wainwright completed his first degree at the University of Leicester, UK, and holds an MSc from the University of Nottingham, UK. Wainwright completed his ESRC-funded PhD in 2009 (University of Nottingham) where he investigated the UK mortgage market, wholesale banking, asset management and the unfolding of the credit crunch within the financial services sector. He then worked at the University of Nottingham as a Research Assistant on projects that examined wholesale-retail bank linkages and wealth management and subsequently as a Postdoctoral Researcher at the Small Business Research Centre (SBRC) at Kingston University, UK. He is currently at Southampton Management School, University of Southampton, UK. His research examines the effects of the credit crunch on small businesses and how older people are turning to 'older entrepreneurship' as a strategy to manage their financial needs in later life.

Kathryn Wilkins recently completed a PhD in historical geography at Durham University, UK. Her PhD combined an historical case-study with contemporary mobilities theory to investigate the importance of movement and networking to the existence of the London Season in the nineteenth century, and the impact this period had on the physical character of London's West End. She is the author of several journal articles and contributions to edited collections.

Michael Woods is Professor of Human Geography and Director of the Institute of Geography and Earth Sciences at the Aberystwyth University,

UK. His research focuses on rural geography and political geography, including work on rural elites and changing power structures, and, currently, on globalization and the emergent 'global countryside'. He is editor of the *Journal of Rural Studies* and author of several books including *Rural* (Routledge 2011), *Rural Geography* (Sage 2005) and *Contesting Rurality: Politics in the British Countryside* (Ashgate 2005).

Foreword: From Kosrae to Kensington: uncovering cartographies of abundance

In 2007 I was fortunate enough to spend six months travelling around the world. And although I had always been intellectually aware of the vast differences in wealth between the planet's rich and poor, the reality of the situation came as something of a shock. The contrast was truly evident as I moved from places like Micronesia (including the island of Kosrae), Central America and Zanzibar, to London and its surrounds, including Sandbanks (near Poole, Dorset) – reputedly one of the most expensive places in the world to buy real estate. Perhaps sensitized by what I had seen so recently elsewhere, I was struck by the vast wealth evident in the south-east of England. From conversations with residents and my own observations, it became apparent for example that there was a good chance the Bentley that rolled by in Kensington was just one of a stable of expensive vehicles belonging to the owner or that there was a possibility that possession of a fine London house was matched by a 'chocolate box' home in Hampshire, Devon or Dorset, not to mention others in more exotic parts of the world. When I returned to work in Australia I began to investigate geographical work on the super-rich. After a lengthy search and very much to my surprise, I found just two publications. One, published by Eric Neumayer in *Applied Economics Letters*, asked the deceptively simple question 'why are there more super-rich people in some countries than in others?' (2004, p. 793). And in the other, published in *Geoforum*, Beaverstock et al. (2004) exhorted geographers to give attention to contemporary geographies of the super-rich. It is now over eight years since those works were printed and yet library shelves and the pages of journals remain largely devoid of geographical work on the super-rich[1] – a startling lacuna this volume sets out to fill.

So, this volume is really the 'first cut' at a book-length project on geographies of the super-rich. As such, it is intended to generate broader academic interest in this work – and perhaps even some lay attention – and to map out some of the territory for any subsequent work that may follow.

The intended audience is largely an academic one – professional scholars – but vitally important too are those student-readers who may find geographies of the super-rich sufficiently exciting to spark future work.

Although the book confines its explicit attentions to matters of geography, the chapters' coverage of specific topics such as art history, private wealth management, property development, city liveability, and tourism signal appeal and relevance to an even more diverse audience of advanced students and scholars in disciplines such as cultural studies, economics, politics, and sociology. The spatial span of the volume from Singapore to St Barts, London to Lexington may be an additional allure or point of connection to a broad range of readers.

ON READERS AND WRITERS; OMISSIONS AND COMMISSIONS

Recruiting authors for a project on an area in which so little has been written was a challenge. In the absence of a large body of published geographical work on the super-rich I arranged sessions at various conferences including those of the Association of American Geographers in Washington, DC (2010) and the joint meetings of the New Zealand Geographical Society and Institute of Australian Geographers held in Christchurch (2010) to expose – and promote – emerging scholarship on the super-rich. Calls for papers associated with those sessions attracted several excellent scholars. Then, having secured a contract with Edward Elgar, I was able to uncover and recruit other authors through an extensive Web-search coupled with 'world-wide' listserve calls for contributions. And finally, one author emerged after I had asked him to referee one of the chapters submitted to this collection! Although there is some international flavour to authorship here, with contributors from Australia, England, France, Germany, New Zealand, Singapore, the United States and Wales, there are some notable absences – particularly for a book on the super-rich. These include, for example, Canada, China, India, Russia, and the various countries of South America, a part of the world with disproportionate numbers of the ultra-wealthy. But having acknowledged these unfortunate absences and being cognizant of publishing deadlines, I am afraid I can do little more at this stage except hope that if there is ever a second edition of this book or a successor of some kind, it will be possible to repair this flaw in coverage – maybe even drawing on new work this volume might stimulate.

Perhaps as a consequence of the author-recruitment method I found myself obliged to adopt, and as is so often characteristic of edited collections, this volume has chapters of varying 'densities' and complexity. For this, I make no apology: it is a fact of life that different ideas and authors require different forms of expression. However, I know that in every case the authors whose work is set out here have worked to present material as clearly as possible. And as an editor with a career interest in effective communication, I have devoted considerable attention in this volume to matters of clarity. One objective of this has been to help ensure that chapters are accessible to as wide a range of prospective student and professional academic readers as possible, as well as to interested lay readers.

Over and above each chapter's readability another of my critical concerns, not surprisingly, has been credibility in this new area of work. So, for that reason, every chapter in this collection has been reviewed by experts in relevant fields. Referees have been kind with their time and energy and have offered sensible, comprehensive and critical opinion. I owe a great deal of thanks to each of them, listed alphabetically here, together with their institutional affiliation: Neil Argent (New England), Tim Butler (King's College London), Eric Compas (Wisconsin – Whitewater), David Crouch (Derby), Keith Halfacree (Swansea), Roy Jones (Curtin), Karen Lai (National University of Singapore), Richard Le Heron (Auckland), Ute Lehrer (York), Cheryl Morse (Vermont), Dieter K. Muller (Umeå), Chris Paris (Ulster – Magee), Martin Perry (Massey), Mike Roche (Massey), Matthew Rofe (South Australia), Bruce Ryan (Cincinnati), Regina Scheyvens (Massey), Neelu Seetaram (Bournemouth), Eric Sheppard (Minnesota), Jim Walmsley (New England), Saskia Warren (Sheffield) and Steffen Wetzstein (Western Australia). I also thank Michael Scott (Flinders) and Barney Warf (Kansas) for their comments on earlier drafts of the book's introductory chapter. And before concluding I would also like to express a special note of thanks to contributors to this volume not only for their patience with my particular style of editing but also for their fine work establishing this exciting field.

Iain Hay

NOTE

1. Notable exceptions include the 2010 work of Ley; 2011 work of Pow; and Beaverstock, Hall and Wainwright's 2011 paper. Aside from David Ley, each of these scholars has contributed to this volume.

REFERENCES

Beaverstock, J.V., Hall, S. and T. Wainwright (2011), 'Servicing the super-rich: new financial elites and the rise of the private wealth management ecology', *Regional Studies*, 1–16.

Beaverstock, J.V., Hubbard, P. and J.R. Short (2004), 'Getting away with it? Exposing the geographies of the super-rich', *Geoforum*, **35**, 401–7.

Ley, D. (2010), *Millionaire Migrants: Trans-Pacific Life Lines*, Chichester: Wiley.

Neumayer, E. (2004), 'The super-rich in global perspective: a quantitative analysis of the Forbes list of billionaires', *Applied Economics Letters*, **11**, 793–6.

Pow, C-P. (2011), 'Living it up: super-rich enclave and transnational elite urbanism in Singapore', *Geoforum*, **42**, 382–93.

1. Establishing geographies of the super-rich: axes for analysis of abundance

Iain Hay

> Of all classes the rich are the most noticed and the least studied.
> J.K. Galbraith, *The Age of Uncertainty*, 1977, p. 44.

This book sets out to give and encourage geographical attention to the super-rich. There is perhaps a misguided sense among geographers that work on the super-rich constitutes a frivolous focus of passing interest and little real significance. Or there may be a sentiment abroad that instead of wasting time looking at the lifestyles of the rich and famous, we should – as serious social scientists – devote our attention to much more solemn social justice, cultural and economic issues that command social intervention (see, for example, Shaw 1997). And so our focus as geographers has typically been on the lives and challenges of the disenfranchised, the dislocated and the poor majority. Yet, other social scientists and commentators have not ignored the super-rich.

For instance, in the past decade or so, a number of economists (Kopczuk and Saez 2004; Saez 2009), historians (Hunt 2003; Rubinstein 2004), political scientists (Hacker and Pierson 2010; Irvin 2008) and political activists (Nader 2009), psychologists (Druyen 2011), sociologists (Gilding 1999, 2002), and journalists (Bernstein and Swan 2007; Frank 2007) have seen fit to give specific attention to the super-rich. Moreover, there has been a broad uprising in the level of public attention given to wealth and to the ways it is distributed. This is has taken form, for example, in central concerns of the 2012 World Economic Forum in Davos, Switzerland about the consequences of the widening gap between 'the super-haves and the have littles' (Preston 2012); extended journalistic interventions about the widening gap between rich and poor in New Zealand and its consequences for health and welfare there (Collins 2012); television documentaries about conspicuous consumption and changing meanings of wealth in North America's new 'gilded age' (Faber 2008);

1

and by recent 'global' online and political activity such as 'Occupy Wall Street' whose slogan "We are the 99 percent" (that will no longer tolerate the greed of the 1 per cent) refers to the growing gaps of income and wealth between the wealthiest 1 per cent and the balance of the population. A good deal of recent and critical attention to the rich and the distribution of wealth might be linked to news of vast bankers' bonuses and corporate bailouts in the midst of the devastating consequences of the Global Financial Crisis (GFC) (see, for example, Abbas 2012 and Schwartz and Kanter 2008) but there lies beneath these high profile matters a more subdued swell in the numbers and wealth of the super-rich that might also underpin emerging concerns. It is this growth to which we turn in the next two sections before moving on to the more substantive part of the chapter, the ambition of which is to set out a number of promising directions for future work on geographies of the super-rich – work this book both introduces and aspires to encourage.

WHAT IS SUPER-RICH? HOW MANY SUPER-RICH ARE THERE? AND JUST HOW MUCH MONEY DO THEY HAVE?

There is no definitive threshold to meaningfully identify the super-rich. Indeed, research on the super-rich is confounded by the interlinked problems of identifying who they are and establishing an appropriate benchmark of wealth (Bloom 1989, p. 177). Not only does wealth take different meanings depending on one's age, culture, ideology and personal point of view (Druyen 2010b) it also depends on one's location. For instance, one million US dollars in Micronesia or Mogadishu is quite different from one million US dollars in New York. Leading European wealth researcher, Thomas Druyen, suggests that the point at which one becomes rich is when it is possible to live comfortably off the interest of one's wealth (Druyen 2010a). In the German-speaking countries where Druyen's Institut für Vergleichende Vermögenskultur und Vermögenspsychologie (Institute for Science of Ethical Wealth and Wealth Psychology) does most of its work, that is currently about €3 million (approximately US$4.2 million). Work in the UK by Barnard et al. (2007) settled on a working definition of very wealthy individuals as those who owned £5 million or more of disposable assets. And in the United States, Frank (2007, pp. 6–12), suggested that in the virtual nation of Richistan, inhabited by the super-rich, there are the residents of Lower Richistan (*household* worth of US$1 million to $10 million); Middle Richistan (US$10 million to $100 million); Upper Richistan (US$100 million to $1 billion[1]); and Billionairesville (households worth more than US$1 billion). Frank suggests that among the rich in these 'neighbourhoods', the residents of Lower Richistan are considered merely 'affluent', not really wealthy (Frank 2007, p. 9). Another journalistic report (Sullivan 2008) suggests the entry level to be regarded as rich in the United States is even higher than Frank indicates, with author Tom Sullivan submitting that it is closer to US$25 million (households, including primary residence).

While context-specific measures of wealth and super-wealth are certainly compelling, they do make it very difficult to gain even a broad impression of wealth levels and distributions globally and to begin prospectively productive international comparisons. So, for the moment, I retreat consciously to measures that have been adopted with the purpose of global reporting and international comparison in mind.

At least two major finance groups have taken up the challenge and now publish global reviews of individual wealth. Since 2010, Credit Suisse (2010; 2011) has produced a useful *Global Wealth Report* which aims 'to provide the most comprehensive study of world wealth . . . across nations, from the very bottom of the wealth "pyramid" to the ultra high net worth individuals.' (2010, p. 3). Credit Suisse regards wealth as the value of financial assets *plus* real assets – mainly housing – fewer debts owned by individual adults (2011, pp. 8–9). Although they do not use the term super-rich, Credit Suisse define High Net Worth Individuals (HNWI) as those with asset holdings in excess of US$1 million and Ultra-High Net Worth Individuals (UHNWI) as those with over US$50 million (Credit Suisse 2010, p. 16). With time, the Credit Suisse reports promise to be a valuable and wide-ranging longitudinal resource for future studies of the super-rich. However, for the moment, Capgemini and Merrill Lynch's annual *World Wealth Reports* stand as a benchmark international resource on global individual wealth. The definitions or general understandings established by Capgemini and Merrill Lynch have been used widely by other wealth analysts (for example, Ledbury Research, International Financial Services, London) and reported against consistently for 15 years.[2] Accordingly, most of the chapters in this book work with explicit or implicit acknowledgment of their understandings of super-wealth.

Capgemini and Merrill Lynch (2010) identify two wealthy groups. The first, who currently number 10.9 million globally – and represent 0.158 per cent of the 2010 global population – are described as HNWI (see Table 1.1). These *individuals* each hold financial assets in excess of US$1 million. This figure includes the book value amounts of private equity holdings, as well as publicly quoted equities, bonds, funds and cash deposits. It *excludes* primary residences, collectibles, consumer durables and consumables. Some might regard this threshold of US$1

Table 1.1   High Net Worth Individuals (HNWI) and value of their wealth
            (1996–2010)

Year	Number (millions)	% change	Wealth (US$ trillion)	% change
1996	4.5	–	16.6	–
1997	5.2	15.6	19.1	15.1
1998	5.9	13.5	21.6	13.1
1999	7.0	18.6	25.5	18.1
2000	7.2	2.9	27.0	5.9
2001	7.1	−1.4	26.2	−3.7
2002	7.3	2.8	26.7	2.7
2003	7.7	5.5	28.5	6.7
2004	8.2	6.5	30.7	7.7
2005	8.8	7.3	33.4	8.8
2006	9.5	8.0	37.2	11.4
2007	10.1	6.3	40.7	9.4
2008	8.6	14.9	32.8	−19.4
2009	10.0	17.1	39.0	18.9
2010	10.9	8.3	42.7	9.7

Source: Capgemini and Merrill Lynch (2008–11).

million to be too low to meaningfully represent the super-rich (for example, Taylor et al. 2009, pp. 4–5) but it is worth noting work by the United Nations University World Institute for Development Economics Research (Davies et al. 2006) which revealed that in 2000 wealth of US$500 000 placed an individual among the richest 1 per cent of adults worldwide and that this group of people collectively owned 40 per cent of global assets.

The second group of super-rich are the UHNWI, who each have financial assets that exceed US$30 million and who numbered 103 000 in 2010 (0.0015 per cent of the world's 2010 population), up from 78 000 in 2009 (Capgemini and Merrill Lynch 2010; 2011). Even among the super-rich these people control a disproportionate amount of wealth. In 2010, UHNWI accounted for 36.1 per cent of global HNWI wealth (that is, about US$15.4 trillion from a HNWI total of US$42.7 trillion) despite constituting just 0.9 per cent of the world's HNWI population (Capgemini and Merrill Lynch 2011, p. 7). Although North America is home to the largest number of UHNWI (40 000 at the end of 2010), Latin America has almost 2.5 times more relative to the overall HNWI population (2.5 per cent compared with the global average of 0.9 per cent) (Capgemini and Merrill Lynch 2011, p. 7).

As Table 1.1 reveals, the number of super-rich individuals world-wide and their wealth have grown quickly over the past 10–15 years.[3] Notwithstanding a falter in 2008 during the global financial crisis (GFC), the number of super-rich more than doubled globally in the period 1996 to 2010. Between them, these High Net Worth Individuals (HNWI) possess investable assets totalling a vast $42.7 trillion (Capgemini and Merrill Lynch 2011, p. 5). To put that sum into some kind of proportion, consider that for the fiscal year 2012 United States' federal spending – including defence, Medicare/Medicaid and social security – is budgeted to total US$3.7 trillion (US Government 2011), or just over 8 per cent of the wealth of the global super-rich. Or ponder the fact that in 2009 the world's ten million richest people had investable assets equivalent to roughly two-thirds of the World's Gross Domestic Product, estimated that year to be $58.26 trillion (World Bank 2011). Alternatively, and by stark contrast, consider that the World Bank estimated that, for 2005 (the most recent year data are available), 1.4 billion people – or one quarter of the popula-tion of the developing world – lived in the extreme poverty of less than $1.25 a day (Chen and Ravallion 2008).

WHERE ARE THE SUPER-RICH?

Perhaps not surprisingly, the world's largest HNWI resident populations are in North America, the Asia-Pacific region and Europe (Table 1.2).

Evidently, the Asia-Pacific region is contributing the greatest recent additions to the numbers of the super-rich and Capgemini and Merrill Lynch (2011) observe, for example, that in the year 2010 the HNWI population in Hong Kong grew by 33.3 per cent; in Vietnam by 33.1 per cent; Sri Lanka 27.1 per cent; Indonesia 23.8 per cent; and India 20.8 per cent.

While the US, Japan and Germany dominate the global HNWI popu-lation (Table 1.3), Capgemini and Merrill Lynch (2011) note that this ascendancy is fragmenting as developing economies continue to grow faster than developed countries.

In terms of wealth held, the remarkable growth of Latin America is worth noting. As Table 1.2 reveals, the fortunes of the super-rich there multiplied five times faster their European counterparts over the period 2000–2010 and more than twice as fast as North America – even though Brazil is the only Latin American country to figure in the 12 largest countries by HNWI population (Table 1.3). More startling however is the apparent concentration of wealth in Latin America, and to a lesser degree Africa. Table 1.2 suggests that, on average, in 2010, HNWI in Latin

Table 1.2   HNWI population and wealth by world region, 2000 and 2010

Region	HNWIs (millions)			HNWI wealth (US$ trillions)		
	2000	*2010*	*% growth*	*2000*	*2010*	*% growth*
Africa	0.1	0.1	0	0.6	1.2	+100
Asia-Pacific	1.6	3.3	+106	4.8	10.8	+125
Europe	2.5	3.1	+24	8.4	10.2	+21
Latin America	0.3	0.5	+67	3.2	7.3	+128
Middle East	0.3	0.4	+33	1.0	1.7	+70
North America	2.2	3.4	+7.5	7.5	11.6	+55
Totals	6.9	10.4	+58	25.5	42.7	+67

Source: Merrill Lynch, Cap Gemini Ernst & Young (2002); Capgemini and Merrill Lynch (2011).

Table 1.3   Twelve largest countries by HNWI population, 2010

Rank	Country	HNWI population
1	United States	3 104 000
2	Japan	1 739 000
3	Germany	924 000
4	China	535 000
5	United Kingdom	454 000
6	France	396 000
7	Canada	282 000
8	Switzerland	243 000
9	Australia	193 000
10	Italy	170 000
11	Brazil	155 000
12	India	153 000

Source: Capgemini and Merrill Lynch (2011, p. 7).

America are more than four times wealthier than their North American counterparts while the super-rich in Africa are, on average, three times wealthier than North America's millionaires and billionaires.

WEALTH FUTURES?

Although recent international economic events such as the GFC point to the challenges of predicting wealth, a 2011 study by the Deloitte Center for Financial Services (2011, p. 6) estimates that the number of millionaire households in 25 major economies[4] will rise from about 38 000 in 2000 to over 65 000 in 2020. In the same period, the wealth of those households is forecast to grow from US$92 trillion to US$202 trillion.[5] The Deloitte work suggests that emerging market economies will grow more quickly than developed markets but that the US and Europe will remain global centres of wealth over the next decade. Moreover, they estimate that 43 per cent of the world's wealth among millionaire households will be in one country – the United States!

Given the enormous disparities between rich and poor, the growing numbers and wealth of the super-rich, and the likely significance of the super-rich and their behaviours for places, spaces and environments, I believe the time has come for geographers to shift at least some of our attention from the people in the biggest part of the economic pyramid and begin to give careful attention to those at the apex. As Beaverstock et al. (2004) pointed out, to fail to do so – to more-or-less ignore the super-rich – is problematic, causing us to overlook potentially valuable insights to the institutions, practices and cultural values of our society, as well as allowing us only a partial view of the consequences of global capitalism.

WHY CARE ABOUT GEOGRAPHIES OF THE SUPER-RICH? SOME DIRECTIONS TO THE ANALYSIS OF ABUNDANCE

There is no shortage of reasons for giving critical and scholarly geographical attention to the super-rich (for introductory discussions see Beaverstock et al. 2004 and Hay and Muller 2012). Among them and by way of some concise rationale for exploring geographies of the super-rich, let me point to eight axes for the analysis of abundance.

First, as we have already seen, the super-rich control a disproportionate amount of the world's wealth in patterns of distribution that are deeply uneven, both intra- and internationally. It is unquestionable that the where and why of these cartographies of abundance merit serious examination over and above the early attention given to those questions by Neumayer (2004). More than this, the vast expansion in the number of millionaires and billionaires warrants detailed investigation. Noted commentator on the super-rich and writer for *The Wall Street Journal* Robert Frank, suggests that growth in numbers of the super-rich in the United States since the early 1990s can be attributed to the convergence of three forces:

It's globalization, and the increasing interconnectedness of countries and markets. It's the explosion, size and sophistication of financial markets. Thirdly, it's the growth in information technology that has greased the wheels, accelerated both globalization and financial markets, and created a kind of perfect storm of wealth creation. (Frank, interviewed in Geracioti 2007)

The geographical dimensions of this informed, but preliminary, explanation are self-evident and point to useful targets for comprehensive examination, work John Rennie Short takes up in his chapter in this book.

Second, as newspapers and websites reveal almost daily (for example, Hembry 2012; McDonald 2012), the super-rich's direct ownership of companies and influence over corporate affairs through stock and shareholding bears unequivocally on a litany of geographical phenomena including investment decisions and landscapes, the opening up or abandonment of transportation routes, the ways and places in which new technological applications are implemented, and emerging patterns of employment and despair ... For example, with the late 2011 opening up of 'Santa's short cut' (the Great Circle route) across the North Pole for twin-engined commercial jets, billionaire Sir Richard Branson made it clear that his company's Boeing 777s and 787s would now be able to fly non-stop from London to Fiji or Tahiti, offering new tourism opportunities – and challenges – for the South Pacific (Massey and Martin 2011). Elsewhere, American industrial giant Caterpillar announced early in 2012 that it was closing its Canadian locomotive plant in London, Ontario and putting 460 workers out of their jobs a little more than a month after they were locked out for turning down pay cuts of up to 50 per cent (Ferguson et al. 2012). These decisions, outcomes, and their connections to the attitudes and activities of the super-rich constitute a valuable and under-researched field.

Third, the super-rich might be regarded as a transglobal community of peers, having more in common with one another than they do with their countryfolk (Freeland 2011), and populating an interconnected constellation of sanitized communities set apart from the rest of the world. This set of ideas bears scrutiny. Let me elaborate.

Circulating globally, the super-rich are said to favour a networked assemblage of 'fast' places (Beaverstock et al. 2004, p.405), such as London, Hong Kong, St Barts, Monaco, and Manhattan. One might conceive these places to be woven together in a global web – a 'virtual country' (Frank 2007, p.3) inhabited by the super-rich. And although most of the residents of this imaginary place may depend on the oil, real estate, mines, software, labour and intelligence of the rest of the world for their continued wealth, in most other regards they exist quite separately from it, developing their own culture of shared wealth, symbolized by cars of the same type (for example, Bugatti, Rolls Royce); ownership of private jets and titanic yachts; favoured holiday destinations or experiences (for example, St Barts, Maldives); personal security arrangements; and patterns of dress (for example, Breguet, Chanel).

But not only have the super-rich created a virtual country from an assemblage of 'fast spaces', arguably on a global scale, they have also sequestered themselves away from the hoi polloi in those fast places (a matter Kathryn Wilkins explores from an historical perspective in her chapter in this volume). Rather darkly, in their remarkable book *Evil Paradises. Dreamworlds of Neoliberalism*, Mike Davis and Daniel Bertrand Monk (2007) present a series of case studies of new geographies of exclusion and the landscapes of wealth which have arisen over the past 20 or so years. Among its other dramatic features, our 'new and greatest gilded age' (p. 1) is one characterized by an 'unprecedented spatial and moral secession of the wealthy from the rest of humanity' (p. 2) where:

> modern wealth and luxury consumption are more enwalled and socially enclaved than at any time since the 1890s . . . . [T]he spatial logic of neoliberalism . . . revives the most extreme colonial patterns of residential segregation and zoned consumption. Everywhere, the rich and near rich are retreating into sumptuary compounds, leisure cities, and gated replicas of imaginary California suburbs. (p. 2)

This set of ideas surrounding mobility and fast spaces woven together as a virtual country and defined by physical and cultural boundaries really does justify examination. And while there has certainly been some work on the geographies of emerging archipelagos of luxury and their consequences (for example, Borsdorf and Hidalgo 2008; Butler and Lees 2006; Lees 2003; Pow 2011; Pow and Kong 2007), there is surely scope for a great deal more, as Pow's contribution to this volume suggests.

Fourth, even if they do not enwall themselves physically, fascinating and enduring transformative effects of the super-rich on the characteristics of places in which they settle or to which they are connected are evident in rural and urban landscapes (for example, see Wilkins' and Schein and Roberts' chapters in this volume). For instance, journalists Adams and Harris (2006) talk of the ways in which the influx of the super-rich to London in particular has had dramatic consequences for the physical form and social fabric of that city:

> Historic areas of London are being taken over by international HNW [High Net Worth] tribes. In Belgravia, it's the Russians; in Chelsea the Americans. They have scant regard for historic codes, and often rub-up uncomfortably with their new neighbours.

> They don't understand things like building consent . . . People who run plan-
> ning groups are finding more and more of these people who have no regard for
> history and just say, 'I've got £1bn I can do what I want.'
> The HNW's interfere with the social structure, change property values, and
> cause the ordinary to disappear. In parts of Belgravia, it is now more or less
> impossible to buy a loaf of white sliced: instead, you must visit Poilâne[6] and
> pay £5 for a baguette.

This example points to some of the specific ways in which the super-rich
can reshape the physical and social characteristics of places they choose
to alight, displacing everyday city dwellers and excluding genuine diversity, preferring instead to experience more sanitized forms of difference
(Butler and Lees 2006). The super-rich are also linked to changes further
afield. For instance, many of the super-rich purchase holiday homes internationally (see Chris Paris' chapter in this volume for a discussion) and
this affects communities around the world. For example, Queenstown,
New Zealand has become a centre for high profile international real
estate buyers who are reported to include singer Shania Twain, actor
Sam Neill, director Peter Jackson, producer Julian Grimmond, and actor
John Travolta (Woods 2010; 2011). Mirroring the kind of controversy
that had occurred earlier in the English countryside as 'Aga[7] louts' sought
to prevent developments that would change the rural aesthetics that had
attracted them, the geopolitics of investment in Queenstown came to a
head early this century when very wealthy real estate owners – some based
overseas – joined *opposition* to development of land within the region.
Their resistance to development 'inadvertently transformed an environmental and landscape conflict into a struggle over *local* control of the
development of the *locality*' (Woods 2010). The Mayor at the time led an
attack on this opposition to the region's 'progress', stating: 'They close
the door, pull the drawbridge up, and leave the peasants outside, to live in
the elitist homes in the rural area.' (Mayor of Queenstown Lakes District
in *The Press*, 11 November 2000 (cited in Woods 2011, pp. 377–8).

The Queenstown example demonstrates the challenge for local communities in which the super-rich, who arguably have little or no day-to-
day attachment to the places where they may own property, are able to
influence and shape development. And yet, their detachment from these
places suggests they may not make any other meaningful contribution
to the local community.[8] For instance, while the global super-rich have
been able to transform areas around the world like Queenstown in New
Zealand, Aspen in the United States, and Puerto Banus in Spain into 'elite
pleasure grounds', and despite their apparent concerns for environment
and aesthetics, their purchases have often not been accompanied by the
full range of economic, political, social and environmental responsibilities

that might once have been taken for granted by wealthy aristocrats who were rooted by family and tradition to those places (Woods 2010). Haseler (2000, p. 79) has even suggested that in the super-rich we may be seeing a 'return to aristocracy' but without the 'noblesse oblige' of the old aristocrats bound to locality and nation. These are matters Michael Woods takes up in his chapter in this volume. As he reveals, the significance of the super-rich for the global countryside is more complex than preliminary speculations might suggest.

So under the banner of the transformative effects of the super-rich on the characteristics of places in which they settle or to which they are connected, there lies a whole range of issues clearly crying out for attention. Evidently the super-rich can transform places substantially. They are reordering inner parts of cities. They are purchasing large properties in their own countryside as well as in other people's. They affect the economics, aesthetics, politics, and culture of these places. I think these are unquestionably matters for geographers to be concerned about and I point to chapters by Woods, Roberts and Schein, and Murphy and McGuirk in this volume as works that take up some of these themes.

Fifth, the super-rich are able to exercise disproportionate political influence – with all that entails for the places we live, the taxes we pay, and the conditions under which we exist. Distinguished political scientists Laurence Jacobs and Theda Skocpol (2006) make the point with clarity: 'Citizens with lower or moderate incomes speak with a whisper that is lost on the ears of inattentive government officials, while the advantaged roar with a clarity and consistency that policy-makers readily hear and routinely follow.' By way of example, Australia's richest person and the 19th most powerful woman in the world (Forbes staff 2011), Gina Rinehart, has taken to using her vast and growing wealth for influence, seeking to change public and political opinion on mining taxes and 'carbon' taxes and by supporting climate-change deniers. Perhaps to support these activities, she has also recently invested US$165 million in a major Australian television network and an additional US$100 million to purchase 4 per cent of Fairfax Media – which produces over 220 publications, including influential newspapers *The Age* and *The Sydney Morning Herald* (Cadzow 2012, p. 8).[9] The links in Australia between the super-rich, the media and political meddling have been highlighted recently by that country's Treasurer, Wayne Swan who, in his accusations that the country's wealthiest residents have demonstrated excessive greed, ruthlessness and abuse of power, has opined: 'The combination of deep industry pockets, conservative political support, biased editorial policy and shock-jock ranting has been mobilised to protect vested interest' (cited in Ansley 2012). He adds that the super-rich are threatening Australian democracy and having 'pocketed a disproportionate share of the nation's economic success now feel they have a right to shape Australia's future to satisfy their own self-interest'.

In the United States billionaires are pumping large amounts of money into the coffers of presidential candidates. For instance, Republican Newt Gingrich's 2011 campaign was almost entirely funded by one man, casino mogul Sheldon Adelson (Shear 2012), who was investing to prevent the 'continuation of the socialist-style economy we've been experiencing for almost four years. That scares me because the redistribution of wealth is the path to more socialism . . .' (Adelson, cited in Bertoni 2012). But perhaps the most notorious, yet secretive, figures in the US political scene are the billionaire Koch brothers. Charles and David Koch have been investing vast sums in projects 'designed to drive the country even more to the right' (Pilkington 2011). Not only have they backed the Tea Party movement, underwritten incubators of radical conservative ideology, and spent over US$55 million funding climate change deniers, but they have also established Themis, a nationwide database connecting millions of Americans who share the Kochs' anti-government and libertarian views, 'a move that will further enhance the tycoons' political influence and that could prove significant in [the next] presidential election' (Pilkington 2011).

Perhaps even more dramatically, in their inflammatory remarks on the self-serving political influence of the super-rich, Davis and Monk (2007, p. 1) observe that 'corrupt insider power, nothing less, that has given away the global commons to a plunderbund[10] that includes Dick Cheney's Halliburton, Boeing, Blackwater, Carlos Slim's Telmex, Yukos, the Abramovich empire, Larry Rong Zhijian's China International Tourist and Investment Corporation, Silvio Berlusconi's Fininvest, and Rupert Murdoch's News Corporation'.

A particular set of views that have been advanced in political and other domains by the wealthy are those that surround neoliberalism.[11] And over the past 30 years, those views which have taken the attention of many geographers (for example, Harvey 2005; Leitner et al. 2007; Peck and Tickell 2002) have come to be a 'dominant global orthodoxy, articulated and acted upon within most corporations, many universities, most state bodies and especially international organizations like the World Trade Organization, World Bank and the International Monetary Fund' (Urry 2010, p. 203). That orthodoxy supports both practically and ideologically the redistributive effects of neoliberalism and the associated growth and power of the super-rich (see, for example, Frank 2007, p. 47 and Petras 2008, p. 327). Yet while geographers have scrutinized the trajectories of neoliberalism, none appear to have delved into the critical links between that form of political-economic governance and its associations with, and consequences for, the super-rich, matters John Rennie Short begins to take up in this volume.

Sixth, as well as shaping political priorities and the social and territorial 'landscapes' of which those are a part, certain groups among the super-rich give shape to consumer preferences[12] (following Veblen 1908) – a matter that has clear community, cultural and environmental significance as individuals compete on a continual and self-defeating quest for standing and relative status through the positional goods[13] they acquire (Hirsch 1976; Frank 1999). John Urry (2010, p. 206) provides a succinct statement of a core part of the relationship: 'dreamworlds for the super-rich provide models of lives that through multiple media and global travel, inflame the desires for similar kinds of often addictive experience from parts of the world's population.' And of course, luxury fever (Frank 1999) and the associated 'arms race' of possessions in which many of us find ourselves now occurs against a crumbling and putrefying environmental backdrop. So troubling is our predicament that it has yielded an uprising of catastrophist thinking in the social and environmental sciences (for example, Diamond 2005; Kolbert 2006; Perrow 2007) and suggestions that the super-rich are core parties to the excessive global consumption that is the prospective 'gravedigger'[14] for twenty-first century capitalism (Urry 2010, p. 191).

Seventh, and in a somewhat different twist on consumption and its consequences, geographies of consumption may be changing in important new ways that truly warrant attention. In a 2005 report to investors, a group of Citigroup analysts led by Citigroup's then Chief Global Equity Strategist, Ajay Kapur, remarked that 'The World is dividing into two blocs – the Plutonomy[15] and the rest' (Kapur et al. 2005, p. 7). They went on:

> In a plutonomy there is no such animal as 'the U.S. consumer' or the 'U.K. consumer', or indeed the 'Russian consumer'. There are rich consumers, few in number, but disproportionate in the gigantic slice of income and consumption they take. There are the rest, the 'non-rich', the multitudinous many, but only accounting for surprisingly small bites of the national pie. (p. 9)

One year later, in a continuation of their work, Kapur and his colleagues (2006, p. 8) observed that in plutonomies – countries like the United States, the United Kingdom, Canada and Australia, driven by huge income and vast wealth inequality – the rich are so rich that their behaviours overwhelm those of the average or median consumer. They point out that in 2004, the top 20 per cent of consumers accounted for almost 60 per cent of income and spending in the United States whereas the bottom 20 per cent accounted for a mere 3 per cent.[16] The point is made more emphatically perhaps by Davis and Monk (2007, p. 1) who remind us that the richest 1 per cent of Americans spend as much as the poorest 60 million![17] And what are we to make of this?

> The conclusion? We should worry less about what the average consumer – say the 50th percentile – is going to do, when that consumer is (we think) less relevant to the aggregate data than how the wealthy feel and what they are doing. This is simply a case of mathematics, not morality. (Kapur et al. 2006, p. 11)

While there are some excellent geographical expositions on consumption (for example, Mansvelt 2005; Goodman et al. 2010) and other reviews of, for example, the broad significance of affluence for environment (Myers and Kent 2004), it would appear from the available literature that geographers have yet to grapple meaningfully with the vast and comprehensively disproportionate spending power of the super-rich. Indeed, taking up Juliana Mansvelt's (2010) theme of 'absent presences' in recent work on consumption, there is a certain irony in geographers' inadvertent marginalization in their research of those who are so central to consumption! I do wonder what might be revealed, for example, if consideration was given to the significance of the super-rich to those matters of sustainability, ethical consumption, fair trade and alternative consumption which Mansvelt notes (p. 235) have recently occupied geographers of consumption.

Eighth, even through their charitable donations, which can amount to billions of dollars,[18] the super-rich are reshaping activity from the level of international development aid (for example, The Bill and Melinda Gates Foundation's commitment to help reach World Health Organization goals to control or eliminate ten tropical diseases) to the local configuration of vital community educational and medical facilities.[19] For instance, in their study of those making donations in excess of US$1 million in 2004 and 2005 in the United States Professor Les Lenkowsky and his team from Indiana University found that almost all of these donations went to schools, hospitals and universities with substantially less going to cultural and art institutions (for example, in 2010, Facebook's Mark Zuckerberg donated US$100 million to improving public schools in Newark, New Jersey [Freeland 2011]). Moreover: '*No* money went to grassroots organizations, to reproductive rights organizations, to community health centers, to domestic violence centers, even to social service organizations . . . [T]his is an instance where philanthropy perpetuates the inequities in our system' (Eisenberg in Hudson Institute's Bradley Center for Philanthropy and Civic Renewal 2008, p. 18. Emphasis in original).

But as Bishop and Green (2009) have alerted us, there is more to the renaissance of philanthropy than just the vast sums of money involved and the places those funds settle:[20] now we have business techniques and ways of thinking applied to philanthropy to produce what they termed in their book of the same name, philanthrocapitalism. It would appear then that neoliberal ideas are not only enmeshed in economic activity and political affairs, but that they have crept into the worlds of beneficence. While a critical geographical review of super-rich philanthropy and its emerging associate, philanthrocapitalism, might be regarded as looking the 'gift horse in the mouth', these disturbing trends in local and global charity plainly warrant close investigation.

These brief directions for future geographical work on the super-rich are by no means a comprehensive statement of reasons for geographers to give attention to the super-rich. My aims in these preliminary paragraphs have simply been to provide some context for the chapters that follow and, with luck, to ignite further interest in the super-rich as a focus of geographical inquiry – pointing to a number of axes of inquiry that appear especially useful. In the paragraphs to follow, and by way of concluding this first chapter, I introduce the other chapters that make up this volume. Some of the distinguished and emerging contributors to this book have advanced ideas discussed here (for example, Pow, Roberts and Schein, Short, Woods), while others have set out work that reflects their own clear thoughts on the geographical significance of the super-rich (for example, Cousin and Chauvin, Fasche, McManus). I hope you find their work as stimulating as I have.

INTRODUCTION TO THE CHAPTERS

The book explores geographies of the super-rich from four main – yet interwoven – standpoints, commencing with explorations of the political/ economic circumstances of which the super-rich are a part (Short, Beaverstock, Hall and Wainwright). It then transitions to consideration of urban matters – both contemporary (Murphy and McGuirk, Paris) and historical (Wilkins) – with Pow's chapter on 'onshoring Singapore' serving as a useful bridge between the political/economic and urban. Then, in quite fascinating accounts, Chapters 8 and 9 take up the role of the super-rich in the transformation of global (Woods) and local (Roberts and Schein) rural geographies. Finally, the book turns to matters that revolve around and flow from leisure pursuits of the super-rich, with chapters by McManus on thoroughbred breeding and racing, Fasche on the role of the super-rich in making new geographies of art history, and Cousin and

Chauvin discussing the dynamics of upper-class segregation in the exclusive French West Indian holiday resort of St Barts.

In his provocative chapter, John Rennie Short suggests that we – and most particularly the United States – are now in a second Gilded Age, a period of concentrated wealth and increased influence of the very rich. Short extends elements of this introductory chapter by setting out some geographic perspectives on the super-rich but focuses most particularly on the discursive reach and impact of the super-rich on political debates, drawing primarily from the US political arena as a case study.

In Chapter 3, Jonathan V. Beaverstock, Sarah J.E. Hall and Thomas Wainwright observe that during this second Gilded Age, the resurgence in the fortunes of the global super-rich has driven the emergence of the retail private wealth management sector in places like London, New York, Hong Kong and Singapore. These wealth management services offer their global super-rich clientele an array of financial products and advisory services to protect and manage their wealth across many jurisdictions. The chapter documents the rise and structure of this sector, through an analysis of the retail products and advisory services of 400 such firms in London.

In his chapter Choon-Piew Pow critically unpacks discourses on urban liveability before turning the attention to Singapore – reportedly a fledging global 'hotspot' for private wealth management with the highest concentration of millionaires in the world (Mahtani 2012). As part of a strategy to attract high net-worth individuals to 'live and bank' in the city-state, the Singapore government is not only promoting the city-state as a secure haven for private banking but also rebranding itself as 'Asia's Switzerland' and the 'new capital of fun and creativity'. In the contemporary world characterized by the rampant offshoring of economic functions from 'first-world' to 'third-world' cities, developments in Singapore could be considered as a way of 'onshoring' cities that aspire to be the lifestyle hub and investment destination for the global super-rich. In this context, the chapter critically examines how recent urban development in Singapore and associated efforts to become a global hub for high net-worth individuals are embedded in the political economy and cultural imaginary of a neoliberal urbanism.

Laurence Murphy and Pauline McGuirk's story of the rise and fall of Irish property developers offers insights into the role of the super-rich in material and symbolic place making. They provide a fascinating account of the rise and impact of super-rich property developers in the Celtic Tiger economy, noting that developers were not only involved in the physical construction of place(s), but were high profile participants in the production of discourses presenting Ireland as a place of opportunity, entrepreneurialism and success. Through two case studies which, not coincidentally, mirror the fortunes of the Irish economy, they also reflect on the role of the developers' conspicuous consumption and personal wealth in mobilizing the huge bank loans on which their urban imagineering was founded.

Chris Paris' chapter considers the many homes of the super-rich and focuses on the impact of global housing markets on prime London real estate. Drawing from a variety of data sources including official UK government data, surveys and market analysis from international real estate agencies, and web-based material Paris explores the ability of hyper-mobile, super-rich individuals and families to purchase and use numerous homes in many locations across the globe, noting the complex spatial interrelations between countries of residence and ownership. He observes that high levels of contemporary personal mobility contrast sharply with the more limited spatial reach of previous cohorts of the super-rich. Moreover, real estate industry and government sources together show that super-rich households own residences in numerous global cities, especially London, where overseas buyers of luxury homes in prime locations are contributing to a de-coupling of parts of the city's housing market from the dynamics of the wider UK housing system.

Kathryn Wilkins takes us back in time to investigate the significance of the activities of the super-rich for the spaces of London's West End during 'Seasons' of the nineteenth century. The Season was an annual phenomenon, which saw wealthy families migrate temporarily to London in early summer to participate in a daily round of extravagant social engagements and dances. Wilkins discusses the importance of the temporal nature of this group's engagement with the capital, suggesting that the West End was made a 'part-time place', influenced as much by the absence of the wealthy for much of the year as by their presence during the Season. The influence of the super-rich during the Season extended to the development of a hard enclave in this pocket of London; gates and bars were erected to restrict the presence of poorer citizens. With a particular focus on Grosvenor Estate in Mayfair, Wilkins goes on to discuss the role of the super-rich in shaping residential development and other physical aspects of the area as a consequence of the Season. She concludes by discussing other aspects of the monopolization of public spaces in the West End giving attention to the case of Hyde Park.

Michael Woods moves us from the urban to the rural. He notes that the transnational super-rich elite are commonly associated with global cities, but they also have a presence and an interest in the global countryside that has antecedents in the global operations of imperial elites. His chapter examines the shifting rural geographies of the transnational super-rich, from imperial elites generating wealth from activities in peripheral rural spaces to support aristocratic lifestyles in the English countryside; to the appropriation of the practices and properties of the country gentry as status symbols by the transnational super-rich in selected rural localities; and the construction of new transnational networks by a new cohort of rural entrepreneurs. In each case, he argues, super-rich elites connect rural localities to the global economy and acts of agents of transformation in the global countryside.

In their absorbing chapter Susan M. Roberts and Richard H. Schein observe that investments of the super-rich in thoroughbred farms in the central Kentucky region known as the Bluegrass Region have been key to the creation of a distinct rural landscape there. This landscape works to solidify the social position of the super-rich, yet because the landscape is understood as a symbol of regional identity and because the thoroughbred industry is an economic cluster, there is considerable support for attempts to preserve the landscape in the face of threats from urban sprawl.

In the final chapters of the book, we turn to leisure-related activity. Phil McManus' chapter focuses on thoroughbred breeding and racing. Drawing on the work of economist and sociologist Thorstein Veblen, and noting the similarities between the leisure class of Veblen's era (late nineteenth/early twentieth century) and today, he explores how and why the super-rich participate in contemporary leisure activities. The chapter outlines some of the implications of the super-rich for the racehorse industry and, following Veblen, McManus concludes that the wealth gap between the leisure class/ super-rich and the rest of society is not simply an economic gap, but is reinforced in a socio-cultural context by the super-rich having time to spend on their leisure activities, and the financial resources to engage in conspicuous consumption around these leisure activities.

Melanie Fasche's intriguing contribution reveals changes in the geography and organization of 'making art history'. She argues that these changes are driven by two interrelated dynamics. First, demand of wealthy private collectors for contemporary visual art is growing especially in new places previously not connected to the Western centred art world such as the former USSR, the Gulf region and Asia. This growing demand is pushing up price levels and increasingly pricing out cash-strapped public museums at galleries and auctions. Second, both in the West and especially in these new places a growing number of private wealthy collectors are abandoning the conventional Western philanthropic practices of supporting public museums. Instead, wealthy private collectors are creating their own private museums and thus performing the legitimating and historicizing role of public museums themselves. The growing influence of new wealthy private collectors and their private museums on making art history causes unease that money may eventually trump art historical scholarship. It is likely that the prestigious art collections of the twenty-first century will no longer be built by public museums in the West but by wealthy private collectors in the East.

And in the final chapter of the book, Bruno Cousin and Sébastien Chauvin discuss Saint-Barthélemy, one of the most exclusive seaside resorts in the world. Three groups interacting locally – historic St Barths, metropolitan immigrants, and super-rich vacationers or villa owners – are all overwhelmingly white. Their cohabitation maintains the elitist character of the island, while obliterating most of its Caribbean heritage. Cousin and Chauvin suggest that St Barts' resort identity is structured around a generic brand of exoticism, a local variation of a global space of upper-class leisure. And by insisting on the multi-class co-production of elite seaside locations, Cousin and Chauvin lay emphasis on the roles of service relations and upper-class dynamics of distinction in the reconfiguration of local cultures within those places patronised by the super-rich.

NOTES

1. Throughout this volume, the term billion is used to refer to one thousand million.
2. In appendices to their annual World Wealth Reports, Capgemini and Merrill Lynch provide an overview of their methodology for calculating HNWI numbers. The model is built in two stages: 'first, the estimation of total wealth by country, and second, the distribution of this wealth across the adult population in that country'. Capgemini and Merrill Lynch (2011, p. 36). The calculations appear to be based on the best generally available data from sources such as the International Monetary Fund, the World Bank, the Economist Intelligence Unit and countries' national statistics and the calculations take account of myriad influences including exchange rate fluctuations and international flows of property and investments. The Capgemini and Merrill Lynch data constitute an accessible, well-scrutinized and widely accepted source of information on world wealth.
3. It is important to note that the recent expansion in the numbers of the super-rich is not an unprecedented phenomenon. For instance, the late 1800s and the 1920s in the United States were eras of considerable economic growth and polarization of wealth, with individuals like Rockefeller, Vanderbilt, Carnegie, and Mellon accumulating vast fortunes. (See Chapter 2 of this volume for a discussion.)
4. The 25 countries surveyed by Deloitte were: *Developed Markets* – Australia, Canada, France, Germany, Hong Kong, Italy, Japan, Netherlands, Norway, Singapore, Spain, Sweden, Switzerland, the United States and the United Kingdom; *Emerging Markets* – Brazil, China, India, Malaysia, Mexico, Poland, Russia, South Korea, Taiwan and Turkey.
5. Household wealth in the Deloitte study includes primary residence. Aside from any other differences in the methodologies of the Deloitte and Capgemini and Merrill Lynch studies referred to earlier, this offers some explanation for the different reports of total wealth held by the super-rich.
6. Pain Poilâne – a stone-ground, naturally-fermented, wood-oven-fired bread – first produced in Paris. The Belgravia district facility opened in June 2000.

7. An Aga is a hand-crafted, cast-iron, heat-storage cooker made in Shropshire, England. They have been built since the late 1920s.
8. By contrast with the tenet of this discussion it is worth noting that Russian billionaire Alexander Abramov's new US$30 million estate at Helena Bay, New Zealand has included sizeable expenditures on environmental protection and restoration measures. The substantial project is also said to be offering 82 full-time jobs plus work for specialist contractors (Gibson 2012).
9. It is interesting to note that on the other side of the Pacific Ocean another billionaire has recently invested heavily in buying political influence. Meg Whitman, former CEO of eBay, spent a record US$144 million of her own reported US$1.3 billion fortune on an unsuccessful run for the California governorship in 2010 (Associated Press/Salon 2011).
10. Plunderbund is a league of commercial, political, or financial interests that exploits the public.
11. A political-economic approach characterized by an emphasis on economic liberalisation, deregulation, privatization, free trade, and open markets.
12. Prince and Schiff (2008, pp. 1–4) make the important point that it is what they call 'middle-class millionaires' (people with a net worth between US$1 million and $10 million including equity in their primary residence) – and not the ultra-rich – who exert influence over the middle class' aspirations, attitudes and consumption patterns.
13. Positional goods are those whose value is linked to their level of desirability. Examples might include a limited edition of a motor vehicle, a Louis Vuitton bag, or a pair of Manolo Blahnik shoes. Positional goods cease to be a luxury when many other people have them.
14. In *Manifesto of the Communist Party*, Marx and Engels (1883, p.483) suggest that 'the development of Modern Industry cuts from under its feet the very foundation on which the bourgeoisie produces and appropriates products. What the bourgeoisie therefore produces, above all, are its own grave-diggers. Its fall and the victory of the proletariat are equally inevitable.' Urry's (2010) argument is that it may not be the proletariat who bring about the demise of twenty-first century capitalism. Instead it may be massive population growth, increased mobility, excessive global consumption, and rising carbon emissions.
15. The term plutonomy was coined by Citigroup's Ajay Kapur and colleagues in 2005. It refers to a socio-economic situation in which wealth and economic growth are controlled by the very wealthiest minority. Contemporary plutonomies are said to include Australia, Canada, the United Kingdom and the United States. Previous eras of plutonomy have embraced sixteenth century Spain, seventeenth century Holland, Industrial Revolution Britain, and the Gilded Age and Roaring Twenties in the United States (Kapur 2006).
16. It is worth noting that the US Federal Government data upon which these figures are based (Census Bureau's 2004 Consumer Expenditure Survey) *does not include* the exceptionally rich! Not surprisingly, Kapur et al. (2006, p. 11) estimate that adding the Forbes 400 richest families to the figures would skew income and expenditure towards the top quintile.
17. According to Frank (2007, p.122) 2005 figures suggest the richest 0.5 per cent of Americans consume at a rate of $650 million per year, equivalent to the total household spending of Italy.
18. *The Chronicle of Philanthropy* noted in its 2012 annual report that the top 50 United States' donors made pledges in 2011 to give a total of $10.4 billion (Di Mento and Preston 2012).
19. In a paper on the geography of *corporate* philanthropy in the United Kingdom, Hurd et al. (1998) found that manufacturing companies tended to donate to communities near their production base whereas service companies tended to disperse their goodwill more broadly. The key element shaping the geography of corporate philanthropy was the audience the company intended to address.
20. Early geographical work on philanthropy by Wolpert and Reiner (1984, p.197) suggested that 'locational factors are important inasmuch as . . . donor-recipient markets

generally function at a metropolitan or smaller scale', it does appear as if more expansive locational patterns are now emerging. Wolpert (1993) went on to write *The Structure of Generosity in America*, a broader analysis of the geography of philanthropy in the United States. Some years later Lambert and Lester (2004) wrote of the transglobal range of reference associated with geographies of colonial philanthropy.

REFERENCES

Abbas, M. (2012), 'Big banker bonuses divide Britain', *Reuters*, 2 February, http://uk.reuters.com/article/2012/02/02/uk-britain-bankers-bonuses-idUKTRE8111 NW20120202, accessed 7 February 2012.

Adams, G. and S. Harris (2006), 'The super rich: Britain's billionaires', *Independent. co.uk*, 17 December, www.independent.co.uk/news/uk/this-britain/the-super-rich-britains-billionaires-428774.html, accessed 22 February 2012.

Ansley, G. (2012), 'Australian Treasurer takes on billionaires', *nzherald.co.nz*, 6 March, www.nzherald.co.nz/world/news/article.cfm?c_id=2&objectid=10790034, accessed 6 March 2012.

Associated Press/Salon (2011), 'Final Meg Whitam tally: $178.5M', *salon.com*, 1 February, www.salon.com/topic/meg_whitman//, accessed 22 March 2012.

Barnard, M., J. Taylor, J. Dixon, S. Purdon and W. O'Connor (2007), *Researching the Very Wealthy: Results from a Feasibility Study*, London: National Centre for Social Research.

Beaverstock, J.V., P. Hubbard and J.R. Short (2004), 'Getting away with it? Exposing the geographies of the super-rich', *Geoforum*, **35**, 401–7.

Bernstein, P.W. and A. Swan (eds) (2007), *All the Money in the World*, New York: Vintage Books.

Bertoni, S. (2012), 'Billionaire Sheldon Adelson says he might give $100M to Newt Gingrich or other Republican', *Forbes* (online), 21 February, www.forbes.com/sites/stevenbertoni/2012/02/21/billionaire-sheldon-adelson-says-he-might-give-100m-to-newt-gingrich-or-other-republican/, accessed 22 March 2012.

Bishop, M. and M. Green (2009), *Philanthrocapitalism: How Giving Can Save the World*, New York: Bloomsbury.

Bloom, L. (1989), 'Well-fertilized family trees', *Contemporary Sociology*, **18** (2), 177–8.

Borsdorf, A. and R. Hidalgo (2008), 'New dimensions of social exclusion in Latin America: from gated communities to gated cities, the case of Santiago de Chile', *Land Use Policy*, **25** (2), 153–60.

Butler, T. and L. Lees (2006), 'Super-gentrification in Barnsbury, London: globalization and gentrifying global elites at the neighbourhood level', *Transactions of the Institute of British Geographers*, **31**, 467–87.

Cadzow, J. (2012), 'The Iron Lady', *Good Weekend* (*The Saturday Age*), 21 January, pp. 8–13.

Capgemini and Merrill Lynch (2010), *World Wealth Report 2010*, www.capgemini.com/insights-and-resources/by-publication/world-wealth-report-2010/, accessed 1 November 2011.

Capgemini and Merrill Lynch (2011), *World Wealth Report 2011*, www.capgemini.com/services-and-solutions/by-industry/financial-services/solutions/wealth/worldwealthreport/, accessed 1 November 2011.

Chen, S. and M. Ravallion (2008), *The Developing World is Poorer than We Thought, But No Less Successful in the Fight Against Poverty*, World Bank Policy Research Working Paper Series, http://ssrn.com/abstract=1259575, accessed 7 February 2012.

Collins, S. (2012), 'Auckland: a city divided by income', *New Zealand Herald* (online), 6 February, www.nzherald.co.nz/simon-collins/news/article.cfm?a_id=135&objectid=10783837, accessed 7 February 2012.

Credit Suisse (2010), *Global Wealth Report*, Zurich, Switzerland: Credit Suisse Research Institute AG.

Credit Suisse (2011), *Global Wealth Report 2011*, Zurich, Switzerland: Credit Suisse Research Institute AG.

Davies, J., S. Sandström, A. Shorrocks and E. Wolff (2006), *The World Distribution of Household Wealth*, Helsinki: World Institute for Development Economics Research of the United Nations University.

Davis, M. and D.B. Monk (eds) (2007), *Evil Paradises. Dreamworlds of Neoliberalism*, New York: The New Press.

Deloitte Center for Financial Services (2011), *The Next Decade in Global Wealth among Millionaire Households* (online), May, www.deloitte.com/us/global wealth, accessed 8 March 2012.

Diamond, J. (2005), *Collapse: How Societies Choose to Fail or Survive*, London: Allen Lane.

Di Mento, M. and C. Preston (2012), 'Most-generous donors gave more in 2011 but still lag their pre-recession pace', *The Chronicle of Philanthropy* (online), 6 February http://philanthropy.com/article/America-s-Wealthy-Made-More/130625/?cid=pe_p50nav12_art, accessed 27 February 2012.

Druyen, T. (2010a), 'Reich ist nicht vermögend' ['Rich is not wealthible'], *Soziologie Heute*, **2**, 6–9.

Druyen, T. (2010b), 'Sind Reiche glücklicher?' ['Are the rich happier?'], Interview with *Rheinische Post*, 21 September 2010.

Druyen, T. (2011), *Happy Princes. The Empowerment of Wealthibility*, Vienna: Sigmund Freud University Press.

Faber, D. (2008), *Untold Wealth: The Rise of the Super-rich*, television documentary screened on CNBC, 26 June 2008.

Ferguson, R., R. Benzie and T. Talaga (2012), 'Caterpillar closes electro-motive plant in London', *thestar.com* (online), 3 February, www.thestar.com/news/canada/politics/article/1125718--electro-motive-to-close-london-locomotive-plant, accessed 8 March 2012.

Forbes staff (2011), 'The world's 100 most powerful women', *Forbes* (online), 24 August, www.forbes.com/wealth/power-women, accessed 8 March 2012.

Frank, R.H. (1999), *Luxury Fever: Money and Happiness in an Era of Excess*, Princeton, NJ: Princeton University Press.

Frank, R. (2007), *Richistan: A Journey Through the American Wealth Boom and the Lives of the New Rich*, New York: Crown Publishers.

Freeland, C. (2011), 'The rise of the new global elite', *The Atlantic* (online), January/February, www.theatlantic.com/magazine/archive/2011/01/the-rise-of-the-new-global-elite/8343/, accessed 27 February 2012.

Galbraith, J.K. (1977), *The Age of Uncertainty*, London: British Broadcasting Corporation/Deutsch.

Geracioti, D.A. (2007), 'Richistan', *Trusts and Estates* (online), 19 September, http://trustsandestates.com/wealth_watch/Wealth_Watch_News_09192007/, accessed 1 March 2012.

Gibson, A. (2012), 'Billionaire's construction helps 82 NZ families', *nzherald.co.nz*, 20 March, www.nzherald.co.nz/business/news/article.cfm?c_id=3&objectid=10793246, accessed 20 March 2012.

Gilding, M. (1999), 'Superwealth in Australia: entrepreneurs, accumulation and the capitalist class', *Journal of Sociology*, **35**, 169–82.

Gilding, M. (2002), *Secrets of the Super Rich*, Sydney, NSW: Harper Collins Publishers.

Goodman, M.K., D. Goodman and M.R. Redclift (eds) (2010), *Consuming Place: Placing Consumption in Perspective*, Farnham: Ashgate.

Hacker, J.S. and P. Pierson (2010), *Winner-Take-All Politics: How Washington Made the Rich Richer and Turned its Back on the Middle Class*, New York: Simon and Schuster.

Harvey, D. (2005), *A Brief History of Neoliberalism*, New York: Oxford University Press.

Haseler, S. (2000), *The Super-Rich. The Unjust World of Global Capitalism*, London: Macmillan.

Hay, I. and S. Muller (2012), '"That tiny, stratospheric apex that owns most of the world" – exploring geographies of the super-rich', *Geographical Research*, **50** (1), 75–88.

Hembry, O. (2012), 'Qantas slashes jobs as skies get rougher', *nzherald.co.nz* (online), 17 February, www.nzherald.co.nz/business/news/article.cfm?c_id=3&objectid=10786049, accessed 22 February 2012.

Hirsch, F. (1976), *The Social Limits to Growth*, London: Routledge & Kegan Paul.

Hudson Institute's Bradley Center for Philanthropy and Civic Renewal (2008), *Is Philanthropy Going to the Dogs?*, Edited transcript of panel discussion held on 5 September at Hudson Institute's Betsy and Walter Stern Conference Center, http://works.bepress.com/ray_madoff/53, accessed 22 February 2012.

Hunt, G. (2003), *The Rich List: Wealth and Enterprise in New Zealand 1820–2003*, Auckland, NZ: Reed Books.

Hurd, H., C. Mason and S. Pinch (1998), 'The geography of corporate philanthropy in the United Kingdom', *Environment and Planning C: Government and Policy*, **16** (1), 3–24.

Irvin, G. (2008), *Super Rich: The Rise of Inequality in Britain and the United States*, Cambridge: Polity Press.

Jacobs, L.R. and T. Skocpol (2006), 'Restoring the tradition of rigor and relevance to political science', *PSOnline*, January, **30** (1), 27–31.

Kapur, A., N. MacLeod, N. Singh, P. Luk, H. Hong and A. Seybert (2005), 'Plutonomy: buying luxury, explaining global imbalances', *The Global Investigator*, Citigroup Global Markets, 14 October.

Kapur, A., N. MacLeod, N. Singh, P. Luk, H. Hong and A. Seybert (2006), 'The plutonomy symposium – rising tides lifting yachts', *The Global Investigator*, Citigroup Global Markets, 29 September.

Kolbert, E. (2006), *Field Notes from a Catastrophe: Man, Nature, and Climate Change*, New York: Bloomsbury.

Kopczuk, W. and E. Saez (2004), 'Top wealth shares in the United States, 1916–2000: evidence from estate tax returns', *National Tax Journal*, **57** (2), 445–87.

Lambert, D. and A. Lester (2004), 'Geographies of colonial philanthropy', *Progress in Human Geography*, **28** (3), 320–41.

Lees, L. (2003), 'Super-gentrification: the case of Brooklyn Heights, New York City', *Urban Studies*, **40** (12), 2487–509.

Leitner, H., J. Peck and E.S. Sheppard (eds) (2007), *Contesting Neoliberalism, Urban Frontiers*, New York: Guildford Press.

Mahtani, S. (2012), 'Singapore no. 1 for millionaires – again', *The Wall Street Journal – South East Asia* (online), http://blogs.wsj.com/searealtime/2012/06/01/singapore-no-1-for-millionaires-again/, 1 June, accessed 6 September 2012.

Mansvelt, J. (2005), *Geographies of Consumption*, London: Sage.

Mansvelt, J. (2010), 'Geographies of consumption: engaging with present absences', *Progress in Human Geography*, **34** (2), 224–33.

Marx, K. and F. Engels (1883), *Manifesto of the Communist Party*, reprinted in R.C. Tucker (ed.) (1978), *The Marx-Engels Reader*, 2nd edn, New York: W.W. Norton, pp. 469–500.

Massey, R. and A. Martin (2011), 'Airlines given permission to fly over North Pole for the first time slashing the hours to exotic destinations', *mailonline*, http://www.dailymail.co.uk/news/article-2078301/Mind-sleigh-Airlines-given-permission-fly-North-Pole-time-slashing-hours-exotic-destinations.html#ixzz1oUWfXunj, accessed 8 March 2012.

McDonald, H. (2012), 'PayPal's bid to create 1000 jobs praised by Irish PM', *The Guardian* (online), 21 February, www.guardian.co.uk/business/2012/feb/21/paypal-create-1000-jobs-irish-pm, accessed 22 February 2012.

Merrill Lynch, Capgemini and Ernst & Young (2002), *World Wealth Report 2001*, www.in.capgemini.com/m/in/. . ./pdf_2001_World_Wealth_Report.pdf, accessed 1 November 2011.

Myers, N. and J. Kent (2004), *The New Consumers: The Influence Of Affluence On The Environment*, Washington, DC: Island Press.

Nader, R. (2009), *Only the Super-rich Can Save Us*, New York: Seven Stories Press.

Neumayer, E. (2004), 'The super-rich in global perspective: a quantitative analysis of the Forbes list of billionaires', *Applied Economics Letters*, **11**, 793–6.

Peck, J. and A. Tickell (2002), 'Neoliberalizing space', *Antipode*, **34** (3), 380–404.

Perrow, C. (2007), *The Next Catastrophe*, Princeton, NJ: Princeton University Press.

Petras, J. (2008), 'Global ruling class: billionaires and how they "make it"', *Journal of Contemporary Asia*, **38** (2), 319–29.

Pilkington, E. (2011), 'Koch brothers: secretive billionaires to launch vast database with 2012 in mind', *theguardian* (online), www.guardian.co.uk/world/2011/nov/07/koch-brothers-database-2012-election, accessed 22 March 2012.

Pow, C-P. (2011), 'Living it up: super-rich enclave and transnational elite urbanism in Singapore', *Geoforum*, **42**, 38293.

Pow, C-P. and L. Kong (2007), 'Marketing the Chinese dream home: gated communities and representations of the good life in (post-)socialist Shanghai', *Urban Geography*, **28** (2), 129–159.

Preston, R. (2012), 'The rich, worried about inequality?', *BBC News* (online), 25 January, www.bbc.co.uk/news/business-16715721, accessed 7 February 2012.

Prince, R.A. and L. Schiff (2008), *The Middle-Class Millionaire. The Rise of the New Rich and How They Are Changing America*, New York: Doubleday.

Rubinstein, W.D. (2004), *The All-Time Australian 200 Rich List*, Sydney, NSW: Allen and Unwin.

Saez, E. (2009), 'Striking it richer: the evolution of top incomes in the United States', www.econ.berkeley.edu/~saez/, accessed 18 May 2010.

Schwartz, N.D. and J. Kanter (2008), 'How many corporate bailouts are too many?', *The New York Times* (online), 8 September, www.nytimes.com/2008/09/08/business/worldbusiness/08iht-big.4.15987307.html, accessed 7 February 2012.

Shaw, W. (1997), 'The spatial concentration of affluence in the United States', *The Geographical Review*, **87** (4), 546–53.

Shear, M.D. (2012), 'Reports show Adelson's enduring support of Gingrich', *The Caucus (The New York Times)* (online), 20 March, http://thecaucus.blogs.nytimes.com/2012/03/20/adelson-continued-to-finance-pro-gingrich-group/, accessed 22 March 2012.

Sullivan, T. (2008), 'Are you rich? How much of a nest egg do you need to join the true elite?', *Barrons* (online), 10 March, http://online.barrons.com/article/SB120493403520820695.html#articleTabs_article%3D1, accessed 5 March 2012.

Taylor, J., D. Harrison and S. Kraus (2009), *The New Elite. Inside the Minds of the Truly Wealthy*, New York: American Management Association.

Urry, J. (2010), 'Consuming the planet to excess', *Theory, Culture and Society*, **27**, 191–212.

US Government (2011), *Budget of the US Government, Summary Tables*, www.gpo.gov/fdsys/search/pagedetails.action?packageId=BUDGET-2012-BUD, accessed 22 December 2011.

Veblen, T. (1908), *The Theory of the Leisure Class: An Economic Study of Institutions*, New York: Macmillan.

Wolpert, J. (1993), *The Structure of Generosity in America*, Washington, DC: Brookings Institution.

Wolpert, J. and T. Reiner (1984), 'The philanthropy marketplace', *Economic Geography*, **60** (3), 197–209.

Woods, M. (2010), 'Rich, rural and rooted? Neoliberalism, neopaternalism and the new transnational geographies of the rural super-rich', paper presented to the annual conference of the *Association of American Geographers*, Washington DC.

Woods, M. (2011), 'The local politics of the global countryside boosterism, aspirational ruralism and the contested reconstitution of Queenstown, New Zealand', *Geojournal*, **76** (4), 365–81.

World Bank (2011), *World Development Indicators 2011*, http://data.worldbank.org/data-catalog/world-development-indicators/wdi-2011, accessed 23 December 2011.

2. Economic wealth and political power in the second Gilded Age

John Rennie Short

INTRODUCTION

The poor are always with us: especially in the discursive spaces of the social sciences where they occupy a position of some prominence. Studies of the marginal are, paradoxically, at the centre of many academic debates. Poverty is a central focus in the social sciences, a concern that compensates for the poor's absence in other discourses yet also reflects issues of positionality and power. Attitudes of deference and authority that work to the advantage and comfort of the researcher are built into the relationship of academics and their impoverished subjects. Status may be further enhanced and reputation burnished by the perception of doing good work, giving voice to the marginalized and perhaps even speaking truth to power. At the end of most academic engagements, however, the sad and dispiriting truth is that the poor remain poor.

There is an asymmetry in our understanding of the contemporary world. We have many more studies of the poor than we have of the rich, especially the very rich. There are many reasons. The rich inhabit spaces not easily accessible to researchers. They restrict access: part of their power is neither to be intimidated nor overly impressed by academic researchers, who invariably have a lower income level and occupy a less vaunted position in the social hierarchy. The rich easily avoid too much scrutiny. The upshot is that while we know a great deal about those at the bottom, the lives of those at the very top of the socio-economic hierarchy remain more opaque (but see Wood 2011). This book is an example of renewed interest in the wealthy. In this chapter I limit my remarks to three areas. First, I suggest that we are in a second Gilded Age, a period of concentrated wealth and increased influence of the very rich. This second Gilded Age – the first came to full force in the late nineteenth century – is intimately connected to globalization and especially financial globalization. Second, I provide some geographic perspectives on the super-rich, arguing that their spatial embodiment is global but still connected to the national and the local. The very rich occupy pivotal positions at a number of spatial scales. Their scalar mobility and multiple spatial connections are both sources and expressions of their wealth. Third, I explore the discursive reach and impact of the rich on political debates, drawing upon the US political arena, but I will also make wider connections where appropriate.

A SECOND GILDED AGE

By any measure we are living in an era where vast riches are concentrated in a few hands. It is legitimate to speak of a superclass of the very rich, who constitute a very influential global elite (Rothkopf 2008). Estimates by Capgemini and Merrill Lynch (2011) indicate that there are close to 103 000 people, classified as ultra high net worth individuals with a net worth greater than US$30 million – an arbitrary figure to be sure but one that is high enough to be suggestive of concentrated wealth. I will refer to them as the super-rich. They can be found all over the world whether it be the incredible wealth of Carlos Slim in Mexico (net worth US$74 billion), Mukesh Ambani in India (net worth US$27 billion) or Bernard Arnault in France (net worth US$41 billion).[1]

At the global level the richest 1 per cent now own almost 40 per cent of global assets, while the richest 2 per cent own 51 per cent (Atkinson 2006). The rich are getting richer in a context of increasing inequality. Some basic facts from the US will function as exemplars of both the concentration of wealth and of growing inequality: in 1985 there were 13 billionaires but by 2008 there were 10 000; a further 49 000 households have a net worth of between US$50 million and US$500 million, while 125 000 have between US$25 million and US$50 million. This is a tiny minority in a country of over 300 million but there are still close to 200 000 households with net worth greater than US$25 million. In the US between 1979 and 2005 the top 1 per cent increased their share of after-tax aggregate income from 7.5 per cent to 14 per cent (Aron-Dine and Sherman 2007). The richest 1 per cent had 9 per cent of national income in the US in 1970, but by 2007, this figure increased to 23.5 per cent. The top 1 per cent of households now controls a quarter of the national income and 40 per cent of its wealth (Stiglitz 2011). Whatever the data used or the measures employed, the result is always the same. The very rich are getting much richer as part of a general redistribution of income towards a small minority. Inequality is increasing as the wealthy and especially the very wealthy capture most of the economic gains of recent decades. Data from the non-partisan Congressional Budget Office (2011) tell the story. Figure 2.1 shows the increasing share of national income held by the richest 20 per cent. Figure 2.2 highlights the

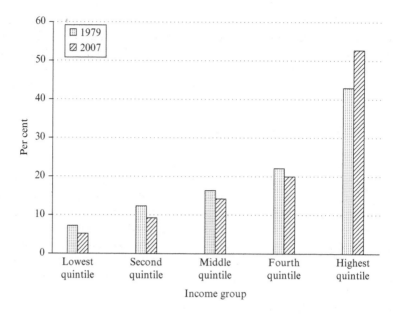

Source: Congressional Budget Office http://www.cbo.gov/doc.cfm?index=12485References.

Figure 2.1   *Shares of income after transfers and federal taxes, 1979 and 2007, USA*

incredible growth of the richest 1 per cent. For the period between 1979 and 2007 the richest 1 per cent increased their after tax income by 275 per cent. For the 60 per cent of households in the middle the increase was 60 per cent and for the 20 per cent in the lowest income group the increase was only 18 per cent. Over the past 20 years more than half of all income growth in the US went to the top richest 1 per cent of households and fully one-third went to the top one-tenth of 1 per cent! The very rich are getting a lot richer in an era of increasing inequality.

It is legitimate to speak of a second Gilded Age (Bartels 2008). The first was the name given to the rapid economic growth and wealth concentration in the US in the last third of the nineteenth century. It is associated with the fortunes of the newly super-rich such as John D. Rockefeller, Andrew Carnegie, John Pierpont Morgan, and Cornelius Vanderbilt. The descriptor also refers to the conspicuous consumption patterns of these wealthy families who were eager to express their new-found riches in the overblown aesthetics of old moneyed European aristocracy, complete with mansions that looked like chateaux, summer lodges that resembled castles and furnishings that included suits of armour and the recently purchased

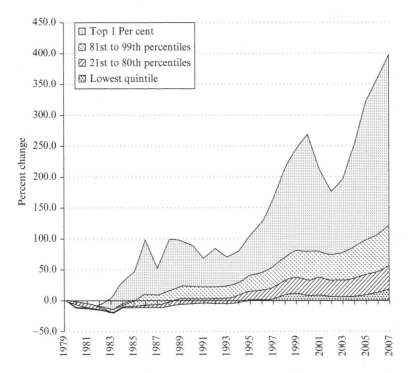

Source: Congressional Budget Office http://www.cbo.gov/doc.cfm?index = 12485References.

*Figure 2.2   Cumulative growth in average after-tax income, by income
group, 1979–2007, USA*

libraries of the impecunious aristocracy of Europe. Economic capital was
turned into cultural capital. Rich American heiresses became sought after
brides for the relatively poor English aristocracy to produce a literal marriage of money and breeding. It was in this setting that Thorstein Veblen
(2007) wrote *The Theory of The Leisure Class*, where he outlined his ideas
of conspicuous consumption and conspicuous leisure. The consumption
of the very rich, he noted, centred on status. Consumption patterns were
less about maximizing utility and more about signifying class position.

Table 2.1 summarizes some of the similarities and differences between
the two Gilded Ages. The table compresses complex arguments into simple
binaries. A more nuanced account could expand them further. A major
difference between the first and second Gilded Age, for example, occurs in
the justification and representation of wealth. In the first it was considered
appropriate, indeed mandatory, for the very wealthy to have a leisured

Table 2.1   Comparing the Gilded Ages

Characteristics	First Gilded Age	Second Gilded Age
Highpoint	1890s	1990–2012
Dominant ideology	Social Darwinism	Neoliberalism
Dominant sector	Industrial capitalism	Financial capitalism
Main sites of old money/new money	UK/USA	USA/China
Aesthetics	Extravagant opulence	Understated opulence
Emblematic figures	Andrew Carnegie	Warren Buffett
Key ideologues	Herbert Spencer	Rupert Murdoch
Important trends	Industrialization	Globalization, deregulation
Social expression	Conspicuous consumption	Wealth as reward for work

life. Distance from work signalled achievement and status. In the second, by contrast, the emphasis is on work. In order for wealth to be justified by something other than itself, notions of hard work, sacrifice and ability are continually invoked. In the discursive space of the second Gilded Age the 'hardworking rich' replace the 'idle rich'. When pressed by British MPs in the summer of 2011 at the height of the phone hacking scandal, Rupert Murdoch (US$7.6 billion) stated that he worked long, hard hours. People earning minimum wage also work long and hard hours. In the second Gilded Age wealth is justified with reference to ability and industry rather than birth, luck or connections.

One similarity between the two Gilded Ages is the ideological under-pinning used to support the massive concentration of wealth. In the first Gilded Age Social Darwinism became a well-used justification for the extremes of wealth. Rather than social outcomes they were the result of 'natural' processes of survival of the economically fittest. Fast forward over a hundred years to the founder of the world's largest hedge fund, Ray Dalio (US$5 billion). He gives each new employee of the Bridgewater Associates hedge fund, with over US$75 billion under management, a 100-page text that he wrote entitled, *Distributed Principles* (Cassidy 2011). It reads as if Herbert Spencer could have written it with its ideas of natural selection as they apply to business. In the first as in the second Gilded Age, wealth is justified not simply as a result of luck or connections, but as a 'natural' phenomenon and hence immune to political change or social debate.

The first Gilded Age owed its wealth to rapid industrialization. In the new Gilded Age, there are both traditional and new forms of wealth pro-duction; we can consider four. The first is in the ownership and control of global commodities. In the carbon-based economy, oil and natural gas provide sources of considerable wealth as global markets' demand for these resources steadily increase and ownership tends to be monopolistic. The entry of China with its huge import demands for energy and raw materials has reinforced the upward arc of global demand. Elites in control of such resources thus have access to huge rewards. The riches of the Saudi royal family are the most obvious example. Prince Alwaleed Bin Talal Alsaud, a nephew of the Saudi King, has a net worth of US$19.6 billion. In primary export-producing countries the greatest wealth lies in the ownership and control of primary commodities. The two richest Australians are Georgina Rinehart (US$9 billion), whose wealth derives from inheritance and high iron ore prices, and Andrew Forrest (US$6.7 billion), a mining tycoon.

The second is the ownership, control and management of finances. Financial globalization has created huge opportunities for super profits to be made. Warren Buffett (net worth US$50 billion) makes his fortune by buying and selling stocks and shares. Money in the concentrated form of capital generates more money. In the early twentieth century, the Austrian economist Rudolf Hilferding (1981) proposed that a new form of capitalism was taking hold. In his book, *Das Finanzkapital* (*Finance Capitalism*), he ventured that the increasing concentration of economic activity and banking into larger and larger combines was effectively producing a new form of capitalism, the finance capitalism of the book's title. Because this new form of capitalism controlled the flow of investment, he suggested that it was displacing competitive industrial capitalism while creating a demand for a centralizing and 'privilege-dispensing state'. According to Hilferding, finance capitalism was always on the lookout for state intervention to prop up its wealth and privilege. Fast-forward almost 100 years and we can see the full unfolding of Hilferding's prescience.

The financial sector in the US has grown both absolutely and relatively, now occupying a position of centrality and dominance. The sector was responsible for only 15 per cent of corporate profits in 1980 but reached 33 per cent in 2003. Not only was the sector as whole growing in size, but so also were the individual firms. By 2007 Citigroup had US$2.2 trillion in assets while Goldman Sachs had US$1.1 trillion. With this concentration of capital came increased compensation. By 2007 compensation in the financial sector was 80 per cent greater than in other business sectors. Twenty years previously they were approximately equivalent.

The financial services sector binds government to its needs and requirements through the slick passages of individuals who move effortlessly and often from finance to government and back again. There is a revolving door of people moving between major financial institutions and senior government positions. Robert Rubin, for example, worked at Goldman Sachs for 26 years before becoming Treasury Secretary under Clinton. He

worked furiously to promote deregulation before moving on to Citibank
where his eight-year tenure netted US$126 million in cash and stock.
Hank Paulson rose to CEO of Goldman Sachs. In 2006 President Bush
appointed him as Treasury Secretary: at the time his net worth was valued
at around US$600–$700 million. Then, after years of calling for less government regulation and involvement in the financial markets, in 2008
he led the effort to give US$700 billion of taxpayer money to financial
institutions through the Troubled Asset Relief Program. Goldman Sachs
received US$10 billion in the scheme. Rubin's colleague at Treasury,
Larry Summers, moved from a lucrative hedge fund position to advising
Barack Obama. Simon Johnson (2009) writes of a quiet coup as the US
government is hijacked by the finance industry. There is the *regulatory
capture* in which the agencies meant to protect the public from financial
misdeeds do little to very little or too little too late. The banks and financial institutions also achieve *cognitive capture*. Their interests were and
still are seen as tantamount to the national interest. Deregulation was
vigorously promoted before the financial crash and regulation is strongly
resisted since the crash.

In his analysis of global inequality Galbraith (2010) finds that inequality increases the more an economy becomes dominated by the financial
services sector. The more the financial sector grows absolutely and relatively in an economy the greater the inequality (Madrick 2011). There is a
synergistic causality between the rise of finance, government deregulation
and rising inequality.

Third, there is the ownership of successful companies. Just as in the
first Gilded Age the fortunes of the second Gilded Age are still made in
the sectors such as steel. India is now a major steel producer and Lakshmi
Mittal (net worth US$31.1 billion) is the richest man in India with his
fortune largely made in the family steel business. Fortunes are also possible in new expanding sectors. In the *Forbes* list of the richest people in
the world, Bill Gates (Microsoft, net worth US$56 billion), Larry Ellison
(Oracle, net worth US$39.5 billion), Larry Page (Google, net worth
US$19.8 billion) and Sergey Brin (Google, net worth US$19.8 billion) are
ranked 2nd, 5th and 24th and 25th respectively, giving us an indication of
the rapid growth and high profits of the computer software sector. Mark
Zuckerman, founder of Facebook has a net worth of US$17.5 billion
making him the 14th richest person in the world.

The fourth and perhaps surest way to be wealthy is to have very wealthy
parents and grandparents. Liliane Bettencourt (US$23.5 billion) owes
her fortune to her father founding the successful cosmetic company of
L'Oréal. Christy Walton (US$26.5 billion), Jim Walton (US$21.3 billion),
Alice Walton (US$21.2 billion) and S. Ronson Walton (US$21 billion)

owe their considerable fortunes, making them 10th, 20th, 21st and 22nd wealthiest people in the world, not to hard work or inventiveness but to the simple fact that their father was Sam Walton, founder of Wal-Mart.

Two interlinked processes aid the concentration of wealth in this second Gilded Age. The first is globalization that allows an upward scalability in turnover, revenue and hence profit generation. As economic transactions are less restricted to individual countries, the very rich become richer with an extension and deepening of their profit sources and a widening of their income streams. As the world flattens, the sources of wealth generation become larger and more lucrative. Karl Albrecht (US$25.5 billion), for example, expanded his grocery chain from southern Germany to the UK, Australia and then the US. New pools of wealth concentration also occur in rapidly expanding economies with increased global connectivities. As China's economy has grown and globalized, so the number of wealthy has increased. In 2004 there were only four billionaires in the entire country; by 2011 there were 95. Globalization powers the upward escalator for the rich, the creation of a new middle class in developing countries and the downward movement of the middle and lower income groups in the developed economies. While globalization has different effects in the middle and lower registers of the income scale of different countries, it tends to have the same effect at the upper levels: the rich get a lot richer.

The second and intimately related process is the implementation of a neoliberal agenda involving privatization of national assets, deregulation of capital controls and encouragement of wealth accumulation (Plant 2009; Steger and Roy 2010). The adoption of neoliberalism leads to privatization of large public utilities, state enterprises and publicly owned assets that provide the opportunity for quick and massive profits. The privatization of public assets is often marked by a cronyism and rigging that aids the already well connected. Many privatizations have not resulted in market efficiencies but in personal enrichment. For example, the majority of Russian billionaires, 101 in 2011, have as their original and major sources of wealth, the privatization of the national resource base. Vagit Alekperov (US$13.9 billion) was a deputy minister in the Soviet oil industry. After 1989 he gained control of three ministry-controlled oil fields and established his own oil company, Lukoil. Roman Abramovich (US$13.4 billion) owes his wealth to the privatization of the Soviet/Russian public oil company that he acquired at a fraction of its real worth. The richest man in the world Carlos Slim (US$74 billion) owes some of his vast fortune to the privatization of the Mexican public telephone system.

Globalization, deregulation and privatization generate a more pronounced marketization – that is, a deepening and widening commoditization of goods, services and products – that in turn generates more profit making opportunities that are appropriated by the wealthy. Neoliberalism is an accelerant to wealth concentration and a cause of growing inequality.

STAYING SUPER-RICH

Wealth begets even more wealth. The super-rich have advantages by virtue of their wealth. In addition to exclusive vacation spots, private jets, personal staff, priority status, and financial perks from credit card companies and retailers, the super-rich enjoy greater economic, social, and political access that allows them to expand and protect their wealth. They often serve on the boards of their business associates, make campaign contributions, and donate to charitable causes – actions that allow them to improve their public image and to expand their social and political influence. They receive special executive perks like stock options, bonuses, and insurance. They are able to network from their passage through elite schools, and they expand their networks through attendance at exclusive international forums and conferences. Because the super-rich are a highly sought-after group of consumers of financial services, they typically pay the lowest fees and have access to customized investment packages upon request from mutual fund managers. The super-rich do not need to understand the increasing complexity of financial markets because they can afford the most qualified financial management teams to diversify and hedge their investments for them. They have access to alternative investments (venture capital funds, private equity funds, and direct commodity investments) that are restricted by law to accredited investors or households with over US$1 million. The super-rich also have access to estate planning services and offshore tax havens, which allow them to protect their wealth across generations. Because of the scale of their holdings, the super-rich have staying power in turbulent economic times when other investors are forced to sell off assets (Steverman 2010).

GEOGRAPHIC PERSPECTIVES ON THE SUPER-RICH

The super-rich inhabit multiple spaces. They occupy the fast lane of the flattened world: not simply flying at the front of commercial aircraft but owning their own planes. Moving through VIP lounges and residing in luxury enclaves, they inhabit transnational spaces that some have called Richistan (Frank 2007). This is not a single place, or individual country; it is a separate universe of privileged sites scattered around the world. The very rich have the lightness of a smooth mobility that allows them to criss-cross the globe but enough political and economic weight to have a heavy influence on their local areas, national societies and global discourses.

One image of the global rich depicts them as free floating above the earth, permanently in first class, or flying the corporate jet or in the private plane. To some extent that reflects their global connectivity, and for many the wealth allows an untethered lifestyle, but for most, their lives are lived at a variety of scales. The ability to live anywhere in the world is counterposed by the need to have a national presence. Georgina Rinehart, who inherited a mining conglomerate and turned it around – helped in no small measure by escalating iron ore prices and China's insatiable demand – has enough money to live anywhere in the world. However, the basis of her wealth is quite literally in the Australian ground. When the Australian government proposed a new super tax she, along with fellow billionaire Andrew Forrest, mounted a campaign against the tax. As Iain Hay notes in this volume, she subsequently purchased an interest in a television network that furthers her anti-tax message. Billionaires who derive their fortune from specific countries need to attend to these countries. Another Australian-born mogul, Rupert Murdoch, had to obtain US citizenship in order to expand his media empire in the US.

The rich have global fortunes and may have national identities but they also inhabit local sites. Their considerable wealth often means that they have a high impact on very local places. Take the case of Roger Ailes. As chairman and CEO of Fox News, he made around US$23 million in 2009. Several years earlier he decided to buy a 9000-square-foot (836 square metres) residence in the small town of Garrison in rural New York State only 90 minutes from Manhattan. Unhappy with the reporting in the local newspaper, he did what any really rich person could do: he bought the two local newspapers, the *Putnam County News and Recorder* and the *Putnam Country Courier*, installing his wife as manager and hiring a new editor and news staff. Disappointed with security arrangements he purchased more property to give him and his family a security buffer. Displeased with the zoning rules he turned up at a local meeting with a high priced attorney and essentially forced the county supervisor to change the land use zoning regulations (Boyer 2011). Roger Ailes had enough money to transform Garrison into his own private and privatized image of small town America.

DISCURSIVE PRACTICES OF THE SUPER-RICH

The wealth of the super-rich is also expressed by their ability to affect global consumption patterns, national communities and local practices.

Their power is reflected both in their location in specific places, and their power to affect space and discourses at the global, national and local levels.

While the very wealthy may or may not secure specific political outcomes they do get to set the terms of the debate. This discursive power resides at multiple levels and exhibits a variety of forms. At the global level we can consider the case of Bill Gates, the second richest man in the world, with an estimated fortune of US$56 billion. Gates gave US$30 billion of his fortune to establish the Bill and Melinda Gates Foundation that focuses on curing tuberculosis, polio and other diseases prevalent in developing countries. Gates' actions highlight some of the progressive strains among the very wealthy and in this particular case their ability to influence the direction of global health policy.

At a continental level, the billionaire Mo Ibrahim tries to shape politics in Africa. He established the Ibrahim Prize in 2006 that awards five million dollars to an elected African leader who promotes democracy, acts honestly and leaves office willingly. The prize also awards a lifetime grant of US$200 000 per annum. Ibrahim, born in north Sudan, made his fortune from establishing a successful company selling mobile phones in Africa. His net worth is estimated around US$2 billion. He lives most of the time in Monaco where there are substantial tax benefits, but also has residences in Monte Carlo, Cairo, London, and Khartoum (Auletta 2011). He embodies how the super-rich are entrenched in the prominent enclaves of privilege yet traverse transnational spaces with frictionless mobility and also influence wider political discourses.

At the national level the very rich are involved directly and indirectly in influencing policies and agendas. Their involvement is particularly visible in the US where there are few restrictions on campaign funding yet often stringent reporting requirements. The US thus provides a transparent example of the political power of the super-rich in democratic societies. For example, Steve Forbes (net estimated worth US$430 million)[2] a former presidential contender whose policies were largely restricted to imposing a flat tax and eliminating all capital gains tax, gives money to the right wing Heritage Foundation that is devoted to promoting 'free enterprise' and limiting government, funds anti-union campaigns and advises Republican candidates for the Presidency and Congress. A contender for the Republican presidential nomination in 2012 was Mitt Romney whose fortune, made working at a private equity firm that symbolizes the power of finance capitalism, was estimated between US$200–250 million The return on his investments provide an annual income of over US$20 million.

Massive wealth does not guarantee political success. Meg Whitman

(US$1.3 billion) made her fortune working for eBay and cashing in lucrative stock options. The financial reward enabled her to run for the governorship of California in the 2010 election. It was her first foray into politics. She had even not voted for 28 years. It is estimated that she spent US$163 million of her own money in the failed bid. Her campaign suffered a setback when it was announced that she employed an undocumented worker as a nanny. After her defeat she joined the boards of Hewlett Packard and Proctor and Gamble.

Meg Whitman's defeat notwithstanding, the rich are also well represented directly in the political process in the US. While the median net worth of members of the US Congress more than doubled from US$280 000 in 1984 to US$725 000 in 2009 (in 2009 dollars), the median family income declined slightly from US$20 600 to US$20 500 (Whoriskey 2011). In other words, over the past 25 years, while members of Congress doubled their incomes, the income of the average US family declined. Income disparity between the governing and the governed has widened into a vast chasm. The governing are getting much richer while the governed are getting much poorer. Take the freshman class of the US Congress, newly elected after the mid-term elections in 2010. While only 1 per cent of Americans are worth more than US$1 million, more than 60 per cent of the Senate freshman and 40 per cent of the House freshman are worth that amount. The new Senator from Connecticut, Richard Blumenthal, has an estimated net worth of US$95 million, while in the House, Dianne Lynn Black of Tennessee is worth close to US$50 million. Neither of these new politicians was close to the top of the Congress' rich list. Darrell Issa, a senior Republican from California, has an average net worth of US$303 million, and another Californian, Jane Harman, a Democrat had US$293 million. The average wealth for all members of the Senate is US$13.6 million and for the House US$3.4 million. Wealth does not influence the specific votes of individual members: the third and fourth richest members of Congress, John Kerry (US$238 million) and Mark Warner (US$174 million) are considered more liberal Democrats. However, the bias in political representation to those with wealth has an impact on how politicians see and understand the world. As Joseph Stiglitz (2011) wryly notes, most members of Congress are in the top 1 per cent, they tend to be financed by the top 1 per cent and invariably are employed by the top 1 per cent after they leave office. As the political class looks more like the economic elites, it is no surprise then that the past thirty years has seen a steady reduction of taxes for the wealthy, regressive social policies and a resultant shift in national income and wealth towards the rich and very rich. Even one of the richest men in the world, Warren Buffett, argued for Congress to stop protecting the super-rich from any notion of shared sacrifice. In an op-ed piece in *The New York Times*, he wrote, 'My friends and I have been coddled long enough by a billionaire-friendly Congress' (Buffett 2011).

The super-rich also fund the popularization of anti-government and small government ideologies in the US. The rise of neoliberalism and its enthusiastic adoption in the US is connected to the discursive and political impact of the super-rich. The largest private company in the US is Koch Industries, owned by two brothers, Charles and David Koch. Each year the company, with interests in oil, paper, timber and textiles generate revenues of around a hundred billion dollars. The Koch brothers' net worth is estimated at US$22 billion each, making them the 18th richest people on the planet. They believe fervently in low taxation, minimal environmental regulation and limited spending on social services (Mayer 2010). As rich owners of a company with a heavy environmental impact their personal interests neatly dovetail with their political philosophies. They are the biggest single donors, even outdoing ExxonMobil, in funding research that questions the basic validity of human-induced global warming. Over the years they have funded extreme right wing groups, including David Koch's run for vice president of the Libertarian Party in 1980. The platform called for abolition of Social Security, minimum wage, all personal and corporate taxes and most of the government's regulatory organizations such as the Department of Energy, and the Securities and Exchange Commission. The only role of government in this manifesto was the protection of individual rights. After this unsuccessful direct entry into the political process the Koch brothers decided to be more indirect and to influence the discourse rather than promote their own candidacy. Their money funds a number of right-leaning organizations and institutions. Between 1986 and 1993 they donated US$11 million to the Cato Institute which according to its own website (2012) is dedicated to 'the principles of individual liberty, limited government, free markets and peace'. They provide financial support to a number of centres that promote deregulation and the abolition of environmental controls such as the Citizens for the Environment and the Mercatus Center at George Mason University in Virginia. They have also used their considerable fortune to fund the Americans for Prosperity Foundation that worked assiduously to promote and fashion the populist, conservative Tea Party movement into a viable political force. Their political philosophy now has the legitimation of a mass movement. Their far right views on small minimal government are now part of the political mainstream and everyday discourse in the US.

Because of the tight nexus in the US political system that links money and politics, the very rich are also involved in specific policy issues. There are many examples of the very rich using their wealth to influence policies that affect their immediate interests. Take the case of the Fanjul brothers, Alfonso and Jose, whose net combined worth is US$1 billion. They own vast sugar interests in the US and overseas. They own Domino Sugar as well as Tate and Lyle. They make major contributions to both the Democrat and Republican parties at the state and federal level. It is not accidental that the sugar industry in the US is a favoured industry with guaranteed price supports, strictly enforced import quotas that keep out foreign competition and labour exemptions that allow the company to use cheap, imported labour on a temporary basis (Johnson 2006). The Fanjul brothers' experience remind us, if we need reminding, that the golden rule of politics is that those with the gold get to make the rules.

Dick DeVos is son of a cofounder of Amway, with a personal fortune estimated at around $500 million. Despite the poor performance of school voucher programmes, the DeVos family has waged an enormously expensive covert political campaign through a network of various think tanks and advocacy groups pushing these programmes. They coordinated a plan to have politicians and advocates refer to public schools as 'government schools'. At a Heritage Foundation conference in 2002, Dick DeVos proposed a behind-the-scenes system of political rewards and punishments to pressure politicians to support voucher programmes. The DeVos family use their wealth to push for the privatization of public education (Tabachnick 2011).

The very wealthy can, in the right circumstances, shift the agenda of political discourse. In a political system like the US where there are no real limits on campaign contributions and a very expensive and constant cycle of campaigns, the very rich through bankrolling candidates and funding campaigns have great political power in electing politicians and influencing the tenor of the political debate. While voters exercise political choice the very rich wield political power. The rise of the very wealthy and the rightward shift in US politics is neither accidental nor random. The very rich, eager to maintain and increase their wealth, have used their power to shift the debate ever rightwards so that even democratic politicians now find it difficult to promote or defend a state concerned with redistribution and the social good against assaults on what is now effectively labelled as 'big government', the 'heavy hand' of government regulations and the 'burdens' of personal and especially corporate taxation.

Of course, for the super-rich, the 'problem' of government can turn into the business opportunity afforded by government. Take the case of billionaire Philip Anschutz (net worth US$ 7 billion) who owns 150 private companies, funds anti-union activity and supports the Koch brothers' American for Prosperity. His ideological resistance to government does not extend to his own business deals. He owns large swathes of downtown

Los Angeles and has worked to get the city to seize the private property (of others) and issue US$300 000 000 worth of bonds to help him build a sports arena for an American football team franchise (Bruck 2012). The bonds will be paid by city funds usually earmarked for essential services such as police and fire departments.

CONCLUSIONS: CHALLENGES AND RESISTANCES TO THE SUPER-RICH

The contention of this chapter is that we are in a second Gilded Age, a period of rising inequality, accumulated wealth and the increasing power of the super-rich to influence political discourses. This power and influence is especially clear in societies such as the US where the direct connections between politics, power and wealth, policy and influence are more transparent. In the US, but also in many other countries the discursive power of the super-rich is evident and embodied in the entrenchment of a neoliberalism that encourages privatization, deregulation, marketization and globalization. These practices, in turn, lead to greater concentration of wealth in the hands of a few and increased inequality.

The first Gilded Age came to an end with the rise of the Keynesian-New Deal compromise that, in the richer countries at least, saw rising standards of living across the social spectrum, a more equal distribution of wealth and greater political democratization. Part of the legacy remains so that the second Gilded Age is not a simple reprise, it unfolds in the resistances institutionalized against the first Gilded Age. This base for resistance and challenge to the increasing power of the super-rich is also being widened and deepened by new social forces across the globe. The Arab Spring that began in December 2010 is too often seen in broad geopolitical terms, the movement often captured in narrative form as a popular rising against despotism. Yet it was also a protest against accumulated wealth and forms of neoliberalization that hardened income inequalities. Protest is also occurring, even in the US where the ideological commitment to market capitalism and individualism is more entrenched. In September 2011 a protest movement with the slogan 'We are the 99%' occupied Zuccotti Park in New York City. Protestors drew attention to increasing inequality and the corrupting influence of the financial service sector. The Occupy movement went national and international as protestors around the world occupied public spaces. Just as the second Gilded Age created the forces that overturned it, we may be witnessing the beginning of global and globalizing social movements that contest the second Gilded Age. From Arab Spring to American Autumn and other movements to come, the trajectory of resistance and contestation continues. The super-rich have more power and influence, but their power is not total, their influence is not all encompassing and their victory is not assured. The second Gilded Age, like the first, will not last forever.

NOTES

1. These and subsequent figures in this chapter are taken from the 2011 list of billionaires (http://www.forbes.com/wealth/billonaires). What it lacks in absolute precision it makes up for in providing an accessible, comparative, global metric of concentrated wealth.
2. Despite owning *Forbes* and publishing the annual list of the world's wealthiest people, he does not list his own asset worth.

REFERENCES

Aron-Dine, A. and A. Sherman (2007), 'New CBO data show income inequality continues to widen: after-tax-income for top 1 percent rose by $146 000 in 2004', Center on Budget and Policy Priorities, 23 January, www.cbpp.org/cms/?fa=view&id=957, accessed 1 August 2011.

Atkinson, A.B. (2006), 'Concentration among the rich', UN University – World Institute for Development Economics Research, www.wider.unu.edu/publications/working-papers/research-papers/2006/en_GB/rp2006-151/ accessed 13 February 2012.

Auletta, L. (2011), 'The dictator index', *The New Yorker*, 7 March, 44–55.

Barkun, M. (2003), *A Culture of Conspiracy: Apocalyptic Visions in Contemporary America*, Berkeley, CA: University of California Press.

Bartels, L.M. (2008), *Unequal Democracy: The Political Economy of the New Gilded Age*, Princeton, NJ: Princeton University Press.

Bowles, S., H. Gintis and M.O. Groves (2005), *Unequal Chances: Family Background and Economic Success*, New York: Russell Sage Foundation.

Boyer, P. (2011), 'Fox among the chickens: Roger Ailes's upstate newspaper war', *The New Yorker*, 31 January, 52–61.

Bruck, C. (2012), 'The man who owns L.A.: a secretive mogul's entertainment kingdom', *The New Yorker*, 16 January, 46–57.

Buffett, W. (2011), 'Stop coddling the super-rich', *The New York Times* (online), 14 August, www.nytimes.com/2011/08/15/opinion/stop-coddling-the-super-rich.html, accessed 15 August 2011.

Capgemini and Merrill Lynch, (2011), *World Wealth Report 2011*, www.capgemini.com/insights-and-resources/by-publication/world-wealth-report-2011/?ftcnt=10120, accessed 1 November 2011.

Cassidy, J. (2011), 'Mastering the machine: how Ray Dalio built the world's richest and strangest hedge fund', *The New Yorker*, 25 July, 56–65.

Cato Institute (2012), 'Cato Institute. individual liberty, free markets, and peace', www.cato.org/about.php, accessed 17 May 2012.

Congressional Budget Office (2011), 'Trends in the distribution of household income between 1979 and 2007', www.cbo.gov/doc.cfm?index=12485, accessed 13 February 2012.

Frank, R. (2007), *Richistan: A Journey Through The American Wealth Boom and The Lives of The New Rich*, New York: Three Rivers Press.

Galbraith, J.K. (2010), 'Inequality and economic and political change: a comparative perspective', *Cambridge Journal of Regions, Economy and Society*, **4** (1), 1–15.

Hilferding, R. (1981), *Finance Capital: A Study of the Latest Phase of Capitalist Development*, London: Routledge and Kegan Paul.

Johnson, J. (2006), *The One Percent*, HBO Documentary Films, www.theonepercentdocumentary.com/, accessed 10 February 2012.

Johnson, S. (2009) 'The quiet coup', *Atlantic Magazine* (online), May, www.theatlantic.com/doc/200905/imf-advice, accessed 9 August 2011.

Lizza, R. (2009), 'Money talks', *The New Yorker* (online), 4 May, www.newyorker.com/reporting/2009/05/04/090504fa_fact_lizza, accessed 1 August 2011.

Madrick, J. (2011), *Age of Greed: The Triumph of Finance and the Decline of America, 1970 to the Present*, New York: Knopf.

Mayer, J. (2010), 'Covert operations', *The New Yorker* (online), 30 August, www.newyorker.com/reporting/2010/08/30/100830fa_fact_mayer?printable=true, accessed 1 August 2011.

Mills, C.W. (1956), *The Power Elite*, New York: Oxford University Press.

Plant, R. (2009), *The Neo-liberal State*, Oxford: Oxford University Press.

Rothkopf, D.J. (2008), *Superclass: The Global Power Elite and The World They Are Making*, New York: Farrar, Straus and Giroux.

Steger, M.B. and R.K. Roy (2010), *Neoliberalism: A Very Short Introduction*, Oxford: Oxford University Press.

Steverman, B. (2010), 'Secret financial weapons of the super-rich', *Bloomberg Business Week* (online), 15 December, http://images.businessweek.com/slideshows/20101214/secret-financial-weapons-of-the-super-rich/, accessed 1 August 2011.

Stiglitz, J. (2011), 'Of the 1%, by the 1%, and for the 1%', *Vanity Fair* (online), May, www.vanityfair.com/society/features/2011/05/top-one-percent201105?printable=true&currentPage=all&wpisrc=nl_wonk, accessed 1 August 2011.

Tabachnick, R. (2011), 'The DeVos family: meet the super-wealthy right-wingers working with the religious right to kill public education', *AlterNet*, posted 6 May 2011, www.alternet.org/module/printversion/150868, accessed 2 August 2011.

Veblen, T. (2007), *The Theory of the Leisure Class*, Oxford: Oxford University Press.

Whoriskey, P. (December 27 2011), 'Congress looks less like rest of America', *The Washington Post*, A1 and A4.

Wood, G. (2011), 'Secret fears of the super-rich', *The Atlantic* (online), April, www.theatlantic.com/magazine/archive/2011/04/secret-fears-of-the-super-rich/8419/, accessed 1 August 2011.

3. Overseeing the fortunes of the global super-rich: the nature of private wealth management in London's financial district

Jonathan V. Beaverstock, Sarah J.E. Hall and Thomas Wainwright

INTRODUCTION

> The upsurge in private wealth in the 1990s, driven by economic growth and buoyant stockmarkets, generated new interest in private clients on the part of asset management firms and other City services providers, notably lawyers and accountancy firms. Many formed (or revitalised) private banking operations in an endeavour to get a piece of the booming market in private wealth management. (Roberts 2008, p. 157)

Up until the early-1980s, the sleepy world of private banking remained a 'gentlemanly' affair serving its traditional clientele: royalty, the landed gentry, industrialists and entrepreneurs and, latterly from, for example, the 1970s, the billionaires and millionaires from the Middle East and other foreign jurisdictions (see Maude and Molyneux 1996). But this cosy world of private banking came under fierce competition following the discovery of the private wealth of individuals by wholesale banks and professional service accounting, legal and insurance firms. Financial deregulation on Wall Street and in London from the mid-1980s, combined with the longest running bull market during the 2000s, created astronomical levels of individual private wealth which needed to be 'managed'. In short, the private wealth management sector grew to service this ever-expanding market. Referring back to Roberts (2008), it is no surprise that many banking, financial and professional services wanted to enter what was to become a new financial services market for the global super-rich, private wealth management (Beaverstock et al. 2012).

Over the last 20 years, London, New York, Singapore and Hong Kong have become the most important onshore international financial centres (IFCs) for the investment and management of private wealth (International Financial Services London [IFSL] 2009). Their prominence as global centres has been produced by both demand- and supply-side factors. On the demand-side, their standing has been shaped by the unprecedented rise in the number of US dollar, euro and sterling million and billionaires, the so-called, 'global super-rich' (Beaverstock et al. 2004; also see Hay and Muller 2012). The recent growth in the global super-rich has been driven by the emergence of a new cadre of financial elites and entrepreneurs from the 1980s, who were central to the development of finance-led capitalism (see Froud and Williams 2007; Hall 2009). In contrast, on the supply-side, these financial centres have enhanced their global significance for the investment of private wealth, which has accounted for the rapid development and expansion of the private wealth management sector (Maude 2006), competing with traditional private banking as a means of providing financial services to the wealthy.

In essence, the role of traditional private banking involved retail banking for the rich, providing current and savings accounts, rudimentary asset management, tax advice and limited brokerage, supplied in a close relationship with one or very few managers (see Maude and Molyneux 1996). In contrast, the contemporary private wealth management sector now transcends private banking involving an array of financial and professional services, reaching across: other banking sectors (retail and investment) and financial services (for example, hedge fund management); accounting; insurance; legal services; real estate; and specialist brokerage firms (see Maude 2006). In addition, in terms of organizational structure, the contemporary private wealth management sector is composed of both transnational conglomerates, who supply a range of the services listed above; and 'single-line', specialist firms, which could be small and medium sized enterprises or transnational corporations (TNCs) (see IFSL 2009). However, while the role of private banking has been widely documented in London and Europe, the growth and functionality of the relatively new private wealth management sector, encompassing global, foreign and investment banks, and a range of professional services like accounting, insurance and law, in London and other IFCs, has been comparatively neglected.

In response, the aim of this chapter is to document the rise and structure of the private wealth management retail financial services sector which has been established to service the burgeoning global super-rich. In order to explain the organizational nature of the City of London's (used to denote the entirety of London's financial district, including the West End and Canary Wharf) private wealth management sector, we draw on an original survey of its retail provision which is specifically tailored for the super-rich (financial products such as yacht and art insurance; and named services such as fund management). The rest of the chapter is organized into four parts. First, we outline a significant demand-side factor in the growth of the private wealth management sector: the rise of the High Net Worth Individual (HNWI) market. Second, we account for the City of London's leading position in the supply of private wealth management. Third, we report an original empirical study of London's private wealth management retail provision in accounting, banking (global/universal, private and investment), legal services and insurance. Finally, we offer several conclusions.

THE RISE OF THE HIGH NET WORTH INDIVIDUAL AND GLOBAL PRIVATE WEALTH

The genesis of the contemporary private wealth management financial services sector is founded on the response of retail financial and professional services to supply expert advice and new products to a rapidly burgeoning pool of private wealthy individuals from around the globe, but particularly from the US and Europe from the mid-1980s. The specific identification of a new financial market for the super-rich, defined as the High Net Worth Market, has become a financial classification in its own right to define and segment the wealthy by their liquid or investable assets (that is, those investments than can be readily converted into cash, excluding primary residential property). Capgemini Merrill Lynch Global Wealth Management [CMLGWM] (2011) identifies the HNWI as a person who has investable assets greater than US$1 million and regards Ultra-High Net Worth Individuals (UHNWI) as those with more than US$30 million in investable assets. Many investment banks' wealth management subsidiaries (for example, Barclays Wealth) and accounting firms (for example, PricewaterhouseCoopers) have their own definitions of the HNW market, which essentially mimics the segmentation of the CMLGWM definition into, 'wealth pyramids'. These many definitions and segmentations of the HNW market are neatly summarized by the IFSL (2009) 'think tank' as:

- Ultra high net worth individuals (NWIs), with over US$30 million of investable assets.
- Very high NWIs with over US$5 million of assets.
- High NWIs with over US$1 million of assets.
- Mass affluent with assets of over US$100 000.

But, after CMLGWM (and *Forbes* magazine's various lists of the most wealthy, see *Forbes*, 2011), a second influential indicator of the market segmentation of wealth and assets under management (AuM) is derived from the Boston Consulting Group (BCG) (2011), who define global wealth as:

- Ultra-high net worth households (more than US$100 million in AuM).
- Established wealthy (more than US$5 million in AuM).
- Emerging wealthy (US$1 million to US$5 million in AuM).
- Affluent (US$100 000 to US$1 million in AuM).

By analysing time-series data on the stock, share and distribution of global HNWIs and private wealth sourced from CMLGWM and intelligence from the financial sector that charts the rise of the 'bonus culture', we illustrate the conditions for an aggregated demand for the provision of a 'new' retail private wealth management market.

CMLGWM's High Net Worth Market: Growth and Geography

In 1996 Capgemini Merrill Lynch (CML) (2007) estimated that there were 4.5 million HNWIs globally, with an accumulated wealth of US$16.6 trillion. By 2010, the number of HNWIs had increased by 142 per cent (6.4 million) to an all-time high of 10.9 million, and the value of global wealth by 157 per cent (US$ 26.1 trillion) to US$42.7 trillion (CML 2007; CMLGWM 2011). The global super-rich have shown significant recovery from the aftermath of the 2007–8 global financial crisis. Between 2008–10, the number of HNWIs increased by 27 per cent, from 8.6 million to 10.9 million, and their wealth grew by almost a third (30 per cent), from US$32.8 trillion to US$42.7 trillion (CMLGWM 2011). These CML and CMLGWM data from 1996 show exceptional year-on-year growth in the HNWI population (except in 2000 and 2008), which averaged approximately 7.5 per cent between 1996 and 2010 (Figure 3.1).

In terms of geographical share of the HNWI market, up to 2008, North America and Europe had always been the major markets in absolute terms for both the number of HNWIs and their accumulated wealth. On average, from 1996 until 2008, North America and Europe normally accounted for about two-thirds of both the total share of HNWIs and value of private wealth (in US$ trillions) (see Beaverstock 2012; CML 2002; CMLGWM 2008, 2011). However, from 2009, while North America heads the pack (accounting for 31 per cent and 27 per cent of the total shares of HNWIs [3.4 million] and wealth [11.6 trillion] respectively in 2010), the global

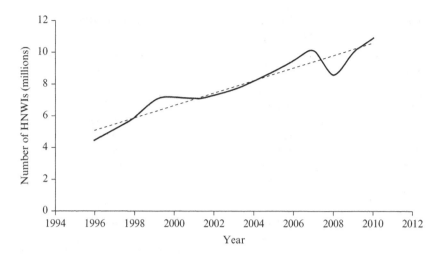

Source: CML (2007), CMLGWM (2008; 2009; 2010; 2011).

Figure 3.1   The HNWI population, 1996–2010

distribution has changed in favour of the Asia-Pacific region. From 2009, this world region surpassed Europe in terms of wealth (US$10.8 trillion compared to US$10.2 trillion, respectively), and number of HNWIs (3.3 million compared to 3.1 million respectively) (CMLGWM 2010, 2011). Across the emerging markets, there has been significant relative growth in the number of HNWIs and value of private wealth particularly in China, Brazil and India, and the Middle East (especially the United Arab Emirates – Dubai and Abu Dhabi) (CML 2007; CMLGWM 2008, 2009, 2010). In 2010, the five top countries by share of HNWI were: US (3.10 million, an increase of 8.5 per cent from 2009); Japan (1.74 million, up 5.4 per cent from 2009), Germany (0.92 million, up 7.2 per cent from 2009), China (0.54 million, up12.0 per cent from 2009) and the UK (0.45 million, up1.4 per cent from 2009). Between 2009 and 2010 the number of HNWIs grew by 20.8 per cent in India, from 127000 to 153000 (CMLGWM 2011).

Executive Remuneration and the 'Bonus' Culture

From the early-1980s, a significant driver in the growth of the global HNWI market was the creation 'new money' millionaires and billionaires derived from three major sources. First, individual private wealth created through so called 'liquid events' (Smith 2001), for example through flotations of private companies, privatization and the exploitation of

*Table 3.1   City of London employment and bonus payouts (April),
              2001–2011*

Year	City jobs[1]	City bonus (£ billions)
2001	312000	3.921
2002	308000	3.329
2003	317000	6.400
2004	325000	6.950
2005	327000	9.653
2006	343000	11.383
2007	354000	11.565
2008	324000	5.332
2009	305000	7.336
2010	319000	6.749
2011	327000	7.154

Note: [1]These are the number of jobs in the London Borough of the City of London that
are related to banking, financial and professional services employment, often referred to as
'City-jobs' (see Beaverstock and Hall 2012).

Source: CEBR (2010, 2011).

natural resources (as in the case of 'Oligarchs' of the Former-Soviet
Union) (*The Economist* 2009). Second, wealth was generated through
the rise of significantly enhanced remuneration for executives at the level
of President, Vice-President, Chief Executive Officer, Chief Finance
Officer, and Chief Operating Officer (Frank 2007; Irvin 2008; North
2005). Third, private wealth was accumulated through the mushroom-
ing of the 'bonus' culture, associated specifically with banking, finance
and professional services occupations in financial centres like London,
New York and Hong Kong (Beaverstock et al. 2012). With respect to
instantaneous wealth being created by enhanced executive remuneration and the bonus 'culture', the rise of these so-called financial elites
(Folkman et al. 2007; Hall 2009) provided a ready-made HNWI demand
for the retail private wealth management sector, as many were senior and
fee-earning employees of the wider banking, financial and professional
services sector (Beaverstock et al. 2012). High base remuneration and the
year-end bonuses are a major facet of all major IFCs. Taking the financial
district of the City of London as an example, in 2007 354000 banking,
financial and related business services (including accounting, insurance,
legal and other financial intermediation) workers received bonuses worth
£11.565 billion (Table 3.1). Post-financial crisis, London bankers, like
elsewhere were back on the bonus trail. The Centre for Economics and

Business Research [CEBR] (2010, 2011) estimated that in 2011, 327000 City-workers would share a bonus pot of £7.154 billion, an increase of 34 per cent (£1.8 billion) from 2008. Wall Street bankers are also on their way back in the bonus stakes. An estimated US$20.8 billion was paid out to Wall Street's financial community in 2010, up 18.2 per cent or US$3.2 billion more than in 2009 (*The Economist* 2011).

Thus, over the last 30 years or so, the size, composition and geography of global wealth have changed dramatically from its 'old' money roots (see Lundberg 1988; Thorndike 1980). In particular, the growth of the super-rich has provided the demand, and often bespoke stimulus, for the development of a broader range of new retail financial products and services to not only manage (as typified private banking) but also enhance their wealth in the form of the private wealth management sector (Beaverstock et al. 2012). Given the ways in which these products and services increasingly tie the super-rich into the international financial system through their investment practices, these individuals can be conceptualized as a financialized market. This develops work on the financialization of 'everyday life' (Langley 2008) that has examined how individuals are increasingly reliant on the international financial system for their own financial well-being and security through, for example, their pension provision and mortgage finance. But, this work has neglected the ways in which the super-rich also increasingly use the international financial system to manage their own financial affairs.

THE CITY OF LONDON AND THE SUPPLY OF PRIVATE WEALTH MANAGEMENT

The City of London is one of the leading IFCs for the investment of private wealth from both domicile and non-domicile (offshore) residents, and the provision of a private wealth management retail financial sector. In 2010, BCG (2011) estimated that US$1.9 trillion of private offshore wealth was managed in the UK (primarily in the City), Jersey, Guernsey, Isle of Man and Dublin, second after Switzerland (US$2.1 trillion). Of the US$1.9 trillion of offshore private wealth held in the UK, 39 per cent originated from mainland Europe (US$0.74 trillion) and 27 per cent from the Middle East (US$0.52 trillion). Indeed, the BCG (2011, p. 16) noted that, 'UK offshore banks, especially those in London . . . are well positioned to attract wealth from China, India, Latin America and the Middle east owing to historical ties.' These historical ties have been well established since the nineteenth century, most notably associated with international trade and merchant banking which linked the City of London with places

Table 3.2   The top 20 global private banks, 2011

Bank/Group	Assets (US$ billions)	Growth 2010 (%)	Primary currency
1. Bank of America	1945	+4	USD
2. Morgan Stanley	1628	+8	USD
3. UBS	1560	+7	CHF
4. Wells Fargo	1398	+15	USD
5. Credit Suisse	865	+12	CHF
6. Royal Bank of Canada	435	+15	USD
7. HSBC	390	+6	USD
8. Deutsche Bank	369	+36	EUR
9. BNP Paribas	340	+46	EUR
10. JP Morgan	284	+5	USD
11. Pictet	268	+10	CHF
12. Goldman Sachs	229	−1	USD
13. ABN Amro	220	+24	EUR
14. Barclays	186	+2	GBP
15. Julius Bar	182	+22	CHF
16. Credit Agricole	172	+4	EUR
17. Bank of New York Mellon	166	+8	USD
18. Northern Trust	154	+6	USD
19. Lombard Odier	153	+8	CHF
20. Citi Private Bank	141	+15	USD

Source: Scorpio Partnership (2011).

like Hong Kong, Shanghai, Mumbai, New Delhi, Kolkata and Rio de Janeiro (see King 1990). The latest available data on UK fund management for the end of 2010, estimated that private clients accounted for almost 10 per cent (£475 billion) of the total UK market (£4839 trillion), which exceeded funds under management in hedge funds (£234 billion), property funds (£140 billion) and private equity funds £112 billion) (TheCityUK 2011a, p. 7).

The establishment of London's global private wealth management sector has been driven by several factors. First, the City's world class reputation in traditional private banking has laid the foundations for the new private wealth management sector (see Bicker 1996; Cassis and Cottrell 2009). London's private banks have been in existence since the end of the seventeenth century (for example, Coutts & Co established 1692), and today the City hosts the headquarters or regional offices of the top global private banks, who still remain significant players in the management of private wealth (see Beaverstock 2012) (Table 3.2). Private banking has not only engrained a tradition of credibility, trust and safety in the deposit of wealth, but it has also created a milieu of expertise, knowledge and financial instruments which spill-over into similar financial sectors. Second, London's position as a fully functional IFC has meant that these firms have been able to take advantage of their location and global service platform to engage with private clients or diversify into wealth management functions. In particular, global universal banks like Citicorp, UBS and Credit Suisse, investment banks like Goldman Sachs, JP Morgan and Barclays Wealth, and professional services (for example, 'magic circle law firms'[1] and the Big Four accounting groups for example, KPMG, PwC) have begun to offer new products and bespoke advice to a high volume HNWI market in competition with traditional private banks and brokerage firms (Beaverstock et al. 2012). Third, London's position as a global financial centre means that it has a global talent pool to draw upon, with a range of specialist financial, professional and expert knowledge (including trusts and taxation), in many jurisdictions and markets, which are second to none (see Beaverstock and Hall 2012; Wainwright 2011; Z/Yen 2011). London is a specialist global centre with a talent pool that can access and manage: conventional funds (for example, cash, bonds and equities); and alternative funds (for example, private equity, hedge funds, equity derivatives, and the trade in fine arts and collectables) (IFSL 2009). Fourth, London is a global centre for specialist banking and investments, such as Islamic finance which is vitally important for the Middle-East and SE Asian HNWI clientele (IFSL 2009). For example, London has 22 banks which supply Islamic products, of which five are fully sharia compliant, and 34 Islamic funds managed from the UK (TheCityUK 2011b). Fifth, over time, London has developed as an important location for managing the UHNWI market primarily through family offices, which offer: specialist advice and planning; investment management; and administration (see Maude 2006). There are over 300 family offices in London, each with assets of over £100 million under management (ISFL 2009). London also hosts Bloomberg's top family office HSBC Private Wealth Solutions (ranked by assets), which manages a total of US$102 billion in its 18 offices around the globe (Effinger and Ody 2011). Sixth, and importantly, London is a residential magnet for the global HNWI and UHNWI population.

A SURVEY OF PRIVATE WEALTH MANAGEMENT IN THE CITY OF LONDON AND UNITED KINGDOM

The authors undertook a web-based survey of 400 leading retail and wholesale private wealth management firms to identify the specialist financial products and services offered to the HNWI market.[2] These firms were categorized into six major providers of private wealth management: (1) accountancy; (2) asset management; (3) banking, including group/ foreign, retail/commercial, private and investment; (4) insurance; (5) legal; and (6) retail Internet-based specialists and 'high-street' providers. Firms were selected for investigation from the major industry and, or professional bodies or societies that represented their banking, financial and professional services sectors, including the: British Bankers Association; Investment Managers Association; Association of British Insurers; Legal 500; and Accountancy Age. All of these sources included both UK-headquartered and foreign firms. In order to compile the database of private wealth provision, each firm's website was scrutinized systematically to capture data on: their supplier type (for example, all individual private banks were grouped together under the field of private banks); the types of products and services that they offered to clients; their 'target' or segmented market for different client types (for example, HNWI up to UHNWI); and the organizational characteristics (for example, location of headquarters, number of international offices and employment size). The products and services offered to HNWI-UHNWI clients on the firm websites were coded to create a series of variables for each firm. These different product and services variables could then be cross-tabulated against other key firm characteristics to provide a bespoke database for analysis. In doing so, it was possible to use descriptive statistics to explore the proportions and frequencies of different services and products offered by different types of firms. This revealed new trends for sub-groups within the HNWI categories. In the following section, we analyse in detail the composition and characteristics of five leading providers of private wealth management (accounting, asset management, banking, insurance and law) to illustrate the nature, functioning and scope of the retail private wealth management sector in London. In so doing, we outline their supply of bespoke banking, financial and professional services to the HNWI market.[3] Our analysis reveals how these services serve to financialize the retail financial provision offered to high net worth individuals by tying their personal affairs more closely into the international financial system.

Accountancy

Forty-eight accountancy firms were investigated in the database including the major transnational corporations – the Big Six (for example, Baker Tilly; Deloitte; Ernst & Young; KPMG; Grant Thornton; PwC) and an array of medium-sized UK providers (for example, Moore Stephens and

Shipleys). An analysis of the products and services on offer from these accounting firms indicated that 92 per cent of their private wealth management business was predominantly to clients in the HNWI to UHNWI market (the remaining 8 per cent were targeted at clients in the Mass Affluent[4] (MA) market). Furthermore, the 'private' products and services most regularly supplied to the HNWI to UHNWI market, accounting for 53 per cent of the total, were advice on personal taxation (including filing returns), financial planning, setting-up and managing trusts (for inheritance) and the management of estates (private property portfolios). The importance of managing trusts which involves investments in international stock markets shows the emergence of a more financialized retail financial sector for the super-rich alongside services that typified private banking such as estate management. The major global accounting firms offered a full portfolio of specialist products and services to clients within and between different jurisdictions through devoted private wealth partnership teams including a more specialized focus on expatriates and 'non-domiciled' residents in the UK and beyond. In contrast, many of the regionally-based firms targeted local HNWIs and large family-run businesses/entrepreneurs primarily focused on personal taxation, trusts and financial planning.

Asset Management

The private wealth management provision of 131 asset management (AM) companies were analysed in the survey. These firms represent one of the new burgeoning segments of the 'private wealth management' sector that mushroomed from the late 1980s and are central to the financialization of retail financial services provision for the super-rich because of the centrality of international financial markets to their operations. Our database of AM firms included: a variety of transnational firms, with domestic and foreign ownership, with offices in other IFCs (for example, JP Morgan Asset Management in New York; USB Global Asset Management in Zurich); those which are subsidiaries of global (for example, HSBC Investment Funds) and investment banks (for example, Credit Suisse Asset Management; Goldman Sachs Asset Management); and specialist SMEs, often one office firms located in the City (for example, Troy Asset Management Ltd), Edinburgh (for example, Baillie Gifford & Co. Ltd) or other regional cities (for example, Liverpool Victoria Asset Management in Liverpool). In AM the majority of firms offered their products and services across the entire range of the wealthy, to the Mass Affluent plus (MA+), HNWI and UHNWI markets (representing over 71 per cent of the products and services on offer). The MA-UHNWI range provides little insight into the particular niche markets. The reasoning behind this is that many financial products, mutual funds and Open-Ended Investment Companies (OEICs) may be recommended for purchase by an MA+ client's accountant, or by the private bank of a HNWI-UHNWI, leading the two to overlap. For example, Credit Suisse and JP Morgan Asset Management offer unit trusts, fund of funds, Individual Savings Accounts (ISAs) and OEIC products to its clients. A closer comparison of the MA+ client products and the HNWIs, reveals products that are deemed to require larger initial investments. While the MA+ consumers products tend to focus on 'traditional' products such as exposures to equity, corporate bond funds and government bonds (accounted for 72 per cent of advertised products), the HNWI-UHNWIs products included 'non-traditional' products including hedge funds, bespoke portfolios and structured funds (which accounted for 22 per cent of HNWI products).

Banking

We surveyed a total of 55 banks. Of these 55, 16 were UK banking groups and foreign banks (for example, Arab National Bank, Bank of India, BNP Paribas, FIBI Bank, NM Rothschild & Sons Ltd), whose targeted markets were their resident national populations and clients who wanted their wealth managed 'offshore' in London. The majority of products and services were offered to HNWI-UHNWI (56 per cent) and MA+ clients (21 per cent). The most common services and products for HNWI-UHNWIs included, financial planning, investment management, current accounts, secured lending and trust services, but also included more diverse services such as tax advice (expatriate), lifestyle advice and art and jewellery advice (for example, storage and insurance).

Twenty-three of these 55 banks were London's leading private banks, and for some, their interests have been in the City for over 100 years (for example, Arbuthnot Latham & Co, Brown Shipley & Co, Coutts & Co), with one being headquartered in Bermuda and two in Zurich. The HNWI-UHNWI client sector accounted for 83 per cent of the services offered by private banks. The most frequently offered services included: current accounts and investment management (13 per cent each); financial planning (10 per cent); trust services (9 per cent); and offshore services (8 per cent) for expatriate and non-domiciled clients with interests in the UK. These private banks also offered a range of specialist lending facilities and products to their clients to address their complex financial requirements (for example, brokerage, yacht finance, secured lending, and pensions).

Finally, our banking survey included 16 investment banks including institutions like Barclays Wealth Management, Mellon Bank, Morgan

Stanley Private Wealth Management, Schroder & Co. Ltd, UBS AG. Eighty-eight per cent of all products and services were targeted at the HNWI to UHNWI market. These banks supplied a diverse range of products and services to their HNWI-UHNWI clients, in a similar way to private banks. The most commonly offered products were: investment management (16 per cent); financial planning and current accounts (15 per cent each); and tax advice, trusts and 'lifestyle' advice. These firms also offered the management of alternative investments like hedge funds and private equity – a group that Folkman et al. (2007) term 'new capital intermediaries' – demonstrating the centrality of these actors who drive processes of financialization to the servicing of high net worth individuals in terms of their retail financial service's needs.

Insurance

The distribution of products offered by 135 insurers, including transnational firms (for example, AIG, Aviva, AXA) and specialists (for example, British & Foreign Marine Insurance), to the wealthy only accounted for 22 per cent of all products targeted at the HNWI+ market, including MA+-HNWI-UHNWI (15 per cent) and the HNWI-UHNWIs (7 per cent). The most frequently advertised products were: home and marine insurance (14 per cent each), followed by an array of highly-specialized insurance products (for example, aircraft, kidnap, jewellery, fine art, classic cars, equine). For example, as part of their HNWI-UHNWI product portfolios, Chubb Custom Insurance Ltd provided specialist products to protect assets such as jewellery and fine art, and AIG UK Ltd offered yacht, aircraft and kidnap products.

Legal Services

Twenty-five law firms, including City-based 'magic' and leading US practices (for example, Allen & Overy LLP, Baker McKenzie LLP, Herbert Smith LLP) and specialist providers (for example, Dawson Cornwell, Manches LLP) were analysed to investigate their service provision. All of these firms offered services to the HNWI-UHNWI markets, with a preponderance of the market share accounted for by the global law firms. The three most important services offered to the HNWI market were: the establishment and administration of trusts and estates (36 per cent), to protect the inter-generational transfer of wealth; taxation advice, especially for those with complicated, cross-jurisdictional financial affairs and earnings; and family law, to minimize the loss of wealth outside of the family following death or divorce. The importance of legal services within the private wealth management in London echoes the wider role of City law firms in shaping processes of financialization through their advice in the development of new financial products and services throughout the 2000s (Wainwright 2011).

CONCLUSIONS

Our unique survey of the rise of the private wealth management services in London has shown how rather than simply *protecting* existing wealth (as typified earlier forms of private banking), this sector also seeks to tie the personal wealth it manages much more closely into the international financial system to enhance wealth. As such, we argue that private wealth management represents a financialized form of retail financial services provision for the super-rich centring on four related generic functions. First, the *preservation of wealth* through products and services which focus on being as efficient as possible in limiting the burden of the state, through for example personal income and inheritance taxes (for example, products and services which provide tax advice, expatriate services, financial planning, the establishment and administration of trusts and estates). Second, *the protection of wealth* and investable assets, through for example specialist insurance policies which cover art and jewellery, classic cars, property, private aeroplanes and yachts, and bespoke advice on family law, trusts and land management. Third, *the accumulation of wealth* through services such as: financial planning, investment strategies, brokerage, FOREX, alternative investments (for example, hedge funds, private equity) and family offices services that rely on investment strategies within international financial markets. Finally, what can be best described as *the 'everyday life' retail provision of wealth*, including privileged current accounts, pensions, credit cards and secured/unsecured loans, savings, mortgage finance, and lifestyle advice, car insurance. Following the growing interest in the geographies of financialization more broadly (French et al. 2011), this private wealth management sector also has a distinctive spatiality focused on a specialist cadre of firms, individuals, technologies and products, primarily located in the pre-eminent IFC, London. Moreover, through offering these services exclusively to the rich and wealthy, where the barrier to entry is a high level of liquid assets (greater than US$1 million), these retail financial services are largely divorced from the rest of the UK population that houses them.

Two significant implications can be tabled from this analysis of the private wealth management sector and the market for HNWIs. First, post-financial crisis, the global super-rich have, to coin a phrase, 'never had it so good'. Their number and stock of global wealth have reached record levels (whether you use CMLGWM or *Forbes* data) in mature markets (US in particular), and unprecedented growth is expected in the Asia-Pacific, notably China and India over the coming decades (see BCG 2011; CMLGWM 2011). For the private wealth sector, these forecasting data are fantastic news as the industry expects to be sustained by a high number of UHNWIs who wish to draw on the bespoke products and services of places like the City of London, Wall Street and Hong Kong/ Singapore to preserve and manage wealth. Second, the UK's wealth management financial services sector is an extremely dynamic and competitive retail financial market. London remains the pre-eminent financial centre for the management of such wealth reproduced through a constellation of global players in private banking, asset management, brokerage, insurance and investment and global banking capacity, and expert labour. But policy-makers and stakeholders must be diligent in their regulatory frameworks as the 'City' remains in fierce competition with 'offshore' jurisdictions and established centres like New York, Hong Kong and Singapore.

ACKNOWLEDGEMENTS

We would like to thank the Financial Services Research Forum, University of Nottingham, UK, for funding this research within the project: Scoping the Private Wealth Management of the High Net Worth and Mass Affluent Markets in the United Kingdom's Financial Services Industry (www.nottingham.ac.uk/business/forum/index.aspx). Also we would like to extend our thanks to Iain Hay and referees for editorial advice and comments which have brought clarity and focus to our main argument and reportage of the secondary data and primary, empirical study.

NOTES

1. These are commonly known as the leading London headquartered law firms, including the likes of Allen & Overy, Linklaters, Clifford Chance, Freshfields and Slaughter and May (see Beaverstock et al. 1999).
2. For a detailed analysis of the methodology for this survey see: Beaverstock et al. (2010).
3. We have excluded retail/commercial banking, and retail Internet-based specialists and 'high-street' providers in this analysis because our survey indicated that these sectors were hardly visible in the provision of private wealth management to the HNWI+ market.
4. The acceptable definition of the Mass Affluent are those individuals with liquid,

investable assets greater than US$100 000, but less than US$1 000 000 (see ISFL 2009; PricewaterhouseCoopers 2009).

REFERENCES

Beaverstock, J.V. (2012), 'The privileged world city: private banking, wealth management and the bespoke servicing of the global super-rich', in Peter J. Taylor, Michael Hoyler, Ben Derudder and Frank Witlox (eds), *International Handbook of Globalization and World Cities*, Cheltenham, UK and Northampton, MA, USA: Edward Elgar, pp. 378–90.

Beaverstock, J.V. and S. Hall (2012), 'Competing for talent: global mobility, immigration and the City of London's labour market in banking, finance and professional services', *Cambridge Journal of Regions, Economy and Society*, **5** (2), 271-87.

Beaverstock, J.V., S. Hall and T. Wainwright (2011), 'Servicing the super-rich: new financial elites and the rise of the private wealth management retail ecology', *Regional Studies*, 1–16.

Beaverstock, J.V., S. Hall and T. Wainwright (2010), *Scoping the Private Wealth Management of the High Net Worth and Mass Affluent Markets in the United Kingdom's Financial Services Industry*, Financial Services Research Forum, Nottingham: University of Nottingham, available from the lead author.

Beaverstock, J.V., P.J. Hubbard and J.R. Short (2004), 'Getting away with it? Exposing the geographies of the super-rich', *Geoforum*, **35** (4), 401-7.

Beaverstock, J.V., R.J. Smith and P.J Taylor (1999), 'The long arm of the law: the globalization of London's law firms,' *Environment and Planning A*, **31** (10), 1857-76.

Bicker, L. (1996), *Private Banking in Europe*, London: Routledge.

Boston Consulting Group (2011), 'Global wealth 2011: shaping a new world', www.bcg.com, accessed 13 March 2012.

Cassis, Y. and P.L. Cottrell (eds) (2009), *The World of Private Banking*, Farnham: Ashgate.

Centre for Economics and Business Research (CEBR) (2011), 'Despite fall in bonuses in 2010/11, growth in City workers' pay packets continues to outpace the rest of the UK', news release, 26 April 2011.

CEBR (2010), 'City jobs forecast revised down – Less than 10 000 jobs created on 2010', news release, 2 October 2010.

Capgemini Merrill Lynch (CML) (2007), *World Wealth Report 10th Anniversary 1997–2006*, www.ml.com, accessed 6 January 2010.

CML (2002), *World Wealth Report 2001*, www.ml.com, accessed 6 January 2010.

Capgemini Merrill Lynch Global Wealth Management (CMLGWM) (2011), *World Wealth Report 2010*, www.ml.com, accessed 13 March 2012.

CMLGWM (2010), *World Wealth Report 2009*, www.ml.com, accessed 6 January 2010.

CMLGWM (2009), *World Wealth Report 2008*, www.ml.com, accessed 6 January 2010.

CMLGWM (2008), *World Wealth Report 2007*, www.ml.com, accessed 6 January 2010.

The Economist (2011), 'Wall Street bonuses', 24 February, www.economist.com/node/18231330, accessed 11 May 2011.

The Economist (2009), 'Spare a dime? A special report on the rich', *The Economist*, 4 April.

Effinger, A. and E. Ody (2011), 'HSBC tops family office list as money firm manage rises 17%', www.bloomberg.com/news/2011-08-08/hsbc-tops-family-office-list-as-money-firms-manage-rises-17-html, accessed 18 October 2011.

Folkman, P., J. Froud, S. Johal and K. Williams (2007), 'Working for themselves? Capital market intermediaries and present day capitalism', *Business History*, **49** (4), 552–72.

Forbes (2011), 'The world's billionaires 2011', www.forbes.com, accessed 12 March 2012.

Frank, R. (2007), *Richistan. A Journey through the 21st Century Wealth Boom and the Lives of the New Rich*, New York: Piatkus.

French, S., A. Leyshon and T. Wainwright (2011), 'Financializing space, spacing financialization', *Progress in Human Geography*, **35** (6), 798–819.

Froud, J. and K. Williams (2007), 'Private equity and the culture of value extraction', *New Political Economy*, **12** (3), 405–20.

Hall, S. (2009), 'Financialised elites and the changing nature of finance capitalism: investment bankers in London's financial district', *Competition & Change*, **13** (2), 173–89.

Hay, I. and S. Muller (2012), '"That tiny, stratospheric apex that owns most of the world" – exploring geographies of the super-rich', *Geographical Research*, **50** (1), 75–88.

International Financial Services London (IFSL) (2009), 'International private wealth management', November, www.ifsl.org.uk, accessed 13 March 2012.

Irvin, G. (2008), *Super Rich. The Rise of Inequality in Britain and the United States*, London: Polity.

King, A.D. (1990), *Global Cities: Post-Imperialism and the Internationalization of London*, London: Routledge.

Langley, P. (2008), *The Everyday Life of Global Finance: Saving and Borrowing in Anglo-America*, Oxford: Oxford University Press.

Lundberg, F. (1988), *The Rich and the Super-Rich*, New York: Citadel Press.

Maude, D. (2006), *Global Private Banking and Wealth Management*, Chichester: Wiley.

Maude, D. and P. Molyneux (1996), *Private Banking*, London: Euromoney Books.

North, R.D. (2005), *Rich is Beautiful. A Very Personal Defence of Mass Affluent*, London: The Social Affairs Unit.

PricewaterhouseCoopers (2009), 'Global Private Banking/Wealth Management Survey', www.pwc.com, accessed 13 March 2012.

Roberts, R. (2008), *The City*, London: The Economist.

Scorpio Partnership (2011), '2011: Global wealth management industry is in neutral as rising AUMs are matched by rising costs while new HNW money inflows remain static', press release: 13 July 2011.

Smith, R.C. (2001), *The Wealth Creators*, New York: Truman Books.

TheCityUK (2011a), 'Fund management', www.thecityuk.com, accessed 13 March 2012.

TheCityUK (2011b), 'Islamic financial services', www.thecityuk.com, accessed 13 March 2012.

Thorndike, Joseph J. (1980), *The Very Rich: A History of Wealth*, New York: Crown.

Wainwright, T. (2011), 'Tax doesn't have to be taxing: London's "onshore" finance industry and the fiscal spaces of a global crisis', *Environment and Planning A*, **43** (6), 1287–304.

Z/Yen (2011), 'The Global Financial Centres Index 10', www.zyen.com, accessed 13 March 2012.

4. 'The world needs a second Switzerland': onshoring Singapore as the liveable city for the super-rich

Choon-Piew Pow

INTRODUCTION

> The World needs a second Switzerland. And that's what Singapore is.
> Widdek, a resident of Sentosa Cove quoted in
> *The Los Angeles Times*,18 November 2006.

In a master-planned community off the southern coast of Singapore, wealthy foreigners comprise the majority of the homeowners. Drawn ostensibly by the high quality of life in the city-state and its liberal immigration policy directed at attracting the global super-rich to reside in country, the residents of the 117-hectare Sentosa Cove planned community have each invested millions of dollars to own a piece of prime waterfront property on the land-scarce island. In the contemporary world characterized by the rampant offshoring of economic functions from 'first-world' to 'third-world' cities, developments such as Sentosa Cove may be considered a way of 'onshoring' for cities such as Singapore that aspire to be a lifestyle hub and investment destination for the global super-rich. The term 'onshoring' is used here in two related senses: first, it refers to the relocation of business functions, in particular economic activities related to private wealth management, into Singapore (as opposed to traditional offshore wealth centres such as Switzerland, London and New York); and second, the attempt by the Singapore government to attract high net worth individuals (HNWIs) to 'live and bank' quite literally 'onshore' in the country. The two processes are of course not distinct and as this chapter will illustrate, strategies to onshore Singapore as a fledging global wealth hub draw, in part, on creating a highly liveable urban environment for the super-rich. In other words, urban spaces and the built environment are being mobilized and packaged for elite/corporate consumption, 'rolling out' what Brenner and Theodore (2002) characterize as 'neoliberal' forms of urbanism distinguished by the creation of privatized consumption spaces and speculative real-estate in city centres; reconfiguring local land use patterns in favour of 'highest and the best use' as the basis for major land use planning decisions; construction of mega urban prestige projects to lure high-rollers; proliferation of gated communities and other purified spaces customized for elite social reproduction; rolling forward of the gentrification frontier; and intensification of social-spatial polarization (Brenner and Theodore 2002, pp. 370–71).

In recent years the Singapore government has been stepping up efforts to promote the city-state as a financial-services hub for private banking, with over 30 private banks now catering to wealthy clients from Asia and Europe. According to Mr Ong Chong Tee, Deputy Managing Director of the Monetary Authority of Singapore (2006), over US$200 billion of private-banking assets are being managed in Singapore and this is set to expand further with the growing, untapped wealth of 'Asian millionaires', in particular, non-resident Indians (NRIs), one of the fastest growing groups among Asia's 'new rich' (Tee 2006). As one business report (Siow 2005) has highlighted, Singapore is favoured by the super-rich for its low taxes, banking secrecy, political stability, strong legal framework and professional workforce, and by 2015 may well become one of the largest offshore financial centres in the world, surpassing even Switzerland.

The comparison with Switzerland is deliberate. Singapore's policy-makers have long been enamoured by the Swiss model of development and that country's high standard of living. Most notably, in the early 1990s, then Prime Minister Goh Chok Tong envisioned that Singapore would be able to achieve a 'Swiss standard of living' within a decade. The 'Swiss model' has loomed large in official and popular rhetoric, and the Singapore government has been relentless in pursuing its aspiration to become the 'Switzerland of Asia'. As Allen (2006) reported, Singapore is taking on a distinctively 'Swiss feel' not only in terms of its banking (de)regulation policies but also through its urban redevelopment projects that aim to create the ambience of Zurich or Geneva. A private banking expert with the Boston Consulting Group who also served as an adviser in the Singapore government's economic review committee, suggested that the Singapore authorities recognize that a key ingredient in the success of Zurich and Geneva is the lifestyle the rich enjoy there and that the Singapore government make massive infrastructural changes modelled on those cities to recreate that ambience (Allen 2006). While it may be an exaggeration to state that Singapore is being modelled explicitly on Swiss cities, the city-state has certainly been transformed in quite dramatic ways and fashioned in the image of 'successful' global cities elsewhere.

Unmistakably, all these efforts are aimed at making Singapore an attractive investment and lifestyle destination for the global super rich.

Table 4.1   *Percentage change of HNWI wealth and population in Asia*
             Pacific countries

Country	Change total Asia-Pacific HNWI wealth 2009–2010 (%)	Change total Asia-Pacific HNWI population 2009–2010 (%)
Other markets	10.8	8.4
Indonesia	24.9	23.8
Thailand	17.3	16.0
Taiwan	14.7	13.7
South Korea	16.5	21.3
Singapore	22.6	33.3
Hong Kong	35.0	15.5
India	22.0	20.8
Australia	12.1	11.1
China	13.3	12.0
Japan	6.2	5.4

Source: Capgemini and Merrill Lynch (2011).

Capgemini and Merrill Lynch's 2011 *World Wealth Report* observes that the number of high net worth individuals (HNWIs)[1] in the Asia Pacific region grew from 3 million in 2009 to 3.3 million in 2010. The 2010 figure also indicates that the HNWI population is now 18.3 per cent larger than in 2007. A more recent report by Knight Frank and Citi Private Bank (2011) indicates that notwithstanding recent global financial turmoil, the collective wealth of HNWIs shot back up in 2010 by 22 per cent as investment markets rebounded. Capgemini and Merrill Lynch (2011) also noted that eight of the world's fastest growing HNWI populations were in the Asia-Pacific markets including Hong Kong, Vietnam, Indonesia, Singapore and India (see Table 4.1). Singapore, in particular, has been highlighted as an emerging 'wealth management centre' with reportedly the highest density of millionaires in the world (approximately one in 30 Singaporean residents is said to be a HNWI) (Gopalakrishnan 2010). By 2015, it is predicted that there will be 129 000 high net worth individuals in Singapore whose wealth will amount to US$616 billion (S$740.84 billion) (Ng 2011).

These HNWIs include locals who have profited from the buoyant property and stock markets in Singapore as well as the more recent influx of wealthy foreigners from the region, including Indonesia, China, India and beyond. It is widely reported (*The Business Times* 17 June 2009) that the city state has attracted super-rich celebrities like Chinese movie star Jet

Li and US 'investment guru' Jim Rogers, both of whom have taken up Singapore permanent residence and enrolled their children in local schools. Jet Li, who also holds United States citizenship, was also reported to have bought a sprawling $20 million bungalow in a prime district of Singapore.

The government's strategy of 'onshoring' Singapore as the global destination for the super-rich entails not only providing a conducive pro-business environment for which the country has long been known but also creating a spectacular and visually seductive urban landscape aimed at attracting HNWIs. In this context, this chapter will critically examine how the ongoing construction of privileged landscapes for the super-rich in Singapore are spatialized in and through the urban built environment to produce new contested geographies of wealth, privilege and exclusion. The discussion is organized in four parts. Following the introduction, the chapter briefly reviews how concerns over 'urban liveability' have emerged as a central policy fixation in many cities around the world and been 'hijacked' by entrepreneurial urban regimes as a means of place-marketing. Not surprisingly, such 'liveability' concerns cater specifically to a select group of privileged urban elites ranging from the 'creative class' to transnational capitalist elites and HNWIs. Insofar as the urban liveability rhetoric provides a way to 'benchmark' cities according to their lifestyle attributes and offerings to the global elites, the third section examines recent efforts to shore up Singapore as Asia's lifestyle capital for the super-rich. As I point out, the extreme makeover of Singapore's new downtown landscape as well as the development of scores of new hyper-luxurious consumption spaces (casinos, seaside mansions, penthouses) are embedded in the political economy and urban(e) imaginary of a privileged neoliberal urbanism that is bound up in Singapore's endeavour to become a 'liveable' place for HNWIs. Yet, as the final section concludes, these recent developments also raise the spectre of an increasingly polarized society that breeds discontent and resentment against the super-rich.

LIVEABLE CITIES FOR WHOM?

In an urban policy world obsessed with benchmarking the relative performances of cities, the periodic release of city liveability rankings (much like global rankings of universities) generates much buzz and excitement among urban officials worldwide. This 'fixation' over the liveability ranking of cities should come as no surprise given the litany of urban liveability indexes that have appeared, fuelled in part by the global media's sensational coverage of 'best cities' and popular urban discourses on 'model cities' and best practices. To be certain, concerns with quality of life and humane and socially sustainable urban environments have also been a perennial concern in the social sciences. As Pacione (2009) points out, quality of life issues have been at the forefront of many urban policy debates since the 1950s due to the large-scale post-war urban development taking place in many cities around the world (Pacione 1982; 1990). Yet, notwithstanding the widespread use of the term, liveability as a concept remains highly ambiguous and contested. Underlining many definitions of urban liveability is the persistent tension between achieving liveable urban places at the local scale and maintaining urban economic competitiveness on the global front. While liveability indexes have traditionally been used by transnational corporations to determine 'hardship allowances' for expatriate staff postings, those rankings underwritten by urban consultancy companies have increasingly been appropriated as a means to brand cities in the midst of intensifying global inter-urban competition.

As McCann (1998) points out, the attempt to fuse urban quality of life issues with the economic imperative of globalizing cities is now routinely understood as a means of gaining competitive advantage – one that bestows upon one group of cities the hallowed status of being highly sought-after 'lifestyle destinations' for global elites and the super-rich. These cities are seen to be able to offer premium consumption spaces for economically valued (footloose) class fractions who now are able to choose the cities in which they want to live or invest in on the basis of specific lifestyle opportunities offered. Most notably, the definition of urban competitiveness in relation to such a narrow understanding of urban liveability is manifested in Richard Florida's (2002) contentious thesis on the rise of the creative class: to be economically successful and to attract the creative class cities must transform themselves into lifestyle hubs and attractive consumption destinations (McCann 2004). Recently, liveability rankings have been appropriated as a way of selling lifestyle destinations to the global super-rich.

In a nutshell, what could be observed is that fuelled in part by the global media's ranking of 'best cities' and popular urban discourses on 'model cities' (McCann 2004), the discourse on urban liveability has been appropriated strategically by entrepreneurial urban regimes seeking to brand cities as liveable in order to attract highly mobile global elites. Popular 'liveability indexes' such as Mercer's *Quality of Living Survey* (2011) and the Economist Intelligence Unit's *Liveability Ranking Report* (2011) have quickly become 'industry standards' that urban authorities readily adopt to benchmark and 'improve' their city's relative performances in the global arena.

Singapore, in particular, has consistently been ranked favourably by international consultancies. For example, the 2011 *Quality of Living*

Survey by Mercer Human Resource Consulting revealed that Singapore offers the best quality of life in the Asia region. In 2008, the city-state was also rated 'The Best Place to Live' for Asian expats by ECA International (Cheam 2008). More recently, the 'Global Liveable Cities Index' commissioned by Singapore's Centre for Liveable Cities (CLC) ranked the city-state as the third most liveable city in the world, only behind the Swiss cities of Geneva and Zurich (Ng 2010).

Beyond these superlative rankings however, it is important to note how the urban liveability discourses have been appropriated by Singaporean government agencies such as the Economic Development Board to market Singapore as a destination for the global super-rich. The Economic Development Board's (EDB) website (2012) for example, proclaims Singapore as 'one of the cleanest and greenest cities in the world', a safe, orderly yet dynamic global city-state with an 'efficient and affordable public transport system' as well as 'world-class healthcare services'. Backing its claim with survey results from Mercer's *Quality of Living Survey* ranking, the EDB further emphasized that Singapore offers a cosmopolitan living environment with varied lifestyle options and the 'best place to live, work and play in Asia'.

In practically all other government ministries and statutory boards such as the newly set up Centre for Liveable City, improving the 'quality of life' of the city has become a mantra that is regularly touted in policy documents and the speeches of government officials. In tandem, promoting a sustainable 'liveable city' has almost become a default mission statement and objective in almost every state-led urban development project.

In its relentless pursuit of the status as a 'highly liveable' global city, the Singapore government has recently embarked on a series of ambitious plans to transform the city-state into a cosmopolitan lifestyle hub for global business elites and the super-rich. As the next section of this chapter examines further, these new landscapes of wealth and power are entrenched in the political economy and cultural imaginary of a neoliberal and privileged urbanism.

ONSHORING SINGAPORE AS ASIA'S LIFESTYLE CAPITAL FOR THE SUPER-RICH

As part of its strategy to attract high net worth individuals to 'live and bank' in Singapore, the government is not only promoting the city-state as a safe money (tax) haven – bolstered in part by a highly selective immigration policy (see Yeoh and Chang 2001) that privileges elite wealthy immigrants – but is also rebranding Singapore as Asia's new 'capital of fun and creativity'. Some recent major initiatives towards this end include staging international events such as the Formula One Grand Prix and building a brand new downtown at Marina Bay, complete with six-star hotels, casinos, luxurious service apartments and waterfront housing such as Sentosa Cove, the first full-scale gated community in the country. In this context, the entire urban landscape at the new downtown in Marina Bay has been re-imaged and transformed into a conspicuous space of hyper-consumerism, centred on extravagant commodity displays and seductive urban spectacles aimed at luring the global super-rich and well-heeled locals.

Designed as a self-contained city-within-a-city, the 360 hectares of new urban spaces at Marina Bay have been projected to house global head-quarters of leading financial institutions and other advanced producer services, ultra-luxurious residences and hotels, as well as entertainment/ retail complexes (Pow 2010). Built almost entirely on reclaimed land, the new downtown is designed to extend Singapore's existing downtown district and further support the city-state's continuing growth as a major business and financial hub in Asia. Among some of the landmark develop-ments in the area are the Marina Bay Sands Integrated Resorts (designed by celebrity architect Moshe Safdie) and iconic cultural infrastructure such as the Esplanade Theatres on the Bay. At the centre of the down-town development is a 3.55-hectare Business and Financial Centre (BFC) comprising state-of-the-art office towers, luxurious hotels and six-star residential developments such as the Sail @ Marina Bay.

Overall, the design of the new downtown is predicated on spectacular landscapes conjuring up imaginaries of global modernity and cosmo-politanism that bear testament to Singapore's unencumbered drive and ambition towards achieving premium global city status while at the same time appealing to the lifestyle and consumption desires of the super-rich who are the key drivers for the demand of luxury goods and collectibles such as automobiles, yachts, private jets, as well as fine art collections, watches and gems. On the global scale, as Davis and Monk (2007, p.xii) remark, the 'spending spree by high net-worth individuals has replaced market deepening (the expansion of mass-consumption entitlements) as the principal piston of economic expansion. Those elite firms who have traditionally scratched the itch of the very rich – Porsche, Bulgari, Polo Ralph Lauren, Tiffany, Hermes, Sotheby's, and so on – cannot open new branches fast enough in Shanghai, Dubai and Bangalore.' At the Marina Bay, this is exemplified by the latest offering from Louis Vuitton – a flag-ship 'island' store that appears to float on the water in front of the Marina Bay Sands. Designed by award-winning architect Peter Marino, this glass-and-steel crystal pavilion with floor to ceiling windows overlooks the Marina Bay and has a private lounge and an art gallery that cater to the immense purchasing power of the super-rich and their penchant for so-called 'investments of passion' (Capgemini and Merrill Lynch 2011, p. 20).

Alongside the new downtown and its luxurious trappings, several upmarket residential projects have also been launched in Singapore in recent years. Most notably, the Sentosa Cove housing resort has attracted homebuyers from around the world. Over 60 per cent of the resort's home-owners are foreigners who have each invested millions of dollars to own a piece of prime waterfront property on the island. Reportedly, a detached house in Sentosa Cove costs between S$16–$20 million while non-landed property such as a condominium apartment unit goes for over S$21 500 per square metre (*The Business Times* 10 January 2009). According to the developers, the well-heeled residents of Sentosa Cove are not only afflu-ent locals who bought their property as a second 'holiday home' but also HNWIs and expatriates working in global banking and financial indus-tries in Singapore and the Asia Pacific region. Many of the foreigners and Permanent Resident (PR) homebuyers hail from neighbouring countries such as Indonesia and Malaysia but others have come from further afield, including Britain, Australia, China, India and to a lesser extent, the United States and Western Europe.

Designed to emulate the idyllic charm of the French Riviera and south-ern California suburbia, Sentosa Cove boasts two golf courses and a 400-berth marina village with 10 berths for mega yachts (Pow 2011). Like many master-planned communities, every aspect of the living environment within Sentosa Cove is highly controlled, manipulated and designed to appeal to the cosmopolitan tastes and lifestyles of its super-rich residents without them ever having to step out of tropical Singapore. Internally, the Cove's streets are designed to be closed off to non-residents and the sur-rounding coastal waters are patrolled by guards and monitored by high-tech surveillance equipment. The appeal of super-rich enclaves such as Sentosa Cove rests on what Knox (2005, p. 34) describes as the 'enchant-ment of suburbia as an object of (and setting for) consumption' that works towards the naturalization of the ideology of competitive consumption and privilege. Characterized by packaged development, simulated settings and conspicuous consumption, what is enchanting about these emblematic cultural landscapes of neoliberal capitalism is not their supposed convivial social life but their 'appeal to people's exclusionary impulses and, above all, to their self-identity as consumers' (Knox 2005, p. 37). For Sentosa Cove, it is precisely the enchantment of such privileged landscapes of exclusivity and luxury that makes the housing enclave immensely popular with its super-rich inhabitants.

In an unprecedented move, the Singapore government lifted the restric-tion on foreign ownership of landed property to allow foreigners to buy and own landed housing in Sentosa Cove. According to the property ownership laws in Singapore, and in an effort to prevent land speculation in the land-scarce city-state, foreigners are effectively barred from buying and owning landed properties. Sentosa Cove is, however, established as a special zone where residents who own a landed property on the island can qualify for special Long Term Social Visit Pass (LTSV) of up to three years which allows them multiple entries into Singapore without restriction. In addition, residents who own bungalow units in Sentosa Cove and have S$5 million worth of total assets held in Singapore can also apply for a fast track application for Permanent Residency under the 'Financial Investor Scheme'. The special status of the property development is further encapsulated in a set of residential rules and bylaws under the 'Sentosa Cove Regulation Act' drawn up by the Ministry of Trade and Industry. As a quasi-self-governed micro-territory, Sentosa Cove effectively functions as an onshore metropolitan enclave for global elites in Singapore.

To the extent that recent developments such as the Marina Bay downtown and Sentosa Cove are designed to target the super-rich specifically, these landscapes of privilege and wealth also raise the spectre of an increasingly polarized society that may breed discontent and resentment against the rich. According to figures released by the Department of Statistics in 2010, the poorest 10 per cent of Singaporean households had an average monthly income of S$1400 compared with S$23 684 for the top 10 per cent. With a Gini coefficient for income inequality of 4.72 – the second highest level of income inequality among 42 nations with very high human development according to the United Nations (Chan 2011) – even the Singapore government has to acknowledge that the rich–poor divide is becoming more accentuated in the country. Indeed, since mid-2000, the widening income gap in Singapore has become a recurring theme in public forums and ministerial speeches, including the Prime Minister's National Day rally address to the country (Li 2007).

WHEN MR CARLOS COMES TO TOWN – SUPER-RICH VERSUS THE REST?

> Supposing the world's richest man, Carlos Slim, comes to live in Singapore. The Gini coefficient will get worse. But I think Singapore will be better off. Even for the lower income Singaporeans, it will be better.
> Prime Minister Lee Hsien Loong, quoted in Chia 2010.

In a dialogue session held with the ruling People's Action Party's 'feedback' unit, Prime Minister Lee Hsien Loong was quizzed by members of the public over Singapore's widening income gap. Concern over that gap is not unexpected given that the Gini coefficient for income distribution has jumped significantly over the last decade due in part to Singapore's selective immigration policy that targets the global super-rich. While the world's richest man Mr Carlos Slim probably has no intention of moving to Singapore, the hypothetical scenario posed by the Prime Minister raises several critical questions over social equity issues and the sustainability of Singapore's economic growth model. According to Lee, the influx of foreigners and especially the super-rich is not a zero-sum game for the locals as 'people like Mr Slim, a businessman and philanthropist, could start businesses here and create more jobs and prosperity for Singaporeans' (Chia 2010).

As several commentators and scholars have long observed, rolling out the red-carpet for the transnational capitalist class is inextricably bound up in the global visioning of Singapore as an oasis of talent and a global private wealth management centre (Yeoh and Chang 2001). However, the state's logic of onshoring Singapore as an investment and lifestyle hub for the super-rich is certainly neither hegemonic nor foolproof. Even the business intelligence report readily points out that in Singapore:

> Having a super-rich pool of foreigners in the city poses the risk of accentuating social tensions. Already, housing prices are rising faster than in the rest of the region. Porsches, Jaguars and Ferraris flash by in the streets. The number of international schools in the city catering mostly to foreigners has risen five-fold in the last decade or so. (Gopalakrishnan 2010)

In the context of global city formation, social polarization has often been seen as an inevitable outcome with an exponential increase in the number of people in both the top and bottom income groups, along with a decrease of those in the middle group (the 'disappearing middle'). This is often accompanied by a widening income gap between the top and bottom percentiles of the population. Arguably, the social polarization thesis is a controversial one as not all cities experience polarization in a uniform manner. As Chris Hamnett (2001) carefully points out, the concept of polarization is often inherently unstable and value laden, characterized more by shifting meanings than by precise definition. Hence there is a danger that social polarization is an often taken-for-granted concept and used loosely as an all-purpose general signifier rather than being subjected to rigorous empirical analysis in specific contexts and locales. Several studies have emphasized the need to consider the decisive roles played by different national institutions in mediating social polarization such as the state's intervention in the labour market.

Scott Baum (1999), for example, has argued that in Singapore the social polarization thesis does not quite hold up due to various state intervention

Table 4.2   Household income distribution in Singapore, Hong Kong and Taipei (1990 and 2000)

Year	Singapore		Hong Kong		Taipei	
	1990	2000	1991	2001	1991	2001
Lowest 20%	4.2	2.4	4.7	3.2	9.45	7.71
Highest 20%	48.1	51.0	49.0	56.5	35.97	38.11
Ratio of average income of top 20% to lowest 20%	11.4	20.9	12.3	17.7	3.8	4.9
Gini coefficient	0.436	0.481	0.476	0.525	0.265	0.304

Source: Tai (2006, p. 1752).

schemes and workfare training programmes which elevated the working low-middle class as a whole. He also suggested that within Singapore, there has been a trend towards a professionalized occupational structure and a growing middle-upper income group rather than the development of a polarized structure. However, more recently, in a survey of Singapore, Hong Kong and Taipei, Tai (2006) argues that accompanying the rise of household income in these three cities have been growing disparities between high-income and low-income families. In particular 'it seems clear that global elites cause the increase in the income gap between the top class and the bottom class in Singapore and Hong Kong' (Tai 2006, p. 1751) (see Table 4.2).

Resonating with the above argument on a widening income gap driven by the arrival of the global rich in the city-state, Seah Chiang Nee, a veteran Singaporean journalist wrote in a critical commentary published in the Malaysian newspaper *The Star* that: 'The influx of foreign wealth is not welcomed by all Singaporeans. Some see their cake becoming smaller and more expensive. Many of working class citizens living in the heartland do not see much benefit from having so many rich people around – but they feel the pain of rising costs' (Seah 2010).

Yet, despite the growing disparity of wealth and income, the Singapore government has resolutely maintained that the poor have been well served by the state through special provisions such as the ComCare Fund which provides financial assistance to the needy, the Workfare Income Supplement which supplements the income of low-wage workers, and other measures like rebates on household utilities bills. Indeed, the Prime Minister went so far as to claim that: 'A poor person in Singapore fares much better than the poor in Asia or the West' (Chia 2010). Due in part to the economic downturn, the number of needy Singaporeans applying for financial assistance has increased substantially, with applicants for ComCare funds jumping by 25 per cent in July and September 2011. Significantly, it is not only members of the low-income group that are in financial difficulties but now middle-lower income households are facing the pinch from rising costs of living. This has prompted the government to increase the monthly household income ceiling for those who are eligible for financial assistance from S$1800 to S$3500 (Heng 2011). Hardship among the poorest 10 per cent of Singapore's population is often hidden behind the platitudes of inclusive growth. As sociologist Chua (2011, p. 46) argues, the aged living alone and the hunger of children from low-income families are only 'visible' to the 1800 voluntary welfare organizations catering to more than 100 000 families in need of some form of charity. These urban poor, Chua argues, are 'poorly served by a very rich state with a massive foreign reserve locked up in sovereign wealth funds which relentlessly eschews redistributive social welfare because the government insists that redistributive welfare destroys the work ethic amongst its people' (Chua 2011, p. 46).

To the extent that social inequalities are becoming increasingly salient in Singapore, these disparities are often manifested in the urban landscape through the juxtaposition of highly valorized global spaces of consumption (such as the Marina Bay downtown, luxurious shopping malls in the Orchard shopping district and exclusive gated communities like Sentosa Cove and other high-end condominiums in the city centre) versus pockets of low income and ageing neighbourhoods with predominantly one-room rental flats in the HDB (Housing and Development Board) heartlands. Notwithstanding the 'success story' of Singapore's universal public housing programme, the number of homeless people picked up by welfare officers has doubled in recent years. In 2010 alone, a total of 339 people were picked up by government officials, an increase from 123 in 2007. More than half were found sleeping in void decks of Housing Board blocks as well as on beaches and in public parks (*The Straits Times* 6 July 2011). Though relatively small in numbers compared to other cities, the growing frequency of vagrancy in Singapore offers a stark reminder of the contrasting way of life in the city-state between the urban poor and the super-rich.

CONCLUSION

In a recent paper, Hay and Muller (2012) argued that geographers' academic preoccupation with studying the marginalized lives of the poor (and to some extent, the middle-class) has led us to overlook the geographies of the super-rich, and in particular, their relationship and role in reshaping places; links between their wealth and (geo)politics as well as the social and environmental consequences of 'luxury fever'. For Hay and Muller (2012, p. 75): 'it is past time for geographers and other social scientists to overcome the distaste or misplaced values that divert our attention from those who profit the most from the contours and character of contemporary global capitalism'. Earlier, Beaverstock et al. (2004) observed similarly that there is a dearth of research focusing on the seriously affluent despite their clear significance in the global economy, and they called on researchers to expose the contemporary geographies and transnational lifestyles of these global super-rich. In particular Beaverstock et al. argued that the huge disparities (both perceived and real) between the incomes of high net worth individuals and the majority of the world's population are not at all surprising given the extreme inequality and exploitation that drives the capitalist world system. What is noteworthy, however, is the apparent ability of super-rich individuals to constantly manipulate the state and market to their own benefit, often by positioning themselves in offshore havens (for example in the Cayman Islands, Channel Islands and Luxembourg) beyond the jurisdiction of particular nation-states and benefiting disproportionately from market deregulation and enhanced investment schemes offered in established financial centres such as London, New York, Frankfurt and Singapore. This is of course not to suggest that the super-rich are completely beyond the purview of nation-states for they are after all, still citizens (even nominally) and holders of nationally issued passports. Rather, what is being alluded to here is the paradox of the global super-rich as strategic *homo economicus* operating both *within* and *beyond* nation-state jurisdictions. Unquestionably, these global super rich are highly mobile and constantly on the move to exploit and seek out spaces of profit extraction in the crevices and loopholes of nation-state regulations, particularly in unregulated regional economies where they thrive. As Ley (2010, p. 9) argues, the acumen of the super-rich in capital accumulation has been associated with the 'bamboo networks' of transnational (Chinese) business families or 'territorially ungrounded' cosmopolitan capitalists (Ong and Nonini 1997; Hamilton 1999; Yeung and Olds 2000).

However, in contradistinction to Beaverstock et al.'s (2004, p. 406) assertion that the contemporary super-rich are able to devolve from local national politics and benefit from (and exploit) the withdrawal of state regulation, this chapter has discussed Singapore's specific place-based strategies to court and 'onshore' the global super-rich. These strategies have included a highly customized set of urban policies creating a favourable tax (-free) environment and 'fast-tracked' permanent resident status, coupled with the deployment of real estate products and development of super-rich enclaves such as Sentosa Cove. As this chapter suggests, strategic efforts to 'onshore' Singapore as the investment and lifestyle capital for the global super-rich are entrenched in the political economy and cultural imaginary of a neoliberal privileged urbanism. Such onshoring urban strategies, however, also risk creating an increasingly polarized society and uneven geographies of extreme wealth and exclusion. As Davis and Monk (2007, p.xv) warn, on a planet where more than two billion people subsist on two dollars or less a day, such neoliberal dream-worlds of the super-rich 'not only inflame desires for infinite consumption and promises of total social exclusion and physical security but are also clearly incompatible with the ecological and moral survival of humanity'.

NOTE

1. As noted in Chapter 1 of this volume, Capgemini and Merrill Lynch (2011) define 'high net-worth individuals' (HNWI) as people having investable assets in excess of US$1 million, excluding primary residence, collectibles, consumables and consumer durables (with ultra-HNWI owning over US$30 million in assets).

REFERENCES

Allen, M. (2006), 'Swiss financial blueprint inspires Singapore', *swissinfo. ch* (online), 13 October, http://www.swissinfo.ch/eng/Home/Archive/Swiss_ financial_blueprint_inspires_Singapore.html?cid=682448, accessed 15 March 2012.

Baum, S. (1999), 'Social transformations in the global city: Singapore', *Urban Studies*, **36** (7), 1095–117.

Beaverstock, J., Hubbard, P. and J. Short (2004), 'Getting away with it? Exposing the geographies of the super-rich', *Geoforum*, **35**, 401–7.

Brenner, N. and N. Theodore (2002), 'Cities and geographies of actually existing neoliberalism', *Antipode*, **34** (3), 349–79.

Capgemini and Merrill Lynch (2011), *World Wealth Report 2011*, www.capgemini. com/insights-and-resources/by-publication/world-wealth-report-2011/, accessed 15 March 2012.

Chan, J. (2011), 'Singapore's fast growth creating rich-poor divide?', *CNBC Asia Pacific* (online), www.cnbc.com/id/42891768/Singapore_s_Fast_Growth_ Creating_Rich_PoorDivide, accessed 15 March 2012.

Cheam, J. (2008), 'Expats rank S'pore as world's best place to live', *The Straits Times* (online), 25 July, www.straitstimes.com/Free/Story/STIStory_261111. html, accessed 21 May 2012.

Chia, S.A. (2010), 'Singapore doing a lot to help needy: PM', *The Straits Times* (online), 28 March, http://app.mfa.gov.sg/pr/read_content.asp?View,14727, accessed 21 May 2012.

Chua, B.H. (2011), 'Singapore as model: planning innovations, knowledge experts', in Roy, A. and A. Ong (eds), *Worlding Cities: Asian Experiments and the Art of Being Global*, London: Blackwell, pp. 29–54.

Davis, M. and D. Monk (2007), 'Introduction', in Davis, M. and D. Monk (eds), *Evil Paradises: Dreamworlds of Neoliberalism*, New York and London: The New Press.

Economic Development Board (Singapore) (2012), *EDB Singapore* (online), www.edb.gov.sg/edb/sg/en_uk/index.html, accessed 17 May 2012.

Economist Intelligence Unit (2011), *Liveability Ranking Report August 2011*, www.eiu.com/site_info.asp?info_name=The_Global_Liveability_Report&rf=0, accessed 15 March 2012.

Florida, R. (2002), *The Rise of the Creative Class: And How it's Transforming Work, Leisure, Community, and Everyday Life*, New York: Basic Books.

Gopalakrishnan, R. (2010), 'Singapore swing: playing for wealth crown', *Reuters* (online), 30 September, http://in.reuters.com/article/idINIndia-51860520101002, accessed 15 March 2012.

Hamilton, G. (ed.) (1999), *Cosmopolitan Capitalists: Hong Kong and the Chinese Diaspora at the End of the Twentieth Century*, Seattle, WA: University of Washington Press.

Hamnett, C. (2001), 'Social segregation and social polarization', in R. Paddison (ed.), *Handbook of Urban Studies*, London: Sage, pp. 162–76.

Hay, I. and S. Muller (2012), '"That tiny, stratospheric apex that owns most of the world" – exploring geographies of the super-rich', *Geographical Research*, **50** (1), 75–88.

Heng, J. (2011), 'More people apply for ComCare help', *The Straits Times*, 19 November 2011.

Knight Frank and Citi Private Bank (2011), *The Wealth Report*, www.knightfrank.com/wealthreport/, accessed 15 March 2012.

Knox, P. (2005), 'Vulgaria: the re-enchantment of suburbia', *Opolis: An International Journal of Suburban and Metropolitan Studies*, **1** (9), 33–46.

Ley, D. (2010), *Millionaire Migrants: Trans-Pacific Life Lines*, Chichester: Wiley-Blackwell.

Li, X.Y. (2007), 'PM Lee to address income gap', *The Straits Times*, 19 August 2007.

McCann, E.J. (1998), 'Livable city/unequal city: The politics of policy-making in a "creative" boomtown', *Interventions Economiques* (online), http://benhur teluq.uquebec.ca/rie/2008001/doss_2_McCann.html, accessed 15 March 2012.

McCann, E.J. (2004), '"Best places": inter-urban competition, quality of life, and popular media discourse', *Urban Studies*, **41** (10), 1909–29.

Mercer (2011), *Quality of Living Report 2011*, www.mercer.com/articles/quality-of-living-survey-report-2011, accessed 15 March 2012.

Ng, G. (2010), 'Singapore is third-most-liveable city', *My Paper*, 20 June, www.asiaone.com/News/AsiaOne+News/Singapore/Story/A1Story20100630-224468.html, accessed 21 May 2012.

Ng, M. (2011), 'High net worth value in Singapore to hit $740.84b', *The Straits Times* (online), 1 September, www.straitstimes.com/BreakingNews/Singapore/Story/STIStory_707984.html, accessed 21 May 2012.

Ong, A. and D. Nonini (eds) (1997), *Ungrounded Empires: The Cultural Politics of Modern Chinese Transnationalism*, New York: Routledge.

Pacione, M. (1982), 'The use of objective and subjective indicators of quality of life in human geography', *Progress in Human Geography*, **6**, 495–514.

Pacione, M. (1990), 'Urban liveability: a review', *Urban Geography*, **11** (1), 1–30.

Pacione, M. (2009), *Urban Geography a Global Perspective*, London: Routledge.

Pow, C-P. (2010), 'Recovering from the "Promethean Hangover"? Critical reflections on the remaking of Singapore as a global city', in T. Chong (ed.), *The Management of Singapore Revisited: A Critical Survey of Modern Singapore*, Singapore: Institute of Southeast Asian Studies, pp.400–416.

Pow, C-P. (2011), 'Living it up: super-rich enclave and elite urbanism in Singapore', *Geoforum*, **42** (3), 382–93.

Seah, C.N. (2010), 'Super-rich come to Singapore', *The Star* (online), 16 October, http://thestar.com.my/columnists/story.asp?file=/2010/10/16/columnists/insight downsouth/7231648&sec=insightdownsouth, accessed 15 March 2012.

Siow, L.S. (2005), 'Singapore's private banking rides crest of Asian boom Europeans – non-resident Indians add to growing clientele', *Business Times* (online), 8 April, www.business.smu.edu.sg/MWM/. . ./20050408sg_private_banking.pdf, accessed 15 March 2012.

Tai, P. (2006), 'Social polarisation comparing Singapore, Hong and Taipei', *Urban Studies*, **43** (10), 1737–56.

Tee, O.C. (2006), 'Speech by Mr Ong Chong Tee, Deputy Managing Director, Monetary Authority of Singapore, at Private Wealth Management Conference' (online), www.mas.gov.sg/news_room/statements/2006/Private_Wealth_Management_Conference.html, accessed 15 March 2012.

The Business Times Singapore Press Holdings, Singapore, www.businesstimes.com.sg/.

The Straits Times Singapore Press Holdings, Singapore, www.straitstimes.com/.

Yeoh, B.S.A. and T.C. Chang (2001), 'Globalizing Singapore: debating transnational flows in the city', *Urban Studies*, **38** (7), 1025–44.

Yeung, H. and K. Olds (eds) (2000), *Globalization of Chinese Business Firms*, Basingstoke: Macmillan.

5. 'Super-rich' Irish property developers and the Celtic Tiger economy

Laurence Murphy and Pauline McGuirk

INTRODUCTION

Ireland, long a backwater in the European economic system, underwent a profound economic transformation from the early 1990s. Within the context of sustained political support for foreign direct investment, the Irish economy experienced rapid and continuous economic growth (Drudy and Collins 2011). The metamorphosis from a struggling economy characterized by endemic out-migration into the Celtic Tiger fundamentally altered the country's self-image and physical infrastructure. The rise of the Celtic Tiger was expressed materially in new urban landscapes. Urban renewal programmes, relying on substantial tax incentives for property investors and developers, transformed the inner-city areas of large and, later, smaller cities around the country. Inner-city Dublin, long viewed as a locus of crime, drug abuse and poverty (Punch 2005), became the focus of large-scale apartment development for the new middle-classes. The derelict warehouses of Dublin's docklands area were transformed into the gleaming office blocks of the very successful International Financial Services Centre (Murphy 1998). In tandem with the economic miracle, the combination of rising real incomes and a deregulated mortgage market unleashed a latent demand for property ownership (Kitchin et al. 2010). As the property boom gathered momentum, small-scale property developers increasingly assumed the role of super-wealthy entrepreneurs. On the back of massive land price inflation, a banking system enthralled with property markets and a facilitative planning system, Irish property developers became members of the super-rich.

While Ireland and the Irish have long been associated with property development and construction, as manual workers and labourers, the rise of the Celtic Tiger property developer marked a significant change in the practices, positioning and discourses surrounding property development and developers. In common with those in other countries, Irish developers had in the past been viewed as rapacious and the harbingers of soulless architecture. However these new developers were characterized by a new scale of operations and ambition. Enmeshed in the rhetoric of success, property developers were increasingly portrayed as influential place-makers, sophisticated participants in complex financial arrangements, and global operators. Throughout the early part of the twenty-first century, property developers, politicians and bankers formed a powerful triad of interests at the heart of a thoroughgoing political-economic and socio-cultural transformation of the country.

In its turn, the unravelling of the global property boom and the legacy of the global financial crisis had a profound impact on Irish economy and society. In a dramatic turn of events the Irish banking sector tottered on the edge of collapse and the state intervened to guarantee all bank debts in September 2008 (Drudy and Collins 2011). At the core of the banks' problems was a vast mountain of debt underpinned by poorly performing property deals and a property market in free-fall. To rescue the banks, the state established a government agency, the National Asset Management Agency (NAMA), to buy €81 billion of property loans off the banks at heavily discounted prices and subsequently the state became the largest property company in the world.

The story of the rise and fall of the Celtic Tiger property developers offers insights into the role of the super-rich in material and symbolic place-making. Irish developers were not only involved in the physical construction of place(s); they were very public actors in the construction of discourses of Ireland as a place of opportunity, entrepreneurialism and success. In contrast to the relative anonymity of high-rolling financial traders, property developers were celebrated media stars. Indeed, as the property boom gathered pace, stories of past property successes arguably became an essential prerequisite for mobilizing new rounds of property investment. Developers with the 'Midas touch' were feted by the general and business media (both local and international) and courted by politicians. In this chapter we provide an account of the rise and impact of super-rich property developers in the Celtic Tiger economy. Two case studies of the changing fortunes of developers are presented which, not coincidentally, mirror the fortunes of the Irish economy. In the case studies, we reflect critically on the role of the developers' conspicuous consumption and personal wealth in mobilizing the huge bank loans on which their urban imagineering was founded.

GEOGRAPHIES OF THE SUPER-RICH PROPERTY DEVELOPER

In reflecting on the need to examine the geographies of the super-rich, Beaverstock et al. (2004) and Hay and Muller (2012) both comment on the rise of a new wealthy class. This class derives its wealth not from inheritance but from work. Beaverstock et al. argue:

> More recent theorisations identify the existence of a global bourgeois class who are somewhat different in the source of their wealth: rather than having it passed on through inheritance, their wealth is primarily derived from *working* to their fortunes and *investments*, with the very richest having significant investments in real estate businesses, stock and financial securities, as well as the growing market in luxury collectibles (wine and art). (Beaverstock et al. 2004, p. 402)

They go on to examine issues relating to '"new money" activities (in software, finance and publishing and media) as the growing source of wealth' (p. 402) and address issues relating to the 'extreme global mobility' (p. 404) of the super-rich. The focus on 'new money' activities discursively locates the super-rich in a fast world of hyper-mobile capital. While ultra-high net worth individuals clearly operate in the context of mobility, some of their sources of wealth are nonetheless embedded in specific locations (Beaverstock et al. 2011), particularly the wealth generated from real estate. Consequently, we argue in this chapter that a focus on wealthy property developers offers insights into the processes involved in the amassing of wealth but also insights into the ways in which the super-rich can affect the materiality of contemporary urban spaces and urban life, as well as the symbolic space of urban imagineering. These 'city builders' (Fainstein 2001) are different from the 'masters of the universe' who inhabit the trading floors of the core global cities. They are important not just for their conspicuous consumption (see Hay and Muller 2012) but also for their production activities. The outputs of a property boom – the office towers, mega-malls, industrial parks and housing estates – remain standing and their remaking of urban space endures, even after property values have crashed and fortunes have been lost.

Developers orchestrate the multiple interests required to produce a building. These include land, construction, user, investor and financier interests. In common with financial and currency traders, property developers are essentially risk takers. They assemble large sums of capital, usually non-recourse bank loans, in order to create specific spaces/buildings in anticipation of a future demand. The long lead times involved in creating new office, retail or industrial spaces add to the costs and risks of property development. Yet, in Ireland the local and global property booms created the conditions whereby the perceived risks of property development were diminished and the returns were enhanced. If capital, as Harvey (2010) asserts, is the architect of the built environment, property developers are the conduits of money flows. During the spectacular property boom of the 2000s, Irish property developers, buoyed by highly facilitative national fiscal and planning regulation regimes (Kitchin et al. 2010), were instrumental in guiding vast flows of money into Irish and international property markets, whilst amassing vast personal fortunes and vast financial liabilities.

In the Irish context, the way these personal fortunes were drawn upon in the financing of property deals both elevated the peaks of the property boom and underscored its vulnerability. In contrast to the sophistication of residential mortgage-backed securities and collateralized debt obligations, much of the debt underpinning the Irish property boom was derived from relatively straightforward bank lending. During this property boom banks availed widely of personal guarantees from developers to secure loans, augmenting the role of property as security for the loans by the personal wealth of the developer. In effect, the banks were treating developers not just on the economics of each property deal, but also on the wealth of the individual developer. The personal wealth of developers was viewed as a hedge against any downside risk of development, notwithstanding the fact that the developers' wealth was inextricably linked to successful development outcomes. In effect being super-rich afforded developers a form of credit enhancement in their dealings with the banks and increasingly super-rich developers were strategically placed to engage in large-scale development projects.

Key developers became instrumental in the transformation of urban spaces in Ireland. Liam Carroll, a developer of apartments and office buildings, created a substantial development footprint that led one commentator to state 'Dublin is Carroll's City' (NUIM Geography 2009). Treasury Holdings, in developing Spencer Dock in the Dublin Docklands, undertook one of the most ambitious urban renewal projects in Ireland (Moore 2008). As these developers created new material landscapes they helped to reshape urban landscapes and transform perceptions and meanings of the nation as a place/society/economy. Their developments and their deal making had material and symbolic importance. Their capacity to mobilize capital to support their deal making reflected the rise of the wealthy Irish property entrepreneur and points to their power to engage in urban imagineering.

THE CELTIC TIGER AND PROPERTY

Between 1993 and 2000, Ireland's gross domestic product grew by 8 per cent per annum (Drudy and Collins 2011). This strong export-oriented growth resulted in rising employment levels, increased real incomes and a reputation for success. Unemployment, long viewed as an intractable problem, dropped to just 4 per cent in 2002 (Drudy and Collins 2011). Rising employment and incomes translated into a significant demand for new housing that supported rapid house and land price appreciation. By 2000 the momentum of the residential market became more speculative and increasingly the resources of the economy and finance were directed to property markets. Whereas in 1997 housing contributed between 4 and 6 per cent of gross national product (GNP), by 2007 housing contributed 13 per cent of GNP (Kelly 2009). Reflective of the increasing dominance of the property sector, housing and construction contributed 20 per cent of GNP and construction employed 13.4 per cent of the workforce; the highest proportion in Europe (Kelly 2009; CSO 2008).

The role of property debt within the Irish banking sector also increased rapidly during this period. In addition to increasing mortgage business, the banks became more exposed to construction and property development debt. In 2006, the two largest banks in the state had significant exposure to construction and property sectors. Over 30 per cent of Allied Irish Bank's loan book, and 15 per cent of Bank of Ireland's, was to construction and property deals (Regling and Watson 2010). Among the smaller and more aggressive banks, the exposure to the property sector was even more significant. Property loans accounted for over 70 per cent of the total loans of Anglo-Irish Bank and the Irish Nationwide Building Society (Regling and Watson 2010). For the banking sector as a whole lending to property rose to 60 per cent of bank assets and, by early 2008, Irish borrowing (mainly for property) made up 60 per cent of GDP (Honohan 2010, p. 26).

It was during this period that individual property developers amassed considerable personal wealth and assumed an increasingly prominent role in Irish society. Table 5.1 lists the peak personal wealth of a prominent set of construction and property developers in Ireland prior to the global financial crisis. From relatively obscure and modest backgrounds, property developers had become ultra-high net worth individuals. Sean Quinn, originally a farmer with a quarry on his land, rose to head a set of business interests built around insurance and property interests, and was estimated to be worth over €4 billion in 2007. Liam Carroll, a developer of what the media termed 'shoebox' apartments, was believed to have a net worth of €800 million. Johnny Ronan and Richard Barrett, founders

Table 5.1   Irish property developers' peak wealth

Name	Industry	Net worth – Euro million	Year
Sean Quinn	Quarrying, property Insurance	4621	2007
Liam Carroll	Construction	818	2007
Gallagher family	Construction	348	2007
Sean Mulryan	Property	344	2006
Bernard MacNamara	Construction	280	2007
Gerard Gannon	Construction	231	2007
Johnny Ronan	Property	174	2006
Richard Barrett	Property	174	2006
Sean Dunne	Construction	103	2007
Garrett Kelleher	Property	62	2006

Note: Sean Quinn's wealth was strongly aligned with the insurance sector rather than property.

Source: *Sunday Times Rich List* various years.

of multinational property development company Treasury Holdings, had individual fortunes in excess of €170 million.

In contrast to the relative anonymity of securities traders, developers assumed a significant public profile either willingly or reluctantly. The alignment of developers with their developments, and the highly politicized nature of property development within the Irish planning/political system, ensured that developers were known to the public through intense media attention to their dealings and their lifestyles. In spite of his modest lifestyle and desire for a low profile, Carroll featured prominently in public debates over the poor design of new urban developments and the proliferation of small 'shoebox' apartment developments. In contrast, other developers were feted for their personal extravagance and ambitious developments. Sean Mulryan had a personal jet and two personal helicopters which he reputedly used 'like a bus service' (McDonald and Sheridan 2009, p. 227). Sean Dunne celebrated his marriage to Gayle Killilea in a high profile event on board the *Christina O*, the luxury yacht once famously owned by Aristotle Onassis, and invited an old friend Bertie Ahern, the then Irish Taoiseach (Prime Minister). Media profiling of the riches and influence to be amassed through property dealings arguably fuelled the wider wave of speculative development that seized the national economy, housing sector and, indeed, the national psyche through the 2000s. In the decade leading to December 2005, more than half a million (553 267) housing units were built. By 2007, compared to the rest of Europe, Ireland was building twice as many housing units per head of population (Kitchin et al. 2010).

The rise of the Irish 'property developer celebrity' accords with wider accounts of developers as egotistical 'risk takers'. Fainstein (2001, p. 67) writing on New York and London property markets, recounts one developer's view of himself as a type of movie impresario, relying on his reputation to assemble a cast of property interests to 'create' a building. Like movie directors, a developer's reputation carries weight in the investment decisions made by property investors. And that reputation, in turn, relies on public perception and profile. Within the Celtic Tiger economy, the public perception of the property developer acquired new associations, quite different from older perceptions of the 'Irish Builder', tinged with cultural cringe. Increasingly these developers were linked to an emergent sense of Celtic entrepreneurialism as Irish property developers began pursuing international strategies that were both audacious and symbolically meaningful. Irish developers purchased iconic buildings in London (The Savoy Hotel Group, Battersea Power Station) and invested in Russia and China. They were influential in shifting both internal and external understandings of Ireland, from an image as EU's welfare-dependent poor cousin to an image as an entrepreneurial global success story, ripe with business and investment acumen (*The Economist* 2005).

The booming Irish property market provided the financial backing for developers to leverage more debt to pursue international investment. In particular, the UK became a significant target of investment flows for Irish property developers and it is here that the symbolic import of the new Celtic entrepreneur became evident. Key property deals 'woke up' the market to a new cadre of super-rich Irish developers and cemented them as key players in the London market. Three projects are particularly noteworthy. In 2004, an Irish syndicate led by Derek Quinlan, purchased the Savoy Hotel group (including the Savoy, the Berkeley, Claridge's and the Connaught) for £750 million (McDonald and Sheridan 2009). The scale of the deal and the iconic nature of the hotels meant that Irish developers were now placed at the heart of the London property market. In 2006, Johnny Ronan and Richard Barrett's Real Estate Opportunities (REO) company purchased the Battersea Power Station, the largest single urban regeneration site in central London, for £400 million (Kollewe 2011). The purchase of another iconic landmark building and the scale of the potential redevelopment plans clearly positioned Irish developers as key players in London's urban regeneration programmes. Finally, in a deal rich with historic symbolism, in 2007 Patrick Doherty's Harcourt Developments purchased from the British Conservative Party their former headquarters on Smith Square for £30 million (McDonald and Sheridan

2009). Although the Conservative Party was no longer resident, and Harcourt Developments on-sold the building quickly, the purchase caught the media's attention. In total, the rising tide of Irish property ownership in London, the heart of the old colonial foe, marked a significant economic and symbolic moment in the growth of the Celtic economy and a resonant moment in the progressive transformation in the international perception of Ireland and the Irish. In many ways this flow of investment represented an inverted case of the 'Empire strikes back' with super-rich Irish developers at the vanguard of the assault.

DEVELOPERS AND PLACE-MAKING

Large and elaborate property deals, such as those outlined above, have the capacity to remake urban space, its social relations and its imaginings. We contend that developers' personal wealth and lifestyles have been instrumental in enabling these deals to be actualized, though the developments themselves may have unravelled in the aftermath of the global financial crisis and the Irish banking crisis more specifically. Irish developers created new physical places and as global deal-makers, attracting the attention of the global media (*The Economist* 2005), they helped to refashion Ireland's and Dublin's place in discourses of the global economy. Reflecting on the activities of key players in the boom is instructive on this point, so we briefly explore two indicative examples: Sean Dunne's property activities and the rise of Richard Barrett and Johnny Ronan's Treasury Holdings. These case studies are used to illustrate different facets of the 'rich developer'/deal-making nexus. Dunne represents the rise of the lone, 'small time' developer who became a celebrity deal marker. Dunne's capacity to secure financing on what was then the most expensive land purchase in Ireland highlights the power of the individual developer to mobilize large volumes of capital and to engage in urban imagineering. In contrast, Treasury Holdings are corporate players that leveraged their Irish property portfolio to fund an international development portfolio. Treasury represented a new wave of Irish entrepreneurs competing in the global centres of London, Paris and Shanghai. Significantly, both Dunne and Treasury's development activities generated considerable national and international media attention (Thomas 2009) and developers were at the forefront of new discourses of Irish entrepreneurs (*The Economist* 2005).

Sean Dunne's rise to prominence, and indeed the subsequent downturn in his fortunes, embodies key elements of the dynamic underpinning the property boom in Ireland. Born in the small rural town of Tullow, County Carlow, as one of five children, Dunne started work at 12 because, as he put it, 'we had to' (McDonald and Sheridan 2009, p. 198). Having worked as a quantity surveyor, he established Mountbrook Homes, which undertook its first housing development in 1983. Initially involved in building social housing, Mountbrook expanded to become a large-scale mixed use developer responsible for developments such as Whitewater Shopping Centre (the largest centre built outside of Dublin) and the Riverside IV development in Dublin's Docklands. During the peak of the property boom Dunne was responsible for some of the most spectacular property deals in the country. In 2005, he purchased the Jurys Berkeley Court Hotel site in Ballsbridge, a prestigious central suburb known for its expensive residential streets and as a centre of foreign embassies, for a then record €379 million (Kelly 2011). The Jurys purchase price equated to a then unprecedented €54 million per acre. Dunne's subsequent purchase of Hume House, an office block adjacent to the Jurys site for €130 million raised his investment in the site to over €500 million. These purchases were funded with loans from Ulster Bank (a subsidiary of RBS) which syndicated the loan, bringing in other overseas banks including the Icelandic Kaupthing Bank. While the bulk of the funding for the Jurys site was secured from banks' loans, it was reported that Dunne contributed €130 million of his own money (Quinlan 2009). In the following year, he purchased the AIB Bankcentre site, again in Ballsbridge, for €207 million.

The high price paid for the Jurys site necessitated that the scale of any development be significant and Dunne certainly envisaged a grandiose project aligned to his professed desire to transform the area into 'a new Knightsbridge' with a 'Manhattan-like lifestyle'. His initial €1 billion masterplan included a 37 storey, glass-clad residential tower (cut like a diamond), 14000 square metres of retail space, a 232-bedroom hotel, an 18000-square-metre embassy complex and a 28000-square-metre office complex (Mountbrook 2007). Notwithstanding the fact that the development breached the local planning regulations, and was out of character with the local residential environment, the Council initially approved the development minus the 37-storey tower. Thereafter, Dunne entered into a protracted and contentious set of planning appeals. In September 2011, a much scaled-back €300 million development, minus the embassy complex and with a 12-storey tower replacing the original 37 storeys, was eventually approved (Kelly 2011).

The planning saga surrounding Dunne's Ballsbridge adventure played out against the backdrop of a massive banking crisis in Ireland arising from the global financial crisis (see below). Dunne's property empire began to disintegrate from 2008 onwards and he has subsequently been enmeshed in restructuring debts and unwinding deals. In 2011, NAMA appointed receivers for Dunne's businesses that owned money to Irish banks. The Jurys Berkeley Court site, was estimated to have a value of only €50 million in 2011 (Kelly 2011), a loss of 86 per cent of its value. Dunne's property dealings have had a significant impact on his personal wealth and a profound impact on his public standing. In 2011 the most expensive house in Ireland, reputedly owned by Dunne (Dunne's wife Gayle is the beneficial owner) and bought for €58 million in 2005, was placed on the market for €15 million. Dunne has moved his residence to the US in an attempt to escape the public scrutiny placed on him in Ireland (Curran 2011). Significantly, in March 2012 he was ordered by the Irish Courts to repay €185 million to NAMA, of which €150 million related to personal guarantees that he gave in order to secure loans for a number of developments (McDonald and O'Donovan 2012).

If Dunne represents one facet of the super-rich developer and the actual and imagined transformations of Ireland's urban landscapes and place identity, the rise of Richard Barrett and Johnny Ronan marks another significant moment in the rise of the transnational Irish developer. Barrett, a barrister, and Ronan, an accountant, set up Treasury Holdings in 1989. By 2009 Treasury had 131 individual real estate projects with a combined value in excess of €4.6 billion and a gross development value (GDV) estimated to be over €19 billion (Treasury 2010). Treasury leveraged off the Celtic property boom to construct a property portfolio that included properties in the UK, Russia and China to become genuinely trans-national Irish developers and to further reposition Ireland's place in the global imaginary. The centrality of the Celtic boom to the Group's success was highlighted on their website:

> Capitalising on over a decade of burgeoning economic growth, the Group's Irish portfolio has underpinned much of the Group's success and has led to a property empire valued in excess of €3.4 billon in Irish assets alone. (Treasury 2010)

Barrett and Ronan, as the driving force behind Treasury, represented the professional and corporate face of the Irish property boom. Treasury's purchase of the Battersea Power Station in London reflected the financial ambitions of the group and firmly positioned Treasury in the eye of the media. The proposed masterplan for the site, involving the largest ever planning application in central London, includes approximately '3400 new homes, 161 000 sqm of office floorspace, 64 000 sqm of retail, restaurants, a hotel, leisure space and community facilities' (REO 2011).

In contrast to the secrecy of financial services, Treasury was not a faceless corporation as both Barrett and Ronan had high public profiles and, respectively, audacious and flamboyant personalities that, arguably, shaped Treasury's development (McDonald and Sheridan 2009). Barrett, a self-confessed wine connoisseur, is known for his attention to legal details. His view that 'certain opponents of ours have underestimated our ability to cause legal chaos to their detriment' is reflected in the more than 40 legal actions Treasury has taken, often against other developers (McDonald and Sheridan 2009, p. 169). Ronan's larger-than-life personality is associated with a 'ferocious drive and hotheadedness' (McDonald and Sheridan 2009, p. 161) and with a lavish lifestyle of conspicuous consumption. Ronan owned a helicopter, a Hummer, a €640 000 Maybach car and several houses. In 1998 Treasury held a party in Modena for 50 guests, entertained by Luciano Pavarotti (McDonald and Sheridan 2009).

But the extravagant lifestyles of Barrett and Ronan were not simply the product of their property deals. They were also important ingredients in the deal-making process. In securing the Battersea deal, Barrett undertook a number of lavish dinner meetings with the Hong Kong developers who owned the site, George and Victor Hwang, and discovered a shared passion for wines with George. On reflection Barrett viewed this process as important in developing the relationship that later resulted in the finalized property deal (McDonald and Sheridan 2009). Personal wealth and its trappings, flanked by reputational clout, enable the various elements of 'the deal' to be orchestrated.

Nonetheless, neither symbolic nor personal capital could shield these super-rich developers from the tremors of the global financial crisis, nor its mirror in the Irish banking crisis. As with all developers in Ireland, Treasury Holdings were seriously affected by the crisis. The debt on Treasury's Irish and UK property portfolio was taken over by NAMA and the developers are now working with NAMA to pay off their loans. While their debts have been effectively nationalized the developers continue to be employed in order to turn these projects into profitable concerns.

The business and social trajectories of Dunne, Barrett and Ronan are reflective of a range of personal narratives of the rise of super-rich developers in the Celtic Tiger economy. In common with other Irish property developers their conspicuous consumption was a mark of success that was read by the 'market'. Being wealthy provided not just symbolic and social capital but real capital that secured bank funding. The willingness of bankers to underwrite grandiose development projects reflected not just the present value of projected income streams but also an evaluation of the extent to which developers had 'skin in the game' or money in the development. The wealth of developers was materially incorporated into property deals though the use of personal guarantees. Dunne's purchase of the Jurys site and his use of personal guarantees was symptomatic of this process. In theory, the large houses, helicopters, jets and expensive cars were developers' personal assets that offered the opportunity for banks to chase down any bad debts. These guarantees were a backstop against any deal that went sour. They were not, however, designed to deal with a systemic property market collapse. Significantly, since the crash NAMA has pursued developers such as Dunne and Carroll for payment of personal guarantees. For NAMA, and the courts, these guarantees from wealthy developers represent material assets that were central to the property deals that they were employed in, and need to be recovered (McDonald and O'Donovan 2012).

THE BANKING CRISIS AND THE SOCIALIZATION OF PROPERTY DEBT

The Irish banking sector boomed during the Celtic Tiger years and bank shares hit record levels in 2007. However, the unfolding US subprime mortgage market debacle and the resultant liquidity crisis and global financial crisis dealt a severe blow to the Irish banking sector. In September 2008, in the face of a potential collapse of the sector, the government introduced a blanket bank guarantee covering €400 billion of liabilities owned by Irish banks. The perilous state of the banks became increasingly obvious and in January 2009 the government nationalized Anglo Irish Bank, a bank that had taken a major position in funding large property developments. Ireland became the first European country to enter recession and the dual financial and economic crises had a huge negative effect on the Irish property market. As in all downturns, declining rental values and rising yields resulted in significant falls in capital values.[1] As capital values of properties dropped, loan to value ratios on development projects rose and developers faced the prospect of breaching their loan covenants. Under pressure, developers had to generate more income at a time when refinancing was impossible. Increasingly developers were unable to sustain their debt repayments and the banks were left with more and more worthless property debts. As the banks tottered on the brink of disaster, the government responded by establishing NAMA as a 'work-out' vehicle designed to recapitalize the banks and deal with the property crisis. NAMA was set up to purchase €81 billion of property loans from the banks at a heavy discount or 'haircut', based on 'current values' (NAMA 2010). Having taken on the banks' bad debts its objective is to recover, for Irish taxpayers, all that it paid for the loans and all that it invests to enhance the underlying assets. In effect the banks' property problems have been socialized.

NAMA's relationship with developers is double-edged. Developers are liable for the debts they have incurred yet, given the poor state of property markets, NAMA is required to work with developers to ensure that the state's investment is recovered. Just how NAMA discharges its duty is of particular public concern. Reflective of the sensitivities surrounding this issue the Chairman of NAMA stated:

> any borrower who expects the taxpayer to assume his or her debt burden clearly misunderstands what NAMA is about. We have been *assiduous in acquiring personal guarantees provided by borrowers to the institutions* even if such guarantees are currently worthless and we have, therefore, not paid for them. (Daly 2010. Emphasis added)

Reflective of the key role of personal guarantees given by super-rich developers, the state has acted to acquire these guarantees as a means of accessing developers' assets.

And so, in the unfolding drama of what is colloquially known as NAMA-land, developers have increasingly had to deal with the new government agency as it pursues the personal fortunes on which the super-rich property developers could once leverage their bank loans. NAMA placed companies owned by Sean Dunne into receivership in 2011, even as the Jurys Berkeley Court development was receiving planning permission. Significantly, the Jurys development is outside of NAMA as it was funded by a non-Irish bank. Yet in the wake of the downturn Dunne is subject to being pursued for his personal assets and although he has shifted to live in the US, he remains a target of considerable media scrutiny (O'Farrell and Hanley 2010). Treasury have also entered NAMA and the agency is pursuing strategies designed to secure a return on its investment. Part of this strategy involves bankrolling the development company to ensure its solvency. At the time that Treasury was being bailed out by NAMA, Johnny Ronan was involved in a high profile overnight holiday to Morocco that cost €60 000 (Bar-Hillel and Bar-Hillel 2010) and generated considerable public disquiet. The continuing saga of these 'super rich' developers points to their enduring effects on the post-boom urban landscape.

CONCLUSIONS

The genesis of the Irish Celtic Tiger economy was based on export-led manufacturing growth and a low corporate tax regime. Over time the performance of the Irish economy became increasingly enmeshed with the fortunes of the property sector (Drudy and Collins 2011) and, most spectacularly, with the machinations of a cadre of super-rich property developers. In this chapter we have traced the connections between the property boom and the rise of these super-rich property developers, and suggested that the vast sums of money loaned by the banks to the property sector reflected the confidence that bankers placed in wealthy developers. Personal extravagance, audacity and high media profiles became important ingredients in successful deal-making. Developers, traditionally viewed as disreputable and potentially crooked, assumed a symbolic role as key Celtic Tiger entrepreneurs; particularly the case in Irish developers' forays into the UK property market. Significantly, in contrast to technology and high finance entrepreneurs, property developers' investment strategies were inherently focused on place-making and the creation of new built environments, and as such they were responsible for generating new geographies of urban development. Their gleaming office towers and residential apartments became the physical embodiment of the boom, even if some of the most elaborate plans did not materialize. Developers mobilized vast flows of capital in order to implement their 'city visions' and these visions reshaped the socio-economic geographies and imaginings of cities around Ireland and overseas. In addition, the capacity of these super-rich developers to engineer large-scale financial deals and to undertake audacious global investments helped to transform the economy and reposition Ireland, and Irish entrepreneurs, in the global space economy.

The fall from grace of the developer–banker–politician triad that was responsible for the Celtic property boom was rapid and has had profound implications for Irish economy and society (see Kitchin et al. 2010). The socialization of the bankers and developers failed deals via NAMA, combined with the implementation of economic austerity measures to meet the demands of the ECB and the IMF, have impacted upon all elements of the Irish citizenry, but especially the poor.

Developers are no longer feted as dynamic entrepreneurs but are viewed as key authors of the crisis. Liam Carroll, who once had a net worth of almost €1 000 000 000, is now bankrupt. Sean Dunne, the 'squire' of Ballsbridge, admitted to *The New York Times* that he was technically insolvent (Thomas 2009), and is increasingly struggling to secure his future (McDonald and O'Donovan 2012). Johnny Ronan's 'larger than life' character traits that were once viewed as endearing are now viewed as inappropriate and damaging to the future development of the company. Notwithstanding the public opprobrium levelled at developers, they continue to maintain that with time and money they can weather the crash and, in a Faustian deal, NAMA is continuing to support larger developers as a way of generating a return on its, and the taxpayers', portfolio. The specific character of the Irish property boom, with its emphasis on personal guarantees, places the super-rich at the heart of property deals. As super-rich developers have scrambled to secure their assets, the Irish economy and people have paid a huge price for their extravagance. As property values have crashed, one in three household mortgages in the state are in negative equity and mortgage arrears rates are soaring (Kitchin 2012), it is clear that Ireland's super-rich property developers have left a dubious legacy.

NOTE

1. The direct capitalization approach to valuing commercial property investment is based on the equation: Capital value = Rent/Yield. The yield is derived from market transactions and is affected by price cycles. During a property boom the price of buildings rise and therefore, for a given rent, the yield falls. In effect, during a boom buildings are viewed as less risky and investors are willing to take a lower yield. During a slump prices fall and, for any given rent, the yield increases (see Whipple 2006).

REFERENCES

Bar-Hillel, P. and M. Bar-Hillel (2010), 'Will the antics of Battersea Power Station's Irish playboy owner jeopardise the £5.5bn project?', *London Evening Standard* (online), 19 March, www.thisislondon.co.uk/standard/article-23816907-will-the-antics-of-battersea-power-stations-irish-playboy-owner-jeopardise-the-pound-55bn-project.do, accessed 14 December 2011.

Beaverstock, J., Hall, S. and T. Wainwright (2011), 'Servicing the super-rich: new financial elites and the rise of the private wealth management retail ecology', *Regional Studies*, Doi:10.1080/00343404.2011.587795.

Beaverstock, J., Hubbard, P. and J. Short (2004), 'Getting away with it? Exposing the geographies of the super-rich', *Geoforum*, **35**, 401–7.

Central Statistics Office (2008), 'Construction and housing in Ireland', www.eirestat.cso.ie/releasespublications/documents/construction/current/constructhousing.pdf, accessed 16 April 2012.

Curran, R. (2011), 'Dunne gave €150m in guarantees', *The Sunday Business Post* (online), 24 July, www.sbpost.ie/news/ireland/dunne-gave-150m-in-guarantees-57688.html, accessed 29 July 2011.

Daly, F. (2010), 'NAMA – the objectives, progress and challenges', address by Frank Daly, Chairman of the National Asset Management Agency, to the CPA Annual Conference 2010, www.nama.ie/publications/?wpfb_list_page=4, accessed 16 April 2012.

Drudy, P. and M. Collins (2011), 'Ireland: from boom to austerity', *Cambridge Journal of Regions Economy and Society*, **4**, 339–54.

Fainstein, S. (2001), *The City Builders* (2nd edn), Lawrence, KS: University Press of Kansas.

Harvey, D. (2010), *The Enigma of Capital and the Crises of Capitalism*, London: Profile Books.

Hay, I. and S. Muller (2012), '"That tiny, stratospheric apex that owns most of the world" – exploring geographies of the super-rich', *Geographical Research*, **50** (1), 75–88.

Honohan, P. (2010), 'The Irish banking crisis: regulatory and financial sta-
bility policy 2003–2008', Irish Central Bank, www.bankinginquiry.gov.ie/
The%20Irish%20Banking%20Crisis%20Regulatory%20and%20Financial%20St
ability%20Policy%202003-2008.pdf, accessed 12 April 2012.
Kelly, M. (2009), *The Irish Credit Bubble*, UCD Centre for Economic Research,
working paper series, WP09/32, UCD School of Economics, Dublin.
Kelly, O. (2011), 'Approval for Dunne's Ballsbridge proposal', *Irish Times*
(online), 17 September, www.irishtimes.com/newspaper/ireland/2011/0917/
1224304267437.html, 16 April 2012.
Kitchin, R. (2012), 'Prospects for the Irish property market', www.ucd.ie/geary/
static/podcasts/ieconf/. . ./RobKitchin.pdf, accessed 8 February 2012.
Kitchin, R., J. Gleeson, K. Keaveney and C. O'Callaghan (2010), 'Haunted
landscape: housing and ghost estates in post-Celtic Tiger Ireland', NIRSA
working paper 59, National University of Ireland, Maynooth, www.nuim.ie/
nirsa/research/documents/WP59-A-Haunted-Landscape.pdf, accessed 16 April
2012.
Kollewe, J. (2011), 'BPS pushes another developer into administration', *The
Guardian* (online), 12 December, www.guardian.co.uk/business/2011/dec/12/
battersea-power-station-administration, accessed 3 February 2012.
McDonald, D. and D. O'Donovan (2012), 'Bankruptcy fear as Dunne must repay
NAMA €185m', *Independent.ie*, 10 March, www.independent.ie/national-news/
bankruptcy-fear-as-dunne-must-repay-nama-185m-3045904.html, accessed 16
April 2012.
McDonald, F. and K. Sheridan (2009), *The Builders: How a Small Group
of Property Developers Fuelled the Building Boom and Transformed Ireland*,
London: Penguin Books.
Moore, N. (2008), *Dublin Docklands Reinvented: The Post-Industrial Regeneration
of a European City Quarter*, Dublin: Four Courts Press.
Mountbrook (2007), 'Vision for Jurys Berkeley Court site fact sheet: factual
extract from planning documents', 4 September, www.mountbrook.ie/wp-
content/themes/mountbrook-wp/pdf/factsheet.pdf, accessed 26 June 2010.
Murphy, L. (1998), 'Financial engine or glorified back office? Dublin's International
Financial Services Centre going global', *Area*, **30**, 157–65.
National Asset Management Agency (NAMA) (2010), 'National Asset
Management Agency: a brief guide 2010', www.nama.ie/?s=haircut, accessed
3 February 2012.
NUIM Geography (2009), 'Carroll's city: Mapping the Zoe developments', http://
nuimgeography.wordpress.com/tag/zoe/, accessed 16 April 2012.
O'Farrell, M. and V. Hanley (2010), 'Sean Dunne's life in Nama: as the Irish
shiver ahead of €6bn in budget cuts, the bailed-out builder lives in this $8m US
mansion – while his wife builds another next door', *Mail Online*, 6 December,
www.dailymail.co.uk/news/article-1336211/Sean-Dunne-lives-8m-US-mansion-
wife-builds-door.html#ixzz1de9tLmWb, accessed 14 November 2011.
Punch, M. (2005), 'Problem drug use and the political economy of urban restructuring: heroin, class and governance in Dublin', *Antipode*, **37**, 754–74.
Quinlan, R. (2009), 'Dunne's D4 dream falls victim to harsh reality', *Independent.
ie*, 1 February, www.independent.ie/national-news/dunnes-d4-dream-falls-
victim-to-harsh-reality-1622977.html, accessed 2 November 2011.
Regling, K. and M. Watson (2010), *A Preliminary Report on The Sources of
Ireland's Banking Crisis*, Dublin: Government Publications.

REO (2011), 'Real estate opportunities', www.realestateopportunities.biz/, accessed 1 November 2011.

The Economist (2005), 'The Celtic reconquest: Irish property groups are bursting out of their island across Europe', 21 April, www.economist.com/node/3899143, accessed 12 October 2010.

Thomas, L. (2009), 'The Irish economy's rise was steep, and the fall was fast', *The New York Times* (online), 3 January, www.nytimes.com/2009/01/04/business/worldbusiness/04ireland.html?pagewanted=all, accessed 10 May 2010.

Treasury (2010), 'Treasury Holdings; Treasury Ireland', www.treasuryholdings.com/treasury_ireland.aspx, accessed 19 March 2010.

Whipple, R.T.M. (2006), *Property Valuation and Analysis*, Sydney, NSW: Thompson Lawbook Co.

6. The homes of the super-rich: multiple residences, hyper-mobility and decoupling of prime residential housing in global cities

Chris Paris

INTRODUCTION

The year 2010 was good for billionaires. In March 2011 the *Forbes* list of the world's billionaires reported a new record number, over 1200, and combined net worth of US$4.5 trillion, providing ample opportunities to shop globally for additions to their portfolios of homes. Mexican Carlos Slim stayed on top of the pile, with a reported fortune of US$74 billion; the number of billionaires in China had doubled since the 2010 list; and Moscow was home to more billionaires than any other city.

This chapter develops ideas and arguments sketched out in Beaverstock et al. (2004) and Iain Hay's introduction to this book, through a focus on the residences of the super-rich and their impacts on housing markets in London, the second homes capital of the world. Two issues are explored in detail: (1) the ability of hyper-mobile super-rich individuals and families to purchase numerous homes in many locations with complex spatial interrelations between countries of residence and ownership; and (2) the impact of super-rich overseas buyers of luxury homes in prime locations, contributing to a de-coupling of parts of London's housing market from the general dynamics of the UK housing system.

BACKGROUND

Hay draws attention to the rapid increase in the numbers of super-rich individuals and families, with the global financial crisis accentuating the massive differences between them and the rest of society. Such differences are particularly marked in the housing circumstances of the super-rich, and their impacts on urban form and regional housing markets. Beaverstock et al. (2004, p.405) suggested that the spatial impacts of the super-rich had largely been overlooked by geographers, who 'have rarely (if ever) questioned the immense claim that the super-rich make on the landscapes of contemporary cities'. Like most other social scientists, and especially housing research specialists, more attention had been paid to the circumstances and problems of the poor and disenfranchised. Beaverstock et al. (2004) found a huge literature on gentrification of formerly run-down parts of New York and London, but silence regarding the domination by the rich of prime residential areas in those cities. These issues are central to this chapter which considers how the super-rich are affecting residential property markets in hot locations and how their investment decisions are re-shaping housing markets on an *international* scale.

Housing researchers have largely ignored the impact of globalization and typically conceive housing markets as sets of interactions contained by national boundaries. By way of contrast, Beaverstock et al. (2004, p.403) criticized the assumption that the super-rich dwell within specific nation states, rather they 'must be regarded as transnational', sharing a global rather than national orientation; they are hyper-mobile and 'most of the super-rich have multiple residences' (Beaverstock et al. 2004, p.404).

The identification of specific members of the global super-rich is typically through various lists published by *Forbes* magazine and *The Sunday Times* Rich List. These lists provide detailed information on super-rich individuals and families and their homes. There is also other good evidence about their homes deriving from industry and media sources, including research and commentary by financial institutions and organizations such as Halifax Bank, housing market organizations, and up-market UK estate agents. Two firms in particular, Knight Frank and Savills, provide regular market analysis and commentary with a range of survey-based data on housing and other property markets in major countries. Government departments in the UK regularly publish a range of housing data, including disaggregated house price changes by dwelling type and region, and the Land Registry has excellent data on house price variations at small enough scales to identify sub-regional and local differences. There are also good sources of data on second homes owned by English households and the spatial distribution of second home ownership in England. By way of contrast, Irish housing data are much less useful and private sector agencies do not provide the same level of detailed analysis or information as in Britain.

Many websites and magazines are devoted to the super-rich and global celebrities, including their homes, with many fascinating clips on YouTube.com. The reliability of much web data may be in question, and sites contain diverse mixtures of envy, contempt, anger and lust over property pornography, but they also contain some brilliant commentary (see Beatthewolf 2011).

THE SUPER-RICH AND THEIR HOMES: HERE, THERE AND EVERYWHERE

Affluent global elites include business magnates, energy and minerals barons, financiers and investors, artists and dealers, royalty, show business and sporting superstars, and some celebrity politicians. They own multiple dwellings in many countries as well as fleets of luxury yachts, and can take their pick of additional homes in many locations *and* their nominal country of residence. Unlike the super-rich of pre-industrial societies, or even the richest families of the 1930s, our contemporary subjects have almost unlimited mobility, typically in their own or chartered airplanes, or first-class on premier airlines.

The *Forbes* and *The Sunday Times* lists cover sources of wealth, confirming the view that many of the contemporary super-rich have acquired their fortunes rapidly through industry, finance and 'new money' including software, publishing and the media. To some extent contemporary sources of affluence differ from the classic ways of becoming rich in pre-industrial societies: through royal birth, by benefaction from emperors or kings, colonialism and/or military conquest and plunder (Beresford and Rubinstein 2007). Such sources of wealth are largely absent from recent rich lists, though some fortunes amassed in the former USSR may have involved plunder (see John Rennie Short's chapter in this volume).

Beaverstock et al. (2004) noted that those who acquired wealth by inheritance were a smaller proportion of the richest in 2003 than in 1984, but dynastic inheritance remains a great way to become super-rich. For example, the richest British-born person on *The Sunday Times* Rich List in 2011, Gerald Grosvenor 6th Duke of Westminster, inherited massive London property estates. He grew his fortune by widespread property development and other investments in the UK and overseas; his total wealth includes 'vast estates in Lancashire and Cheshire, great swathes of central London, in Mayfair and Belgravia, and tracts of land in Scotland, Canada and around the world' (Beresford and Rubinstein 2007, p. 183). One of his predecessors, Hugh Lupus Grosvenor, had inherited property wealth in Mayfair in 1869, when he became the 3rd Marquess of Grosvenor. Also a property developer, his loyalty to the then-Prime Minister was rewarded with the conferring of the dukedom of Westminster in 1874; he died in 1899 leaving a fortune estimated to have been worth the equivalent of nearly £10 billion in 2007 values (Beresford and Rubinstein 2007). Unlike the current Duke, his property holdings were confined to England. Even his fortune almost fades into insignificance beside the estimated worth of the richest-ever Briton, Alan Rufus. Born in Brittany, he served with William the Conqueror and was amply rewarded, made Earl of Richmond and had Richmond Castle built as his home and stronghold. He died in 1093 owning huge amounts of land across England estimated to have been worth over £80 billion at 2007 values (Beresford and Rubinstein 2007). But he never travelled far from France and Britain, being limited to horse-drawn surface transport and wind or muscle-driven oar power at sea.

The super-rich typically own spacious homes as investments and sites of luxury consumption, often within heavily secured environments in guarded and fortified estates and plutocratic metropolitan enclaves. The second-richest couple in the world, Bill and Melinda Gates, own a luxurious mansion worth about US$150 million beside Lake Washington in Medina, WA. By way of contrast, the richest of all, Carlos Slim, lives in a relatively modest six-bedroom house in suburban Mexico City (Alexander, H. 2011). When asked by Larry King why he did not have a much bigger home, Slim replied that he saw no point in owning massive empty mansions (King 2010). However, his home contains original works by Michelangelo, Van Gogh, Renoir, El Greco and Rodin; he owns a huge yacht; and had recently bought a US$44 million dollar mansion in New York as an investment (Admin 2010).

Many own *lots* of trophy homes and some may be unsure how many homes they own. During the 2008 presidential campaign in the US, Republican candidate Senator John McCain could not answer a question about how many houses he owned for his own and family use; he responded 'I'll have my staff get to you'. His staff subsequently said that the McCains' owned 'at least four (homes)' though a watchdog organization, Politifact.com (2008), claimed that they probably owned eight, including a high rise condo in Virginia, a 6 acre (2.4 hectares) ranch in Arizona and condos in Colorado, Texas and Oklahoma.

One distinguishing feature of the homes of the super-rich is that the majority are *unoccupied* for most if not all of the time, apart from security personnel and other staff. Super-rich media stars Tom Cruise and Katie Holmes own numerous properties, including one each in London and Telluride, CO, and a US$35 million mansion in Beverly Hills.

Such hyper-consumption in itself is not particularly new and many great historic English country houses were funded by the fruits of colonialism and overseas trade or through revenues generated by vast landholding. For example, colonial adventurer and mining entrepreneur Cecil Rhodes once owned the magnificent Dalham Hall estate in Suffolk, England. The ability of the super-rich to own many properties in different countries and be able to use them at will however, is much more recent. They have almost unlimited choice in the types of homes they buy and where they buy them, together with virtually unlimited capacity to travel between their homes. The current owner of Dalham Hall is the ruler of Dubai, Sheikh Mohammed bin Rashid al-Maktoum; he already owned part of the estate for his racing horses and bought the hall in 2009 for £45 million (Conradi 2009). The high degree of contemporary mobility between the residences of the super-rich contrasts sharply with the circumstances of the super-rich in earlier periods, when mobility was much more limited. Wealth now facilitates choice of countries in which to be based, to minimize tax obligations and/or enjoy desires and fantasies. John Travolta has even combined a luxurious home with a personal aircraft terminal.

I have argued elsewhere that housing scholars have attached too much significance to ideas of 'the home' as a special place (Paris 2011). Rather, large numbers of middle and higher income households, as well as the super-rich, own *more* than one dwelling for their personal and family use[1]; thus affluence, mobility and *multiple* home ownership undermine the concept of 'home' in the singular (Hall 2005; Paris 2011). The many homes of the super-rich show how residential properties are *investment* items containing spaces that may be used or not as convenient at various times of the year, or forms of asset-sheltering and money laundering rather than dwellings in which they actually live. They are also potential bolt-holes should political or other problems emerge in their owners' countries (Caesar 2008).

The Sunday Times Rich List for 2011 showcased the extreme mobility of the global super-rich and their ability to switch countries of residence with ease, while taking advantage of 'non dom' tax status (that is, being the national of a certain country while not actually living there) wherever possible. Only two of the UK's richest 12 people were born in the UK and two others had UK citizenship (see Table 6.1). The list was topped by Lakshmi Mittal, an Indian citizen, and included two other Indian families and three Russians. Mittal was ranked sixth in the world in 2011 by *Forbes* and had also topped the UK Rich List in 2006, at which time Chelsea FC owner Roman Abramovitch was second and Grosvenor came third. Mittal owns numerous homes in the UK (mainly in Kensington), and in India.

Other super-rich Indians have concentrated their housing wealth more at home than overseas. The most expensive home ever reported was recently completed in Mumbai for Mukesh Ambani, ninth on the 2011 *Forbes* global list of billionaires. The 27-storey mansion, 'Antilla', dominates the Mumbai skyline, soaring above the chaotic mixture of sparkling

Table 6.1   The Sunday Times *UK Rich List 2011*

Rank	Wealth (million)	Name	Citizenship	Sources of wealth
1	£17500	Lakshmi Mittal and family	India	Steel
2	£12400	Alisher Usmanov	Russia	Steel, mining
3	£10000	Roman Abramovich	Russia	Oil, industry
4	£7000	Gerald Grosvenor, 6th Duke of Westminster	UK	Inheritance, land, property
5	£6800	Ernesto and Kirsty Bertarelli	Switzerland & UK	Pharmaceuticals
6	£6237	Leonard Blavatnik	Russia	Industry
7	£6200	John Fredriksen and family	Norway	Shipping
8	£6176	David and Simon Reuben	UK	Property
9=	£6000	Gopi and Sri Hinduja	India	Industry and finance
9=	£6000	George and Galen Weston and family	Canada	Retailing
11	£5400	Charlene de Carvalho-Heineken and Michel Carvalho	Netherlands	Inheritance, banking, brewing
12	£4900	Ravi Ruia	India	Energy

Source: Sunday Times (online) 2011 http://www.thesundaytimes.co.uk/public/richlist.

modern new buildings and festering slums (Mawani 2011). Another Indian business tycoon, Vijay Mallya, was reported to be building a penthouse mansion in Bangalore City; the 'White House in the Sky' will top a 34-storey tower block with around 80 apartments, 10 of which are for members of Mallya's family (Bangalore Property Updates 2011).

Abramovitch has an extraordinary portfolio of homes, yachts and aeroplanes, described by Smith (2006) as a 'hidden world' which then included a £28 million house in Belgravia, an £18 million estate in West Sussex, a £10 million St Tropez villa, two super yachts and a Boeing 767. Three years later, having divorced and remarried, Abramovitch paid £54 million for a 'stunning Caribbean hideaway' on the small island of St Barts (Todd 2009, p. 3).

The spatial mobility of the super-rich was explored in a global property wealth survey by Knight Frank (2010), focusing on 'cross-border, non-domestic, luxury residential market trends'. The survey covered an extensive network of international wealth and property professionals in 33 countries and generated more than 350 responses. The survey explored where the main purchasers came from, where they were buying, reasons

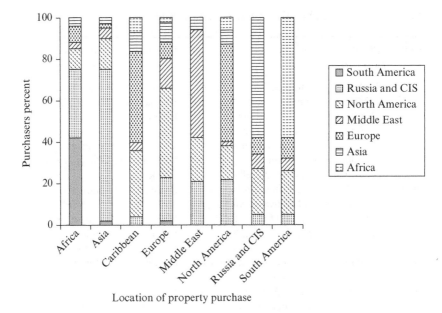

Location of property purchase

Note: [1] Luxury or prime property refers to the top 1 per cent of properties in each location.

Source: Knight Frank (2010).

Figure 6.1   Transnational luxury residential[1] purchasers – split of cross-border luxury residential purchase by region

for purchase, and expected future trends. It showed that the largest groups of current buyers were European, Asian and North American (together comprising around two-thirds of buyers), followed by the Middle East and Russia[2] (together almost 30 per cent), with very small numbers from South America and Africa. The three most important reasons for buying property were 'lifestyle', 'security' and 'investment' (together about 60 per cent); business and education also featured but taxation advantage was the *least* important factor. Future growth in demand was expected most strongly from the 'BRICS' countries,[3] especially China and India, the Gulf States and Eastern Europe. Future demand would be strongest for already-established European areas, including Tuscany and the Alps, 'Anglo-sphere' countries with strong links to the UK, and emergent Asian cross-border hubs. Figure 6.1 shows that there was much strong likelihood of transnational residential property investment into Europe from all other regions, rather than vice versa, with little anticipated cross-border purchase into Russia, Africa, the Middle East or Asia.

The *Wealth Report* by Knight Frank (2011a) also explored the mobility, diversity and complexity of the residential purchase strategies of super-rich households, both in terms of where they are buying and where they choose to define their country of residence. The UK was the site of most second home purchases, topping the preferences from Europe, the Middle East, Africa and India; the other most popular European countries were France, Spain and Italy. Russians rated France first, with the UK and Italy also favoured, though other sources suggest growing Russian demand for prime New York properties (Anon 2011). Affluent East Asian second home purchasers expressed a wide range of preferences, topped by the US and Singapore (also favoured by Indians), but including China, Canada, the UK and Australia. Key factors affecting where people buy include exchange rates, the relationship between plans for children's education and lifestyle dimensions of second (3rd, 4th . . .) homes.

The preferred countries for relocating primary residence varied substantially. The UK was first preference among buyers from the Middle East and Africa, Switzerland was ranked highly by Europeans and Russians, and Singapore ranked first for Indians and Chinese. Many East Asians also favoured Australia so, with continued growth in the number of super-rich Chinese and other Asians, there may be strong growing demand both for second homes and relocation to Australia. This dense and complex global network of preferences can be satisfied on the basis of the wealth of these individuals and families, but can also *change* in response to changing circumstances in host countries.

Property developments catering for the super-rich have had massive impacts on all kinds of places, from high amenity areas in mountains or coasts to inner areas of the world's most prosperous cities, as listed in the international reviews by Knight Frank (2011a) and Savills (2011). Many developments are just additions to already-glittering arrays of exclusive homes: mansions in ritzy areas of London and New York, palaces on the French Riviera, ski lodges in the Alps and exclusive Caribbean island retreats. But other completely new 'communities' have been developed to attract wealthy owners of multiple dwellings to new spaces for hyper-consumption, thereby transforming both landscapes and population characteristics (see Pow, this volume).

Such changing international property markets generate new spatial patterns and inequalities, with overlaps between leisure and pleasure, household members' education, investment and business-related multiple residential ownership at a *global* rather than merely transnational scale (Hall 2005; Urry 2007). The ownership of many dwellings by affluent elites, especially in London and south-east England, thus requires a consideration of *international* dimensions of 'national' housing markets.

THE BOOMING PRIME LONDON RESIDENTIAL PROPERTY MARKET: DECOUPLING AND CASCADING

A new geography of international property markets is emerging, with growing disconnection or 'de-coupling' between sites of investment by the global super-rich and the dynamics of 'national' housing and leisure markets. A large proportion of transnational multiple home ownership and associated air travel is focused on the world's most expensive residential areas, and international estate agencies dealing with luxury property sales focus on *cities*, rather than countries. Savills (2011) launched a new 'global billionaire property index' showing high average property price growth across 10 'global' cities,[4] attracting super prime 'global billionaire' property investors.

This industry-based analytical concept of a 'new global super class of real estate' is consistent with sociological commentary on this dimension of globalization, especially Sassen's (2006) key analysis of global cities:

> The rapid development of an international property market means that real estate prices at the center of New York City are more connected to prices in central London or Frankfurt than to the overall real estate market in New York's metropolitan areas. In the 1980s powerful institutional investors from Japan, for example, found it profitable to buy and sell property in Manhattan or central London. In the 1990s, this practice multiplied involving a rapidly growing number of cities around the world. (Sassen 2006, p. 10)

Many analyses of social exclusion and differentiation in Britain have explored differences between urban and rural areas and it has become increasingly clear that house prices are significantly higher in general in the country than in cities. This is largely a function of the British town and country planning system, designed and used to preserve vast aristocratic acreages of the British countryside, with its post-productivist settlements, from encroachment by city dwellers. The middle classes gentrified the villages, country towns and attractive coastal areas, while the poor are contained inside metropolitan green belts (Paris 2011). The planning system, combined with the continuing absence of tax on land or property, ensures the continued domination of land ownership by the rich and higher land prices than in a free market. The influx of super-rich overseas buyers may be an *unintended* consequence of the restrictive planning regime, but the massively-protected land and property market provides an extremely attractive environment for well-advised mobile overseas investors, able to benefit from capital gains and avoid British taxes.

During the housing boom up to 2007, Britain was identified as 'a haven for the international super-rich' with the prices of mansions in London or country estates in south-east England reflecting the fortunes of global actors rather than the UK economy as a whole (Woods 2007). The world's super-rich were 'queuing up to buy in the capital, with billionaires from India and China joining the Russian oligarchs and the oil sheikhs who have overheated the market in the past five years' (Partridge 2006). Almost half of the country homes in south-east England over £5 million were bought by foreigners as 'Russian oligarchs and tycoons from Asia and the Middle East . . . emulate the lifestyle of Britain's landed gentry' and up to 75 per cent over £10 million were bought by overseas investors (Gadher and Davies 2007). Luxury housing in London is so attractive that many super-rich overseas buyers do not simply buy *one* property in the most expensive areas, but wealthy families from the Middle East or India buy 'a cluster of houses or apartments for themselves, their children and small teams of personal staff' (Phadnis 2011).

As the global financial crisis emerged, international estate agents were confident 'that the market for mansions should be relatively unscathed (because) the high end of the market operated under different rules' and the 'boom for top London properties seems to go on for ever' (Shearer 2007). Indeed it does! Luxury home prices in central London rose faster during 2009 than 2008 in London's buoyant prime residential market (Knight Frank 2009). The strongest sector comprised properties selling in the £5–10 million range, with the London market 'benefitting [sic] from substantial inward investment from overseas buyers looking to take advantage of the weak pound and lower overall prices' (Knight Frank 2009). Rich buyers from Russia, Italy and the Middle East were especially active and 'the revival of the City economy has brought more traditional buyers from the banks, hedge funds and private equity houses back into the market' (Knight Frank 2009). Despite a new tax on banker's huge bonuses, four of Frank Knight's central London offices exchanged contracts on 22 deals, with aggregate sales prices over £60m, and agreed terms on another £45m worth of sales' (Knight Frank 2009).

House values were falling elsewhere in of the UK after 2008, as shown clearly in Figure 6.2, but the London prime residential market continued to boom. The sale of £1 million-plus homes in the UK surged in 2010, with over 80 per cent located in London and south-east England (Lloyds TSB 2011), in dramatic contrast to prices in 'normal' housing markets across most of England, Wales, Scotland, and Northern Ireland. Figure 6.2, derived from government house price statistics, shows house prices in England consistently higher than in Scotland, Wales or Northern Ireland, except for a wild speculative boom in Northern Ireland between 2003 and 2007. Figure 6.2 also shows *growing* regional gaps, as prices in London

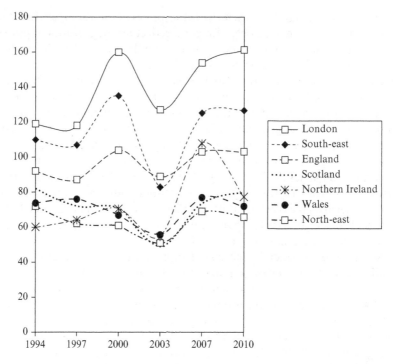

Note: ¹ This refers to mix adjusted average house prices. Sub-national units have been calculated annually taking the average house price for all dwellings in each region and expressing this as a percentage of the average house price for all dwellings in the same year.

Source: Derived from Department for Communities and Local Government Live Table 507, http://www.communities.gov.uk, accessed 2 December 2011.

Figure 6.2   Average¹ house prices UK countries and selected regions 1994 to 2011 (expressed as a percentage of UK average prices)

and south-east England pull further away from other UK regions, especially the depressed north-east. The UK Land Registry house price index (2011) also showed falling house prices across the UK at the county level during 2011, except in Greater London, where prices rose by 1 per cent, and two southern coastal areas. Prices in prime inner London Boroughs, however, increased much more rapidly: 7 per cent in Westminster and 5 to 6 per cent in Islington, Kensington and Chelsea, and Hammersmith and Fulham.

The boom in luxury London house sales accelerated in 2011 and Knight Frank partners shared a £73 million bonus pot in October 2011 'after the frenzied interest in luxury London homes helped push profits to pre-crunch levels' (Shah 2011, p. 3). Turmoil in many countries during the 'Arab Spring' of 2011, plus mounting unrest and fear of fiscal collapse in euro-zone PIIGS[5] countries, added to the attraction of London as a safe haven for mobile affluent families. Estate agents reported an influx of rich Greeks relocating their assets and buying £3 million-plus homes in London: 'Last year Greeks accounted for one in 30 purchases of prime property in London. So far this year they have snapped up almost 50 top-range flats alone' (Davies 2011, p. 7).

Knight Frank's review of London's housing markets (2011b, p. 2) suggested that 'there is no escaping the fact that the prime London sales market has de-coupled from the wider UK residential market and economy'. Exploring the same issues as Sassen and Savills, the report asked whether this represented the beginning of *global* de-coupling. Knight Frank's own data indicated that the annual growth of prime central London house prices was 10 percent higher than in the wider UK market, with affluent overseas buyers identified as the key driver of the continuing trend. Exchange rates and currency movements had favoured overseas buyers after March 2008, the pre-crash market peak (Knight Frank 2011b, p. 3). Strong demand during 2011 was expected to continue through 2012 as 'the strength of the market in London appears to be untroubled by the latest bout of the financial crisis, although a full-scale decoupling is a little too early to call' (Knight Frank 2011b, p. 3).

One development, 'One Hyde Park' has stimulated extensive commentary and criticism, some no doubt inspired by envy. Described as 'the most expensive apartment block ever built anywhere on Earth' (Arlidge 2011, p. 18) it is actually located at 100 Knightsbridge, so the name is more of a trademark than an actual address. Linked to the Mandarin Oriental Hotel in Knightsbridge, it combines supreme luxury, security and amenities:

> One Hyde Park, the first European Residences at Mandarin Oriental, will be the most exclusive address in the world. Its unique location, with the elegance and excitement of bustling Knightsbridge to the south and the glorious romance and serenity of Hyde Park to the north, offers an incomparable London living experience for those who want the ultimate in elegance, peace and style. The exceptional collaboration between leading architects, designers, artists and hoteliers ensures that One Hyde Park delivers ultimate perfection and a unique experience on every level. (Knight Frank 2012)

It is difficult to establish just how much of One Hyde Park had been sold by the end of 2011, but *The Sunday Times* estimated that a third of the apartments remained unsold. It also revealed that most of the apartments that had been purchased were registered to companies based in offshore tax havens including Guernsey, the Isle of Man, Liberia, Belize and the

Cayman Islands (Arlidge 2011), thus removing future liability for sales tax. The developer, Project Grande, is a joint venture between the prime minister of Qatar and a Guernsey-based company and commentators have described the whole development as a form of 'offshore island' functioning largely outside the UK tax system, as 'largely an empty shell for overseas investors to park their assets' (Arlidge 2011, p. 23) and 'a stunning symbol of the excess, raw cynicism, artificiality, market distortions and sheer opaque lifelessness of offshore finance' (Shaxson 2011).

Widespread purchase of luxury London housing by affluent overseas buyers, whether for use or simply to park assets, has helped to sustain the wealth of truly rich local landholders, such as the Duke of Westminster. But it has squeezed some merely-rich British families out of some of the most attractive areas in Mayfair, Bishops Avenue in Hampstead or Kensington Palace Gardens in Knightsbridge (Caesar 2008). There has been a spatial cascade into adjacent areas, fuelling further price inflation there and stimulating yet more luxury development in prime areas and gentrification outside the inner core.

> As overseas cash buyers squabble over the tiny number of ultra-expensive Central London homes on the market, the Brits who would once have spent their City bonuses in Kensington and Chelsea are lowering their gaze to Notting Hill, Fulham and Islington. In turn, residents of these areas find that they cannot afford to move within their neighbourhood and up sticks for Putney, Chiswick or Kentish Town. (Alexander, L. 2011)

CONCLUSIONS

The many homes of the super-rich are predominantly sites of hyper-consumption, and are investment items typically unoccupied for most of the time. In this regard, there is continuity with centuries if not millennia of self-indulgent luxurious display. The distinctively *new* geography is found in their spatial reach: their homes are increasingly spread across the globe in complex networks accessed with ease by these hyper-mobile individuals and families. This capacity was not available to previous super-rich cohorts due to much more limited and slower travel options. The globalization of finance and liberalization of residential requirements enables the ownership of homes in most countries of the world.

The super-rich can pick and choose their country of residence as much as their residential properties. The evidence from Knight Frank (2011a), in particular, highlights a complex and kaleidoscopic mosaic of property purchases and residential relocations. The super-rich occupy and move through spaces that are inaccessible to the vast majority of global inhabitants, both due to the sheer cost of property and also the widespread privatization and securitization of space. Their locational choices and investment decisions are re-shaping the intimate details of urban residential mosaics, de-coupling developments in key locations from national factors. The case of inner west London shows that prime real estate is increasingly de-coupled from wider developments in the UK housing market, as the continuing boom in prime house prices contrasts with widespread stagnation in other UK regions and even parts of London. Similar stories may be told in most, if not all, of the global cities reviewed by Savills (2011) *World Cities Review*. Such reports show clearly how businesses are responding to, and helping to shape, what have become global property markets. As prices soar in prime areas, so there are ripple effects across global city housing markets, affecting adjacent areas and stimulating further gentrification and redevelopment.

ACKNOWLEDGEMENTS

I am grateful to Liam Bailey, Head of Research at Knight Frank, for permission to reproduce material from various Knight Frank reports.

NOTES

1. *Not* including properties rented out as part of rental real estate portfolios.
2. Russia and the Confederation of Independent States in the report, referred to here as 'Russia'.
3. BRIC – Brazil, Russia, India and China.
4. Hong Kong, London, Moscow, Mumbai, New York, Paris, Singapore, Shanghai, Sydney and Tokyo.
5. Portugal, Italy, Ireland, Greece and Spain.

REFERENCES

Admin (2010), 'World's richest man buys Manhattan house for $44 million', *Real Estate News & Information at Tampa Bay* (online), 6 August, http://garyand-nikkiteam.com/2010/tampa-bay-news/world%E2%80%99s-richest-man-buys-manhattan-house-for-44-million, accessed 20 October 2011.

Alexander, H. (2011), 'Carlos Slim: at home with the world's richest man', *The Telegraph* (online), 19 February, www.telegraph.co.uk/finance/8335604/Carlos-Slim-At-home-with-the-worlds-richest-man.html, accessed 20 September 2011.

Alexander, L. (2011), 'Brits take flight in the face of foreign wealth', *The Times*, Bricks & Mortar supplement, 26 August, p. 4.

Anonymous (2011), 'Russians buy up New York real estate', *International*

Residence (online), www.internationalresidence.ru/eng/news/n5473.html, and www.telegraph.co.uk/finance/8335604/Carlos-Slim-At-home-with-the-worlds-richest-man.html, accessed 12 December 2011.

Arlidge, J. (2011), 'Anybody home', *The Sunday Times*, Magazine section, 20 November, pp. 16–23.

Bangalore Property Updates (2011), 'Mallya's white house in the sky', *Bangalore Property Updates* (online), 15 October 2011, http://bangalorepropertyupdates. blogspot.com/2011/kingfisher-towers-bangalore.html, accessed 2 December 2011.

Beatthewolf (2011), 'The world's most luxurious celebrity homes', 15 March, http://beatthewolf.co.uk/blog/index.php/2011/03/worlds-most-luxurious-celebrity-homes, accessed 2 December 2011.

Beaverstock, J., Hubbard, P. and Short, J. (2004), 'Getting away with it? Exposing the geographies of the super-rich', *Geoforum*, **35**, 401–7.

Beresford, P. and Rubinstein, W. (2007), *The Richest of the Rich*, Petersfield: Harriman House.

Caesar, E. (2008), 'A street named desire', *The Sunday Times* Magazine (online), 22 June, http://property.timesonline.co.uk/tol/life_and_style/property/article 4164403.ece, accessed 29 January 2009.

Campbell, P. (2011), 'Luxury property booms in London with £3.7m average price as rest of UK slumps' *Daily Mail* (online), 2 August, www.dailymail.co.uk/ news/article-2021343/Luxury-property-booms-London-3-7m-average-rest-UK-slumps.html?ito=feeds-newsxml#, accessed 3 December 2011.

Conradi, P. (2009), 'Racing king buys piece of empire', *The Sunday Times*, 5 July, p. 6.

Davies, H. (2011), 'Greeks in UK homes odyssey', *The Sunday Times*, 23 October, p. 7.

Gadher, D. and Davies, H. (2007), 'Shires fall to foreign land rush', *The Sunday Times* (online), 28 October http://timesonline.co.uk/tol/life_and_style/property/ article2753535.ece, accessed 17 May 2012.

Hall, C.M. (2005), *Tourism: Rethinking the Social Science of Mobility*, Edinburgh: Pearson.

King, L. (2010), 'See the richest man in the world's house (his name is Carlos Slim)', *Larry King Live*, www.youtube.com/watch?v=z57HaInKz94, accessed 2 April 2012.

Knight Frank (2009), 'London's luxury residential sector ends the year on a high', Press release 18 December, www.knightfrank.co.uk/news/London% E2%80%99s-luxury-residential-sector-ends-the-year-on-a-high-084.aspx, accessed 20 February 2010.

Knight Frank (2010), *Global Property Wealth Survey 2010*, http://my.knightfrank. com/research-reports/global-property-wealth-survey.aspx accessed 30 November 2011.

Knight Frank (2011a), 'The Wealth Report, a global perspective on prime property and wealth 2011', www.knightfrank.com/wealthreport, accessed 30 November 2011.

Knight Frank (2011b), *Autumn 2011 London Residential Review*, http:// my.knightfrank.com/research-reports/the-london-review.aspx, accessed 20 November 2011.

Knight Frank (2012), *One Hyde Park, Knightsbridge W1*, http://search.knight-frank.com/gb0203, accessed 4 January 2012.

Land Registry (UK) (2011), *House Price Index November 2011*, www.landreg.gov.
uk/house-prices, accessed 4 January 2012.

Lloyds TSB (2011), 'Million pound home sales rise at fastest rate since 2006', press
release 2 May, www.lloydsbankinggroup.com/media/pdfs/halifax/2011/020511_
Million_pound_sales_rise.pdf, accessed 3 May 2011.

Mawani, V. (2011), 'Larger than life: Antilla Mumbai – the world's most expensive
home', *Industry Leaders Magazine* (online), 19 January, www.industrylead-
ersmagazine.com/larger-than-life-antilla-mumbai-the-worlds-most-expensive-
home, accessed 30 November 2011.

Paris, C. (2011), *Affluence, Mobility and Second Home Ownership*, London:
Routledge.

Partridge, C. (2006), 'Going large in London', *The Times* (online), 29
September, http://property.timesonline.co.uk/tol/life_and_style/property/over
seas/article2543181.ece, accessed 10 October 2008.

Phadnis, S. (2011), 'Desis home in on London in clusters', *The Times of
India* (online), 18 June, http://articles.timesofindia.indiatimes.com/2011-06-18/
india/29673706_1_cluster-savills-london, accessed 2 December 2011.

PolitiFact.com (2008), 'Updated: eight houses for John and Cindy McCain',
St Petersburg Times (online), 20 August, www.politifact.com/truth-o-meter/
statement/635, accessed on 25 January 2009.

Sassen, S. (2006), *Cities in a World Economy*, 3rd edn, London: Sage.

Savills (2011), *World Cities Review*, http://pdf.euro.savills.co.uk/uk/residential---
other/insights---worldclasscities.pdf, accessed 2 December 2011.

Shah, O. (2011), '£73m bonus for Knight Frank partners', *The Sunday Times*,
Business Section, 23 October, p. 3.

Shaxson, N. (2011), 'One Hyde Park: another offshore island in London', http://
treasureislands.org/one-hyde-park-an-offshore-island-in-london/, accessed 30
November 2011.

Shearer, P. (2007), 'Luxury keeps its cool', *The Times* (online), 28 September, http://
property.timesonline.co.uk/tol/life_and_style/property/overseas/article2543181.
ece, accessed 10 October 2008.

Smith, D. (2006), 'Inside the hidden world of Roman's empire', *The Observer*
(online), 24 December, www.guardian.co.uk/world/2006/dec/24/sport.football,
accessed 4 May 2009.

Urry, J. (2007), *Mobilities*, Cambridge: Polity Press.

Todd, B. (2009), 'Roman's £54m retreat', *Daily Mail*, 23 December, p. 3.

Woods, R. (2007), 'Super-rich treble wealth in last 10 years', *The Sunday Times*
(online), 29 April, www.timesonline.co.uk/tol/news/uk/article1719880.ece,
accessed 10 August 2008.

7. A study of the dominance of the super-wealthy in London's West End during the nineteenth century

Kathryn Wilkins

INTRODUCTION

This chapter moves away from contemporary debates surrounding the spatial implications of the super-rich, and instead focuses on the nineteenth century, to a study of the wealthy who participated in the annual 'Season' in the West End of London for several months each year throughout the century. The chapter introduces the Season before using four examples to demonstrate the differing ways in which the super-rich during this period exercised control over the uses of space, and how this control was manifested. Ultimately, the chapter serves as an illustration of the way in which this group of super-wealthy dominated the West End of London during the nineteenth century. It serves as a reminder that while the scale of contemporary activities by the super-rich is significant, their role in transforming space is not new.

THE SEASON

During the eighteenth and nineteenth centuries, a shift in the consolidation of aristocratic power was witnessed within Britain. Country houses and estates of the super-rich were no longer the foci of wealth and influence. Instead, wealth became embedded within urban centres for several months of the year, following the commencement of the 'Season' in London. Social engagements dominated the months spent in London. These served as mechanisms through which the wealthy and powerful in society could congregate and network with each other on a scale not witnessed throughout the rest of the year.[1] Amassed within a small segment of London between May and July each year[2] were some of the world's most influential people at the time (Atkins 1990, p. 56). At the very core of this social mixing was the desire, or in many cases, the necessity, for families to find their children an appropriate marriage proposal, one which would secure the family's fortune and power in the decades ahead (Perkin 1989, pp. 52–3).

Participation in the Season grew throughout the eighteenth century, reaching a peak during the reign of Queen Victoria (1837–1901), the period focused upon most closely in this chapter. Mingay estimated that in the early days of the Season, participants may only have totalled 300 of the most influential families, however, by the last decade of the nineteenth century *Boyle's Fashionable Court Guide* (a publication which listed the names and London addresses of all those participating in the Season) listed no fewer than 26 000 participating families (Mingay 1963, pp. 20–4). This rise in the clustering of the rich and powerful during the Season can be attributed not only to increased sanitization and the improvement in public health witnessed in the latter stages of the nineteenth century, but also to the loosening of strict rules of etiquette which governed who received invitations to the social events of the Season, widening the numbers of wealthy able to take part. While the number of those attending the Season may have increased, this was still a numerically insignificant proportion of the population as a whole. Even in London, with its estimated 2 362 000 residents in 1851, families participating in the Season accounted for only 0.8 per cent of the capital's population (Jackson 2011). It is important at this stage in the chapter to note that scholars differ on ways to define those participating in the Season, as participants ranged from members of old aristocratic families to newly rich industrialists. For the purposes of this chapter, participants are referred to in terms of their wealth, as it was this unifying factor that enabled those participating to dominate space in the West End.

The world of the Season is difficult to summarize in its many forms, however, Thompson (1963, p. 104) has offered a description which highlights the nature of the period:

> This was the world of politics and high society, of attendance at the House [of Lords] and gaming in the clubs, the place where wagers were laid and race meetings arranged, the source of fashion in dress and taste in art, as well as being the world of drawing rooms and levees,[3] glittering entertainments and extravaganzas, soirées, balls and operas.

Events such as balls, dances, concerts and dinners were purposefully designed to allow for social mixing and congregation; opportunities which were clearly taken. Lady Mary Coke launched herself into her first Season, on one day participating in 34 separate events and social activities

(Kennedy 1986, p. 60). The social events of the Season were conducted according to strict rules of etiquette; thereby ensuring barriers to participation were created not only through cost but also through the securitization of events. Hostesses dictated who could attend, prompting Sproule to declare that: 'Everything in the upper class world of the [nineteenth century] needed to be controlled, to fit into its own place of time, to proceed according to established ideas of what was suitable' (Sproule 1978, p. 24).

The evolution of these controlled and prescribed social events of the Season became the ideal machinery for separating the wealthy from those aspiring to join them. Aside from the strict rules of behaviour which governed the practices of interaction, the Season was ruled by money. The expected standard of living during the period was high; suitability was judged on regular displays of wealth. The Duke of Northumberland was thought to have spent over £20000 entertaining guests during the 1840 Season (Sheppard 1971, p. 341), roughly equivalent to £880000 in today's money (according to the National Archives Currency Converter). To sustain his family's participation in the Season, the 2nd Earl of Verulam, meanwhile, reduced his presence in London from five to two months per year, taking the view that a limited presence in London was better than no presence at all (Horn 1992, p. 6). The importance of wealth is perhaps best illustrated by the participation of American debutantes in the latter stages of the nineteenth century. The agricultural depression across Europe and the United States during the 1870s had led to huge financial hardship for many estate-owning aristocrats in Britain. As a result, the Season needed to loosen the rules of participation to include wealth from previously excluded sources. A proportion of this 'new money' was provided by American debutantes, a phenomenon which became known as the 'transatlantic pipeline', owing to the number of wealthy Americans who infiltrated the Season during this time (MacColl and Wallace 1989, pp. 88–93). Rumours circulated in 1876 that American businessman William Vanderbilt spent $10000000 on securing his daughter Consuelo's marriage to the Marlborough Dukedom (Abbott 1993, p. 59). The acceptance of American wealth into one of the oldest aristocratic families in Britain is significant, as it serves as an illustration of the way in which wealth was able to transcend traditional class based exclusionary practices which had dominated the Season during the early decades of the nineteenth century.

SPATIAL IMPLICATIONS OF THE LONDON SEASON

The arrival of many thousands of wealthy families in London every year during the nineteenth century had significant spatial implications. For the months of the Season, the majority of participants would reside in large townhouses in the West End, some owning their accommodation outright, the majority either having leasehold ownership or renting their properties annually. The significance of their relationships to space, however, was exacerbated by the presence of estate ownership of land in this portion of London. Themselves members of wealthy families, these ground land-lords owned vast swathes of the West End, enabling them to control the character and the residents of the area. The Duke of Bedford owned 80 acres (32 hectares) in Bloomsbury, the Duke of Portland was responsible for much of Marylebone, but it was the Grosvenor family, developers of the Grosvenor Estate across Mayfair and later Belgravia, who held the most influence in terms of the Season, as will be discussed later in this chapter. The exact spaces occupied by the Season changed throughout the century in accordance with changes in fashion, but the area loosely spanned Marylebone in the north and Westminster in the south, and from Kensington in the west to Bloomsbury in the east. The central heart of the Season beat in Mayfair, however, as the vast majority of social events were held there, placing the Duke of Westminster, owner of the Grosvenor Estate during much of the nineteenth century, in a powerful position to control space. This geography played a vital part in creating the Season, as participants resided, socialized, shopped and entertained within this rela-tively compact area. This chapter will reflect on four case studies in which this residential clustering affected the West End: temporally, through methods of control, through the dictation of style and design, and through the monopolization of 'public' space.

The Temporal Phenomenon of the West End

Throughout the nineteenth century, the West End of London was subject to the mobility of the Season. Families would arrive in May, bringing with them servants, horses and material possessions. Pullar likened their arrival to spring, suggesting that on 1 May each year, 'the area burst into full bloom, houses would be freshly painted and window boxes filled with flowers' (Pullar 1978, p. 120). It was not just the appearance of the West End which changed, however. The Marchioness of Bath documented that when her family moved to Berkeley Square for the Season, it was usual for them to require 11 horses to transport them, together with the help of 17 servants (Thynne 1951, p. 13). Replicate this experience 26 000 times over, and it is clear that the Season made a significant impact on the fabric and character of the West End. However, it was not just during the bustle of the Season that the elite left their mark. When families returned to their country estates at the beginning of August, the area fell comparatively

silent. Percy Colson likened the area during winter to Pompeii, recollect-
ing that:

> after Goodwood, the last smart racing fixture of the Season, Mayfair and
> Belgravia settled down for their winter sleep. The Streets of Pompeii are not
> more silent than were Berkeley, Grosvenor and Belgrave Squares and their
> surrounding streets. Gone were the gay window boxes, the smart carriages, and
> powdered coachmen and footmen; indeed, almost the only sign of life was an
> occasional caretaker smoking his evening pipe . . . and chatting with a yawning
> policeman. (Colson 1945, p. 24)

While it would be inaccurate to portray every resident of the West End as
a participant of the Season, a significant majority of homes in this area did
house these temporary migrants. Census data proves useful in demonstrating the influence these migrations had on this corner of London. Berkeley
Square was one of the most aristocratic squares in Mayfair, located at
the heart of the Season. In April 1861, census data, collected before the
Season commenced, reveals that only 12 of the total 35 properties surveyed contained members of the wealthy family in question. The rest of
the properties were occupied by a small number of the families' servants.
These figures can be compared with census data captured for the same
square in June 1841, the only decade when data was collected when the
Season was at its height. Of the same total 35 properties, 28 were occupied
by members of the wealthy family and a full complement of their staff
(Lord Grey at number 48 is recorded as employing 23 staff). This increase
illustrates the existence of temporary migration, and caused Atkins to
refer to the West End during the nineteenth century as a 'part time place'
(Atkins 1990, p. 45). The wealthy participants of the Season influenced the
area as much by their absence from it, as they did by their presence in it
during the summer months.

The Enclaved Nature of the West End

The alteration of space in the West End was not only caused by temporal
changes in usage, however. The elite and super-rich were also responsible for controlling who was permitted to use the area. Physical barriers
to entry existed throughout the West End in the form of gates and bars.
Each gate or bar was accompanied by a set of rules; Olsen (1964, p. 147)
described those relating to four gates erected in Bloomsbury:

> The rules for the new gates . . .. permitted 'gentlemen's carriages of every
> description, cabs with fares and persons on horseback' to pass through them.
> They prohibited 'omnibuses, empty hackney carriages, empty cabs, carts,

drays, wagons, trucks, cattle and horses at exercise, or funerals'. The gates were closed to all traffic from 11pm to 7am.

The rules of this particular gate show that only those with private modes of transport were allowed to travel into the area during the day, while at night, the area was entirely sealed off from the outside world. This suggests that during the Season, residents inside these confines were content to be locked into this gilded cage of privilege (Atkins 1993, p. 266): all social events occurred within the confines of the gates and the wealthy had no reason to venture beyond them. This night-time separation of the super-wealthy from other residents in the city is the clearest demarcation of their dominance in London. The fortress-like nature of the West End during the Season permeates the language of the period. In Reginald Colby's account of his life living in Mayfair, Chapter 2 is simply entitled 'Piccadilly Frontier'. This terminology is explained by his recollections of the high walls which guarded large properties in the West End. He writes that they gave the impression of 'hostile and barricaded seclusion as if the noble owner wanted to have nothing to do with the common world outside' (Colby 1966, p. 27).

The erection of these gates, bars and walls were made possible by the nature of landownership in the West End during the nineteenth century: the space was controlled by families who had a vested interest in eliminating those people considered undesirable. Evidence of the desire for landowners to maintain the gates to their estates, despite increasing pressure throughout the nineteenth century to remove them, can be found most clearly in reports from newspapers of the period.[4] On 9 May 1885, *The Times* reported the Duke of Westminster's speech in defence of the barriers surrounding his Grosvenor Estate, suggesting that his 'inhabitants nearly all objected (to the removal of barriers), and the objection, which had the greatest weight with him was that the leaseholders and inhabitants paid large sums of money to builders for their houses, partly because of the quiet condition of the neighbourhood, which they attributed to the gates and bars'. This response infuriated the Earl of Roseberry (the liberal MP and future British Prime Minister), who declared the gated Grosvenor Estate to be the most remarkable tourist attraction in London, owing to the fact that he was convinced that no foreigner would believe that such gates were actually in existence in London in the latter decades of the nineteenth century. The control of space by the super-wealthy living in the West End is significant, and can be understood through the contemporary work of Cresswell (2010), who suggested that spaces are made meaningful through the context of power. Estate owners and their leaseholders and tenants held a powerful position in society, which was in part manifested through their dominance over the spaces in which they resided. Not only is this significant in highlighting the exclusive nature of the Season, but it is also illustrative of the extent to which powerful families had influence over the social composition of this area of London during the nineteenth century.

Private Squares and Landowner Control

Wealthy dominance over the spaces of the West End was not solely confined to the gates around its perimeters, however. Once inside these estates, the design and maintenance of individual residences was also strictly controlled. The ability of the super-rich to alter the character of spaces in the West End was again made possible through the existence of landowning estates in this area and the accompanying systems of leasehold ownership.[5] Whole streets as well as individual houses were redesigned throughout the nineteenth century, as the demands of the Season changed over time and as fashion altered trends in residential appearance and architecture. Ground landlords had the greatest influence over space during this period. They had the money and influence to modify space to their own specifications, controlling not only the way the area looked, but also the activities which occurred there. The Duke of Westminster, for example, who was responsible for the Grosvenor Estate during much of the nineteenth century, was known as 'Daddy Westminster' owing to the influence he held over his tenants.

Upkeep and control over residential buildings was also the responsibility of the landlord and throughout the history of the Grosvenor Estate, much of this control was exercised specifically to maintain the area's status. Originally built in 1725, the Grosvenor Estate, with Grosvenor Square at its heart, was designed for the wealthy. The *Daily Journal* recorded that 'there is now building a Square called Grosvenor Square, which for its largeness and beauty will far exceed any yet made in and about London' (12 July 1725). Even in the Square's infancy, the wealthy flocked to buy leasehold ownerships of properties, paying prices not previously witnessed in the capital. The Earl of Thanet paid the highest recorded price for a new house in London when he purchased 19 Grosvenor Square in 1730 at a cost of £7500 (Kennedy 1986, p. 48). Unsurprisingly, the area continued to attract the wealthiest in society. Almost 150 years later, in 1873, Thornbury alluded to the continued powerful nature of the Square, stating that 'a bare list of the persons of distinction residing in this neighbourhood would comprehend a great portion of the present British peers' (Thornbury 1873, p. 341). The space of the Square formed a private enclave of wealth and power in the heart of London for several centuries.

The Grosvenor Estate's residents used their presence in this enclave to demarcate themselves from the rest of society. Grosvenor Square was the last street in London to convert from oil to gas lighting, finally succumbing to the more modern method in 1842. Thornbury recalled that 'the inhabitants for many years opposed the intrusion of so vulgar a commodity as gas' (Thornbury 1873, p. 339). In accordance with the status of the area, residents were prepared to pay for the privilege of locating there. By the middle of the nineteenth century it was rumoured that the Duke of Westminster enjoyed a rent roll of £1000 per day from properties on the estate (Thornbury 1873, p. 3). Even as the Season's strict rules of participation loosened during the latter stages of the nineteenth century, Grosvenor Square still remained highly desirable to the wealthy. In the 1870s families who had acquired wealth through the industrial revolution gained a presence in the Square for the first time, with high prices paid for long leases to establish their place in the Season. Even in 1885, Margot Tennant (who later became the wife of the future Prime Minister Herbert Asquith) regularly rode her horse around the Square and into the hallway of her house, public streets of London being used as a playground by the wealthy (Asquith 1920, p. 177).

Locating in this most exclusive area of London not only ensured that residents demonstrated their wealth and social status, but it also proved useful during the Season. Using *The Morning Post* newspaper, which listed all the names of those attending each ball or event during the Season, and cross-referencing these with their residential addresses in Boyle's *Fashionable Court and Country Guide*, it is possible to ascertain where the most inexhaustible participants of the Season lived and socialized. Grosvenor Square, unsurprisingly, was one of the most popular residential spaces for those networking with the greatest frequency during the Season. What is striking about this analysis, however, is the effect the Square had on the popularity of surrounding streets. Such was the desire to locate close to the heart of aristocratic London that streets leading from the Square were also immensely popular with participants of the Season, irrespective of the size of property located there. The further away from the square, the less popular the street became with those people attending the events of the Season with any regularity. This is significant, because the events of the Season took place throughout Mayfair, and towards the second half of the nineteenth century, increasingly in Belgravia. Proximity to social events was therefore not the reason Grosvenor Square became popular. Instead, it can be argued that the Square acted as a beacon of the super-rich presence in London. By locating near this hub, participants gained status through proximity. In this way, it is possible to see that the wealthy used space during this period as a marker, as a tool to reaffirm their position in society.

THE MONOPOLIZATION OF PUBLIC SPACE

It was not just residential enclaves which were created and sustained by the wealthy, however. During the Season, public space, particularly in the West End, was also monopolized by the rich. The most significant example of this dominance was Hyde Park throughout the nineteenth century.

Hyde Park became a designated public park in 1637 by the orders of Charles I, yet during the Season it gained significance through its use by the wealthy as a meeting point. Participants in the Season would travel to Hyde Park to simply move up and down a particular strip, known as Rotten Row, in the hope that they would be recognized by advantageous contacts. The daily spectacle which occurred there was a display of power, wealth and social posturing on an unprecedented scale. Although the timings of meeting in Hyde Park varied throughout the nineteenth century, in accordance with the changing fashions of the period, Evans and Evans (1976, p. 52) estimated that by the middle of the century, the park was the scene of three separate meetings each day. Between 9am and 10am the wealthy would ride horses along the Row, 12–2pm saw the occurrence of both riding and driving of carriages; a scene replicated between 5–7pm. On each occasion, there would have been potentially thousands of wealthy people congregated in one small section of Hyde Park, each attending to display their presence. These opportunities were clearly taken; the Countess of Warwick suggested that her horses were so well known in the park that they 'always made a stir when spotted' (Warwick 1931, p. 24). Such was the scale of the mass promenading along Rotten Row that she suggested she was participating in the 'greatest horse show on earth' (p. 24).

Aside from the significance of the wealthy in monopolizing a park for their own use, the reactions to this unsecured, public space by those of lesser wealth demonstrates the extent to which they felt excluded. A social commentator of the day, Captain Gronow, when speaking of Hyde Park, noted that 'the lower or middle classes [did not] think of intruding themselves in regions which, with a sort of tacit understanding were given up exclusively to persons of rank' (Gronow 1877, p. 53). Gronow's observations are clearly supported by other accounts from the period. Mallock recollected that Rotten Row's 'aspect was that of a garden party, for which, indeed, no invitations were necessary, but on which as a fact few persons intruded who would have been visibly out of place on the lawn of Marlborough House' (Mallock 1920, p. 70). Likewise, Miller clearly displays this tacit understanding that he was not welcome, stating that 'there [Hyde Park], the pride and beauty of England may be seen upon their own stage, and on a fine day in 'The Season' no other spot in the world can outrival in rich display and chaste grandeur the scene which is here presented' (Miller in Thornbury 1873, p. 397). What is so significant about Miller's description is that, like Gronow suggested, he clearly feels that Hyde Park, despite being a public space, was the preserve of the wealthy during this period, describing it simply as 'their stage'.

CONCLUSIONS

These examples illustrate the ways in which wealthy participants in the Season dominated the spaces of the West End during the nineteenth century. This chapter moves beyond assumptions that the Season, and its wealthy participants were simply located in the West End, and instead explores the way in which the rich affected these spaces. The temporal nature of their engagement with space illustrates clearly the significant impact the wealthy had on this area of London, which was affected as much by their absence as by their presence. The capacity for this relatively small proportion of London's population to influence a particular area through their annual mass exodus from it, is testament to the importance of this group in affecting the nature of the spaces in which they resided.

More directly, the determination of wealthy, and in particular land-owning families who owned much of the West End, to keep the area prestigious, provides an indication of the dominance the super-rich had during this period. Estate ownership intensified the number of gates and bars which were erected around this area, objects which were designed specifically to limit the ability of the poorer residents to enter. This was a conspicuous tactic employed by the most powerful in society to regulate which citizens used which streets in the capital, ensuring that only the wealthiest used theirs. Likewise, the control exhibited by estate owners modifying houses within their land during the Season is an example of the ways in which the wealthy altered the fabric of the spaces in which they resided, evidence of which can still be witnessed in the residential streets of Mayfair today. This influence over space in the West End extended beyond that of familial estates, however, to communal spaces in the capital. In this chapter, the example of Hyde Park was used to demonstrate the extent to which the wealthy used their power to transform public space into private land for their own activity. This ability to influence the uses and users of certain spaces in London shows how dominant the super-rich were during this period.

It is also important to note that space was also used actively by those participating in the Season as a marker of wealth. As discussed in relation to proximity to Grosvenor Square, certain spaces in the West End were given meaning during the nineteenth century, in accordance with their perceived potential to attract networking opportunities or through their proximity to social engagements. Those who lived in these high profile residences used their geographical position to demonstrate their wealth. During the Season, therefore, space can be viewed as an active agent used by those participating to position themselves in society at the time.

While this chapter sought to illustrate the way in which the super-rich in the nineteenth century dominated particular spaces, this example of dominance has resonance beyond the confines of the Season. The growth of the American debutante tradition in the early twentieth century resulted in the use of wealth to control areas of New York, lasting evidence of which still exists today (Blakely and Snyder 1999, p. 74). Similarly Sheinbaum (2010, p. 79) has charted the lasting historical expressions of wealth segregation in Mexico City. It is not just through historical legacy that comparisons can be drawn with the present, however. This is particularly the case in relation to the enclaving of the rich, which occurred during the Season. Scholars such as Sidaway (2007) and Turner (2010) have examined contemporary examples of enclaving which share many similarities with the gated communities of Mayfair 300 years previously. Further study is now needed to more fully appreciate the inequalities which these historical enclaves created and maintained. By understanding the full extent of the polarization which occurred in historical examples, the role of the contemporary super rich in increasing divisions in society can be more fully appreciated.

NOTES

1. The London Season was only one element of the socializing undertaken by the wealthy during the nineteenth century. Following the Season in London it was common for families to travel to continental Europe to visit the German and French spa towns, before arriving back at their country homes in Autumn to participate in shooting parties. After Christmas, the British winter would commonly be swapped in favour of warmer climates and participation in the Seasons of mainland Europe. The arrival of Summer would draw the wealthy back to Britain for the commencement of the London Season.
2. The timing of the Season was never fixed. However, as a general rule, the months of May, June and July were the busiest, both in terms of the number of participants locating in London and the number of events to which they could attend.
3. A levee was a morning reception held during the Season. The term court levee was also used throughout the nineteenth century to refer to a gathering with members of the Royal family to which only men were invited.
4. It is important to note that while not all residential districts imposed street barricades, major thoroughfares were often the most securitized. It is also important to note that as the nineteenth century progressed, negative public opinion regarding the gates and bars led to the creation of pressure groups who lobbied, largely successfully, for their removal.
5. The issue of ownership during the Season is a difficult one to summarize, as it included

a tangled web of ground landlords, long term leaseholders (made up of both individual families, and housing landlords) and short term residents who leased or rented from longer term leaseholders.

REFERENCES

Abbott, M. (1993), *Family Ties: English Families, 1540–1920*, London: Routledge.
Asquith, M. (1920), *An Autobiography. Volume 1*, New York: George H. Doran Company.
Atkins, P. (1990), 'The spatial configuration of class solidarity in London's West End 1792–1939', *Urban History Yearbook*, **17**, 35–65.
Atkins, P. (1993), 'How the West End was won: the struggle to remove street barriers in Victorian London', *Journal of Historical Geography*, **19** (3), 159–71.
Blakely, E. and M. Snyder (1999), *Fortress America*, Washington, DC: Brookings Institution.
Boyle's Fashionable Court and Country Guide for May 1862, London: Boyle.
Colby, R. (1966), *Mayfair, A Town within London*, London: Country Life.
Colson, P. (1945), *Close of an Era*, London: Hutchinson.
Cresswell, T. (2010), 'Towards a politics of mobility', *Environment and Planning D: Society and Space*, **28** (1), 17–31.
Evans, H. and M. Evans (1976), *The Party that Lasted 100 Days: The Late Victorian Season*, London: Macdonald and Jane's.
Gronow, R. (1877), *Recollections and Anecdotes of the Camp, the Court and the Clubs*, London: Smith, Elder & Co.
Horn, P. (1992), *High Society: The English Social Élite, 1880–1914*, Phoenix Mill: Alan Sutton.
Jackson, L. (2011), 'The dictionary of Victorian London' (online), www.victorian-london.org, accessed 12 August 2011.
Kennedy, C. (1986), *Mayfair: A Social History*, London: Hutchinson.
MacColl, G. and C. Wallace (1989), *To Marry an English Lord*, London: Sidgwick & Jackson.
Mallock, W. (1920), *Memoirs of Life and Literature*, London: Chapman Hall.
Mingay, G.E. (1963), *English Landed Society in the Eighteenth Century*, London: Routledge.
'National Archives currency convertor', available at www.nationalarchives.gov.uk/currency/, accessed 4 September 2011.
Olsen, D. (1964), *Town Planning in London*, New Haven, CT: Yale University Press.
Perkin, J. (1989), *Women & Marriage in Nineteenth Century England*, London: Routledge.
Pullar, P. (1978), *Gilded Butterflies: The Rise and Fall of the London Season*, London: Hamish Hamilton.
Sheinbaum, D. (2010), 'Gated communities in Mexico City: a historical perspective', in Samer Bagaeen and Ola Uduko (eds), *Gated Communities: Social Sustainability in Contemporary and Historical Gated Developments*, London: Earthscan, pp. 79–92.
Sheppard, F. (1971), *London, 1808–1870: The Infernal Wen*, London: Secker and Warburg.

Sidaway, J.D. (2007), 'Enclave space: a new metageography of development?' *Area*, **39** (3), 331–9.
Sproule, A. (1978), *The Social Calendar*, Poole: Blandford Press.
The Daily Journal, 12 July 1725.
The Morning Post, all editions from 1 May 1862 to 31 July 1862.
The Times, 9 May 1885.
Thompson, F.M.L. (1963), *English Landed Society in the Nineteenth Century*, London: Routledge.
Thornbury, W. (1873), *Old and New London (Volume 4)*, London: Cassel, Peter and Galpin.
Thynne, D. (1951), *Before the Sunset Fades*, Longleat: Longleat Estate Company.
Turner, B.S. (2010), 'Enclosures, enclaves, and entrapment', *Sociological Inquiry*, **80** (2), 241–60.
Warwick, F. (1931), *Afterthoughts*, London: Cassell and Company.

8. The elite countryside: shifting rural geographies of the transnational super-rich

Michael Woods

INTRODUCTION

The contemporary wave of neoliberal globalization has given rise to a new class of the global super-rich, whose wealth is based on a global web of financial interests, and whose lives are lived transnationally between various homes, offices and retreats (see Hay and Muller 2012). The geographies of this transnational elite have been conventionally closely associated with global cities; Beaverstock (2005) noted that 'being a member of a transnational elite is fundamentally associated with being embedded within transnational networks, which are both cross-border and highly spatialized in the transnational social spaces of the city' (p. 246) (see also Beaverstock 2002, 2006; Dunn 2010; Sassen 2001; Sklair 2001).

Yet, the very reach and pervasiveness of transnational networks means that the economic and social geographies of transnational elites extend beyond the global city. The rural landscapes of the emergent 'global countryside' (Woods 2007), variously function as sites of wealth-generation for the transnational rich and super-rich (from farming, mining, energy production and property holdings), and as their play-grounds. Fashionable rural resort areas can act as hubs of transnational elite social space just as much as the gated communities and exclusive clubs of global cities.

This chapter positions transnational elite actors as key agents in the transformation of many rural localities under globalization, and the nego-tiation of the emergent global countryside. However, it also recognizes that the contemporary reconstitution of rural localities engages a country-side shaped by previous generations of national and transnational elites. These earlier interventions have left a legacy not only in terms of the physi-cal landscape and economic structure of rural areas, which are the subject of contemporary transformation, but also in establishing cultural and political practices that have a more enduring appeal as symbols of status, including the performance of 'gentryfied' rural lifestyles (Heley 2010).

The chapter draws on unfunded research conducted on rural elites in Britain and on preliminary research undertaken for a project on farmers as transnational actors funded by the Australian Research Council.[1]

TRANSNATIONAL ELITES IN THE IMPERIAL COUNTRYSIDE

The rich have long been associated with rural places. For centuries, the ownership of rural land was the foundation of wealth in European society, first from the rents and produce of the tenants, and later from commercial farming, mining and quarrying. At the same time, rural areas became key sites of social interaction and performance for the elite. Wealthy individuals built country mansions as retreats from the unsavoury and insanitary conditions of cities, and country estates in turn became platforms on which wealth could be ostentatiously displayed. In countries such as England, the construction of elaborate and expensive country houses, follies and landscaped gardens materially embodied wealth, accompanied by the performance of the leisured yet paternalistic lifestyle of the country gentleman (Everett 1994; Girouard 1981). By the late nineteenth century, the strength of the country gentleman discourse in Britain was such that as economic power shifted from the landed aristocracy to the new industrialist class, the acquisition of a country estate, a landed title and other trappings of the established rural elite became a cherished ambition for wealthy industrialists seeking to convert financial capital into political and cultural capital (Woods 1997).

Elite status was primarily enacted at the national or regional scale, but imperial expansion presented opportunities for ambitious entrepreneurs to develop transnational business networks, often based on the exploitation of a distant, resource-rich rural region. European aristocrats funded the establishment of plantations in tropical and sub-tropical colonies and gained from their trade, while adventurers such as Robert Clive, Admiral George Anson and Edwin Lascelles built-up fortunes from the plantation business that bought them entry to the English aristocracy and were invested in English country estates at Claremont, Moor Park and Harewood respectively (Casid 2005). Others invested in mining, or in the creation of large livestock ranches in Australia, North America or Latin America.

Emblematic of the new imperial transnational elite were William and Edmund Vestey, brothers who were sent by their Liverpool merchant father to work in the stockyards of Chicago. Inspired by the scale of the Chicago meat machine, the Vesteys' genius was to pioneer the use of refrigeration to transport meat, eggs and dairy produce from around the world for sale in Britain, creating a truly global industry in livestock products (Freidberg 2009). The wholly-owned company they established in 1897 became the foundation of a family fortune that reached over £2 billion at its peak, based on a global operation that involved over 23 000 employees and 250 000 head of cattle worldwide (Stephens 2007).

The Vesteys' command of the commodity chain pre-figured the 'vertical integration' of modern agri-food conglomerates (Freidberg 2009). They raised livestock on their own farms and ranches, slaughtered the animals in their own abattoirs and processed the meat in their own plants on five continents. They established two of the world's largest shipping lines to transport the goods, and sold the products through their own retail butchers' chain in Britain. The business was based on the demands of the growing industrial cities of Britain, but it was also dependent on tentacles that reached into rural regions as distant and diverse as Venezuela, the Russian Far East and the Northern Territory of Australia. By the end of the First World War, the Vesteys owned extensive land-holdings in Australia, Brazil and Venezuela, and additionally sourced and processed meat from Argentina, Uruguay, New Zealand, Russia, South Africa and Madagascar, and eggs from China.

In 1915, the Vestey brothers left Britain after a dispute over tax payments to live in Buenos Aires, and channelled their finances through trusts in Paris and Uruguay which enabled them to avoid paying British tax (Knightley 1993). The Vestey brothers were nonetheless awarded baronetcies in Britain, and in 1922 William Vestey succeeded in 'buying' a peerage with a political donation of £20 000 (Millar and Brummer, 1999). Lord Vestey bought the 6000 acre (2400 hectares) Stowell Park in the English Cotswolds, while other family members acquired estates in Scotland and East Anglia.

The transnational rural engagement of the Vesteys was hence spatially differentiated. Rural regions outside Europe, usually in poorer nations of Latin America and Africa, or in the more remote and under-developed parts of Australia and Russia, functioned as spaces of exploitation in which the primary activity of livestock farming took place. These activities frequently impacted severely on the localities concerned, environmentally, economically and socially. In Australia, for example, the Vesteys were the largest landowners in the Northern Territory, and played a key role in the settlement and development of the region, including encouraging other agricultural investment with the opening of an abattoir at Darwin in 1917 (and destroying much of this investment when they closed the plant

three years later) (Linn 1999). More notorious was their use of the local
Aboriginal population as quasi-slave labour, culminating in the Gurindji
conflict in 1966, when a strike by Aboriginal stockmen over wages and
conditions escalated into a protest for land reform (d'Abbs 1970; Kelly
1971; Knightley 1981). As d'Abbs (1970, p. 5) comments, 'Vesteys are particularly important in two fields – the economic development of Northern
Australia and the conditions of Aborigines in the North. Neither field
reflects much credit on Australia or Vesteys.'

Back in Britain, however, the rural estates of the Vestey family served as
spaces for conspicuous consumption and the performance of an elite lifestyle following the model of the country gentleman. Sir Edmund Vestey,
grandson of the first Edmund Vestey and later head of the family business,
managed estates in Scotland and East Anglia, served as High Sheriff of
Essex and as a Deputy Lieutenant for both Essex and Suffolk, enjoyed
fox-hunting two days a week, and was Master of the Thurlow Hunt and
Chair of the Masters of Foxhounds Association (*Daily Telegraph*, obituary, 28 November 2007). In this way, the Vesteys elected to exhibit their
new found status by buying into the relatively discrete conventions of
the English landed class, in preference to the more ostentatious practices
of industrialists who named companies, products, foundations and even
towns after themselves – significantly, none of the main companies established and operated by the Vestey family bore the family name.

The Vestey story also illustrates the curtailing of the old imperial
transnational elite at the hands of political reforms that served to create
national regimes of rural regulation during the mid-twentieth century. The
Vesteys had first bought into Australia as a spoiler, to stop an Australian
livestock industry developing as a rival to their Latin American operations. The adoption of the imperial preference system for trade within
the British Commonwealth at the Ottawa Conference in 1932, however,
imposed tariffs on imports to Britain from Latin America. The Vesteys
responded by purchasing more land in the Northern Territory and building up their Australian operation; yet, Britain's entry to the European
Economic Community in 1972 similarly restricted this trade route, and
prompted further restructuring and reorientation. Equally, Vesteys were
challenged by land reform politics in several of the countries in which
they operated. Following the political fall-out from the Gurindji strike in
Australia, they were forced to hand over land in the Northern Territory to
Aboriginal communities in 1973; while in 2005, Venezuelan troops occupied a cattle ranch owned by the Vestey Group before a settlement was
reached which ceded two ranches to the Venezuelan government.

The Vesteys have not been alone in facing these challenges. Many of
the individuals and families who sought to build transnational business

empires based on rural commodities and rural land-holdings in the twilight of the imperial age struggled with the political and economic upheavals of the twentieth century, the development of protectionist regimes in agriculture, the nationalization of key primary industries, the imposition of controls on non-national property ownership, and pressures for political reform both in Europe and in newly-independent ex-colonies.

NEOLIBERALISM AND THE NEW RURAL TRANSNATIONAL ELITE

After a number of decades in which national regimes of rural regulation clipped the wings of transnational elites operating in the rural economy, neoliberal reforms in the 1980s and 1990s created opportunities for a new cohort of global super-rich individuals to re-emerge as key actors in rural localities. These new actors are not aristocratic heads of family business empires, as were the Vesteys and their contemporaries, but rather fall into two overlapping categories. The first group have accumulated wealth (at least in part) through interventions in aspects of rural economies – Russian oligarchs who bought privatized oil and gas concerns; financiers and speculators in land and resources; corporate executives in transnational agri-food, mining and energy companies; and individual entrepreneurs. The second group have achieved their wealth outside the rural economy, but have become investors in rural property – primarily for amenity purposes – and agents in rural localities.

While both groups can be considered as icons of contemporary globalization, their rural engagement is in both cases shaped by legacies of the old imperial elite. The trading connections and transnational distribution of labour of earlier family business empires have been replicated in modern corporate structures; while the globally super-rich buy properties and perform 'rural' lifestyles in order to emulate the cultural capital of the old aristocracy. In some cases, rural business leaders have acquired rural estates and the trappings of landed gentry, and others have assumed neo-paternalistic roles in the localities of their business or amenity investments. As in the Vesteys' transnational network, however, these elite practices are spatially differentiated, with some rural localities enrolled as sites of production for transnational markets, and others transformed as global elite 'playgrounds'.

The Transnational Rural Amenity Class

For most members of the new transnational elite, rural places are more about the exposition of wealth than the acquisition of wealth. The aristocratic lifestyle of the 'landed gentry' still carries cultural capital for members of the transnational elite just as it did for the new industrialist class in the late nineteenth centuries. Rural locations hence become settings for elite performances of status, from hunting and riding on country estates to holidaying and partying in exclusive beach or mountain resorts. The acquisition of property in one of these localities is a particular expression of wealth and status, just as it was at the start of the last century.

Thus, Wightman (2010) records at least 49 off-shore owners of estates of more than 4000 acres (1618 hectares) in rural Scotland in 2010, more than double the number recorded by Cramb (2000) in the late-1990s. Most were owned by holding companies, but they were largely private estates, not production sites, owned primarily as status symbols by individuals such as Arab sheikhs Mohammed bin Raschid al Maktoum and Mahdi Mohammed al Tajir, Anglo-Egyptian entrepreneur Mohammed al Fayed, and European business scions such as Tetrapak heiress Sigrid Rausing and the Belgian brewing family, De Spoelberch (Table 8.1). Although no Russian oligarchs feature at the top of Wightman's list, steel magnate Vladimir Lisin purchased the 3300 acre (1335 hectares) Aberuchill Castle estate in 2005 for a reported UK£6.8 million, while other Russian investors have bought country estates in south-east England.

Similarly, the liberalization of overseas property purchases in New Zealand has attracted elite buyers to rural properties close to attractive mountain resorts. The most high profile, and controversial, transaction has been the NZ$21.5 million sale of the Motutapu and Mount Soho stations near Queenstown – with a combined area of 24 731 acres (61 000 hectares) – to the Canadian entertainer Shania Twain in 2004. Other international investors in the area include actors John Travolta and Sam Neill, film-maker Peter Jackson, and former California governor Arnold Schwarzenegger.

In common with aspiring middle-class pretenders of the 'new squirearchy' (Heley 2010), transnational millionaires have shown more interest in the trappings and lifestyle of the old landed aristocracy than in their paternalistic responsibilities. Some individuals have attempted to cultivate a role as 'lord of the manor', with varying degrees of success – local opposition to absentee overseas landowners has been a driver of land reform in Scotland (Mackenzie 2006; Wightman 2010) – but most have little routine involvement in local politics or society, although perceived lack of interest by landowners in local affairs has also stimulated criticism.

However, transnational elite investors can be seen to have influence in reconstituting rural places in two ways. First, elite investors have mobilized politically when new developments or other changes are perceived to threaten their property interests – as in the Queenstown district of New

Table 8.1   Major foreign landowners in Scotland, 2010

Landowner	Nationality	Business interests	Estate and area
Van Vlissingen family (Clyde Properties BV)	Dutch	Food and energy	Letterewe, 35262 hectares
'Mr Salleh' (Andras Ltd)	Malaysian	Unknown	Glenavon 28910 hectares
Mohammed bin Raschid al Maktoum (Smech Properties Ltd)	UAE	Crown Prince of Dubai	Glomach 25094 hectares
Ulrich Kohli (Argo Invest Overseas Ltd)	Swiss	Banking	Loch Ericht 22887 hectares
Sigrid Rausing	Swedish	Tetra Pak	Coignafearn 16022 hectares
Mohammed al Fayed (Bocardo SA)	Egyptian	Media, trade	Balnagowan 13077 hectares
Roesner family (H H Roesner Ltd)	US	Unknown	Sallachy 9945 hectares
Van Beuningen family	Dutch	Shipping, Private Investments	Foich & Inverlael 9857 hectares
De Spoelberch family	Belgian	Brewing	Altnafadh 9268 hectares
Count Adam Knuth	Danish	Land, Farming	Ben Loyal 8100 hectares
Mahdi Mohammed al Tajir (Park Tower Holdings)	UAE	Retail, Property, Water	Blackford 5900 hectares

Sources: Cramb (2000); Wightman (2010); author's additional research.

Zealand, where opposition by wealthy property owners to the scale of development under a laissez-faire local government was derided by the local mayor as an elitist attempt to create an 'Aspen of the South Pacific', a 'community of millionaires and multi-millionaires' (Woods 2011). Second, elite actors can have a cultural impact in shaping attitudes towards rural life. In 2006, the British magazine *Country Life* placed the American entertainer Madonna in tenth position in its listing of 100 individuals with power over rural Britain, following her purchase of a country estate with then husband Guy Ritchie. In its citation, the magazine commented that:

> Such is her global fame that anything the singer does receives vast publicity and influences trends and behaviour. Her adoption of English country life as the ideal has brought rural living into the metropolitan and international consciousness and highlighted its challenges as well as its pleasures.

She successfully fought access legislation that affected her privacy, her participation in shooting helped boost the rural economy, and her foray into the world
of riding (given extra publicity by her recent fall and broken bones) will surely
provide a welcome fillip to an equine industry increasingly beset by health and
safety, and employment legislation. (*Country Life* 2006, no pagination)

Transnational Rural Entrepreneurs

There is, however, another dimension to the renaissance of transnational rural elite, which is the construction of transnational businesses
by rural entrepreneurs. These are individuals for whom rural localities
are both the source of their wealth as a site of production, and their
home. The development is particularly notable in Australia, where the
combination of large farm sizes, the historical practice of producing for
export, and radical neoliberal reforms that have removed more-or-less all
forms of state support for agriculture, has created conditions in which a
number of farmers have directly invested in transnational business activities (see Cheshire and Woods 2013). Several have become significantly
wealthy as a result.

The 2009 Australian Rich List, for instance, included 16 individuals
in its top 200 whose wealth was derived from rural business interests,
and a further nine families with rural interests in its list of families with a
shared wealth of over A\$150 million (*BRW* 2009). These included Robert
Ingram, Australia's largest poultry farmer at number 28 (A\$1.05 billion),
dairy farmer and food manufacturer Tony Perich at number 46 (A\$714
million) and beef farmer Peter Hughes at number 84 (A\$443 million)
(see Table 8.2).

The rural members of the Australian Rich List are a mixed bunch. Some
inherited their wealth, others operate their rural business interests through
corporations in which they are directors or shareholders, but some are
genuine farmers, with day-to-day involvement in agriculture. Similarly,
some on this list accumulated their wealth on the back of Australian
markets, but many have at least some transnational business operations.
The trend towards transnational engagement is represented at its most
extreme by John Kahlbetzer, number 57 on the list with a fortune of
A\$609 million, who in 2008 sold three of his family's farming properties in
New South Wales to invest in building up his land-holdings in Argentina.
Kahlbetzer had started investing in Argentina in 1982, but moved there
semi-permanently in 2008, while still retaining substantial rural business
interests in Australia as a leading producer of cotton, wheat, rice, wool
and wagyu beef (*BRW* 2009).

More illustrative of the new breed of transnational farmer-entrepreneurs

Table 8.2   *Entries in 2009 Australian Rich List with wealth derived from rural interests*

Rich List ranking	Name	Wealth	Key interests
Individuals			
28	Robert Ingham	A$1.05 bn	Poultry, thoroughbred horses
37	Allan Myers	A$778 m	Rural property
46	Tony Perich and family	A$714 m	Dairy, food manufacturing
57	John Kahlbetzer	A$609 m	Farming
84=	Peter Hughes and family	A$443 m	Cattle farming, property
108	Sterling Buntine	A$354 m	Cattle farming
112	David and Peter Bartter	A$334 m	Poultry
125=	Graham McCamley	A$300 m	Cattle farming
134	Hugh Maclachlan	A$271 m	Wool, cattle, property
139	Sam Sarin	A$258 m	Fish farming
143	Graeme and Evan Acton	A$254 m	Beef
153	Roger Fletcher	A$232 m	Sheep meat
166	Frank Costa	A$202 m	Fruit and vegetables
180=	Harold Mitchell	A$180 m	Beef, media
183	Terry Morris	A$176 m	Wine
190	Hagen Stehr	A$168 m	Fish farming
Families			
13	Menegazzo family	A$682 m	Cattle, potatoes
15	Casella family	A$665 m	Wine
39	McWilliam family	A$311 m	Wine
45	McDonald family	A$272 m	Beef
51	Hyne family	A$236 m	Forestry
55=	Baiada family	A$215 m	Poultry
57	Brown family	A$197 m	Wine
58	De Bortoli family	A$189 m	Wine
61	Kidman family	A$170 m	Beef

Source: *BRW* (2009).

are the brothers Graeme and Evan Acton, who jointly occupy the 143rd position in the Rich List, with a combined fortune of A$254 million. The Actons are partners in the Acton Land and Cattle Company, which holds 3.87 million acres (1.566 million hectares) of land in Queensland and farms 180 000 head of beef cattle. The family started to move into direct transnational activities in the mid-1990s, as neoliberal agricultural reforms in Australia both destabilized domestic markets and removed obstacles to international trade. The Actons' international operations expanded from a contract to directly supply Raffles Hotel in Singapore and 60 per cent of their product is now exported, chiefly to Japan, South Korea, the Middle East and South-east Asia.

In spite of their growing transnational business, the Actons continue to present themselves as farmers foremost, and to describe themselves as being actively engaged in the day-to-day aspects of farm management. This is a discourse that is reiterated by several other 'rural' members of the Rich List (including Tony Perich, who describes himself as 'a simple farmer' (*BRW* 2009)), as well as by many less-wealthy rural entrepreneurs with expanding transnational interests (see Cheshire et al. 2013). As such, they occupy a position described by Pritchard et al. (2007) as 'neither "family" nor "corporate" farming' (p. 75), but 'exceptionally entrepreneurial, market-sensitive, technologically-oriented, knowledge-seeking and highly capitalized' (p. 83).

Although Cheshire et al. (2013) observe that individual entrepreneurial farmers negotiate the tensions between business interests, farmer identity and place attachment differently, the centrality of the farm continues to connect these wealthy, transnational business people to rural localities. For at least some of the farmers who feature in the Australian Rich List, the celebration of deep rural roots and self-advancement is part of their corporate narrative. The Acton Super Beef website, for example, includes detailed descriptions of the seven properties that constitute their farm holdings, together with a map showing their locations, as well as reference to ancestors William and Jane Acton, 'who emigrated from Ireland in the early 1860s' and who 'purchased a parcel of 1000 acres of prime grazing land on the edge of Rockhampton for 25 cents per acre' (Acton Meats Pty 2008, no pagination). The same tale is repeated in media features on the business, including an article in the Brisbane *Sunday Mail* in 2008, which stated that 'Family means everything to the Actons. Backing each other through thick and thin, staying true to their heritage and sharing the workload has been the cornerstone of success for the tight-knit clan running one of Queensland's biggest cattle companies' (Tucker-Evans and Sourris 2008, p. 54).

In presenting themselves in this way, farmer-entrepreneurs such as the Actons articulate a rootedness in rural place that contrasts with the much more superficial and exploitative engagement with the rural of both the historic transnational rural magnates, such as the Vesteys, and the contemporary global super-rich, for whom the rural is primarily a stage for consumption. Accordingly, the spatial relations of the farmer-entrepreneurs allows for a more constructive influence in the rural localities in which they live and work, as wealth generated through their transnational business activities flows back into the region. In some cases a quite explicit link is drawn between transnational business interests of major farmers and local economic development, for example in Balaklava, South Australia, which has become a centre of the hay export industry to Japan. In other cases leading entrepreneurs have become associated with particular localities which are the base for their businesses, and have used this platform to speak out for regional interests. For example, Roger Fletcher, a former shepherd who became Australia's largest sheep meat exporter and occupied 153rd position in the 2009 Rich List with wealth valued at A$218 million, is the key player in the outback town of Dubbo where his business is based, contributing to infrastructural development such as the construction of a private railway line, and advocating the interests of regional towns.

It is in this sense that echoes of paternalism may be heard in the social, political and economic activities and relations of transnational farmer-entrepreneurs empowered by neoliberalism.

CONCLUSIONS

Rural areas are just as much a part of the landscape of the transnational super-rich as global cities, but the rural engagement of the new transnational elite is spatially-differentiated, as well as influenced by the legacies of previous rural elites. In the late nineteenth and early twentieth centuries, families such as the Vesteys built up global business networks in which wealth-generation was spatially separated from wealth-display, with operations in the colonies of the British empire or the emerging nations of South America creating income that permitted family members to buy into the lifestyle and status of the British landed aristocracy.

The spatial differentiation of these elite practices is reproduced in more fragmented fashion by the new transnational elite at the start of the twenty-first century. Oil, gas, mining, forestry and agricultural interests in remote rural regions of Russia, South America, Africa and Australia continue to generate wealth both for established elite families and for new oligarchs and entrepreneurs; but arguably more significant is rural property investment and leisure performance by wealthy individuals – most with no direct rural business interests – who are still drawn to the cultural cachet of a pseudo-aristocratic rural lifestyle.

The shifting rural geographies of transnational elites are therefore expressions of the changing functions ascribed to rural spaces in the corporate and personal networks of the super-rich, and of the flow of wealth through various sites of accumulation, reproduction and display.

Historically, the imperial super-rich exploited rural peripheries as sources of resources to serve metropolitan markets, generating wealth that was accumulated in the imperial core and exhibited through cultural performances in the metropolitan countryside. Today, sites of wealth accumulation and display form a more complex and dispersed pattern of entanglement. Rural entrepreneurs can emerge from perceived 'peripheral' regions to build fortunes from transnational business that they spend through investments in property and lifestyles in similarly 'peripheral' rural resort areas, where they rub shoulders with super-rich individuals whose wealth owes nothing to rural industry and for whom the countryside is purely a place of consumption.

At the same time, the wealth of the contemporary rural super-rich is invariably dependent on the global economy, and thus on financial transactions and management decisions made in global cities. Fluctuations in commodity prices are reflected in the rise and fall of individuals with interests in agriculture, mining, oil and wine-making in newspaper 'rich lists', as well as in the sale of country estates and resort villas between European industrialists, Middle East oil sheikhs and Russian oligarchs. Moreover, the global economic downturn since 2008 has increased the attractiveness of rural land to the super-rich not only as a status symbol, but also as an investment.

The transnational super-rich consequently play a key role in the reproduction of the global countryside as transformative agents who connect rural localities to the global economy. While relatively few of the contemporary transnational super-rich choose to take their adoption of a 'landed gentry' lifestyle as far as assuming the paternalistic responsibilities in rural governance that their predecessors once fulfilled, some exercise a more subtle form of neo-paternalism simply by creating employment, generating income or through the conflation of their own business interests with wider community interests.

All elite investments and interventions in rural localities have a potentially transformative impact, implicitly connecting rural places into transnational webs of inter-dependencies. However, in most cases, elite individuals take no active political or paternalistic role in the locality. Their influence is secondary and indirect. The major exceptions are entrepreneurs who emerge from within rural communities and combine transnational business activities with an ongoing attachment and sense of responsibility to their home community. Consequently, one might identify a second differentiation, between the globally super-rich who perform pseudo-aristocratic rural lifestyles as expressions of wealth and status, and the entrepreneurial rural rich, whose lifestyles may be more muted, but who have inherited more of the paternalistic mantle of the rural landed elite. In both cases, though, the rich and super-rich are key agents in the construction of the global countryside.

NOTE

1. 'Globally engaged? Responses to neoliberal globalization among family farmers in Australia', Lynda Cheshire, Geoff Lawrence, Zlatko Skrbis and Michael Woods (Australian Research Council Discovery Grant DP0984753).

REFERENCES

Acton Meats Pty (2008), 'Acton Super Beef . . . a long and proud history', www.actonsuperbeef.com.au, accessed 10 October 2009.

Beaverstock, J. (2002), 'Transnational elites in global cities: British expatriates in Singapore's financial district', *Geoforum*, **33**, 525–38.

Beaverstock, J. (2005), 'Transnational elites in the city: British highly skilled inter-company transferees in New York's city financial district', *Journal of Ethnic and Migration Studies*, **31**, 245–68.

Beaverstock, J. (2006), 'World city networks from below: international mobility and inter-city relations in the global investment banking industry', in P.J. Taylor, B. Derudder, P. Saey and F. Witlox (eds), *Cities in Globalization: Practices, Policies, Theories*, London: Routledge, pp. 52–71.

BRW (2009), 'BRW Rich 200 List', *BRW*, 28 May–1 July.

Casid, J.H. (2005), *Sowing Empire: Landscape and Colonization*, Minneapolis, MN: University of Minnesota Press.

Cheshire, L. and M. Woods (2013), 'Globally engaged farmers as transnational actors: navigating the landscape of agri-food globalization', *Geoforum*, **44**, 232–42.

Cheshire, L., C. Meurk and M. Woods (2013), 'Decoupling farm and place: recombinant attachments of globally-engaged family farmers', *Journal of Rural Studies*, **30**, 64–74.

Country Life (2006), 'Power 100 of the countryside', *Country Life* (online), no date, www.countrylife.co.uk/countrysideconcerns/power_100.php, accessed 12 October 2007.

Cramb, A. (2000), *Who Owns Scotland Now?*, Edinburgh: Mainstream Publishing.

D'Abbs, P. (1970), *The Vestey Story*, Collingwood, VIC: Australasian Meat Industry Employees' Union.

Daily Telegraph (2007), 'Edmund Vestey' (obituary), *Daily Telegraph* (online), 28 November, www.telegraph.co.uk/news/obituaries/1570710/Edmund-Vestey.html, accessed 18 May 2012.

Dunn, K. (2010), 'Embodied transnationalism: bodies in transnational spaces', *Population, Space and Place*, **16**, 1–9.

Everett, N. (1994), *The Tory View of Landscape*, New Haven, CT: Yale University Press.

Freidberg, S. (2009), *Fresh: A Perishable History*, Cambridge, MA: Harvard University Press.

Girouard, M. (1981), *The Return to Camelot: Chivalry and the English Gentleman*, New Haven, CT: Yale University Press.

Hay, I. and S. Muller (2012), '"That tiny, stratospheric apex that owns most of the world" – exploring the geographies of the super-rich', *Geographical Research*, **50**, 75–88.

Heley, J. (2010), 'The new squirearchy and emergent cultures of the new middle class in rural areas', *Journal of Rural Studies*, **26**, 321–31.

Kelly, J.H. (1971), *Beef in Northern Australia*, Canberra: ANU Press.

Knightley, P. (1981), *The Vestey Affair*, London: Macdonald Futura.

Knightley, P. (1993), *The Rise and Fall of the House of Vestey*, London: Warner Books.

Linn, R. (1999), *Battling the Land: 200 Years of Rural Australia*, St Leonards, NSW: Allen & Unwin.

Mackenzie, A.F.D. (2006), 'A working land: crofting communities, place and the politics of the possible in post-land reform Scotland', *Transactions of the Institute of British Geographers*, **31**, 383–398.

Millar, S. and A. Brummer (1999), 'Heirs and disgraces', *The Guardian* (online), 11 August, www.guardian.co.uk/theguardian/1999/aug/11/features11.g2/print, accessed 6 April 2010.

Pritchard, B., D. Burchand and G. Lawrence (2007), 'Neither 'family' nor 'corporate' faming: Australian tomato growers as family farm entrepreneurs', *Journal of Rural Studies*, **23**, 75–87.

Sassen, S. (2001), *The Global City: New York, London, Tokyo*, Princeton, NJ: Princeton University Press.

Sklair, L. (2001), *The Transnational Capitalist Class*, Oxford: Blackwell.

Stephens, T. (2007), 'The wrong side of history', *Sydney Morning Herald*, 8 December, www.smh.com.au/articles/2007/12/07/1196813916024.html, accessed 7 October 2009.

Tucker-Evans, A. and M-C. Sourris (2008) 'Acton stations', *The Sunday Mail*, 7 September 2008, p. 54.

Wightman, A. (2010), *The Poor Had No Lawyers: Who Owns Scotland (And How They Got It)*, Edinburgh: Birlinn.

Woods, M. (1997), 'Discourses of power and rurality: local politics in Somerset in the 20th century', *Political Geography*, **16**, 453–78.

Woods, M. (2007), 'Engaging the global countryside: globalization, hybridity and the reconstitution of rural place', *Progress in Human Geography*, **31**, 485–507.

Woods, M. (2011), 'The local politics of the global countryside: boosterism, aspirational ruralism and the contested reconstitution of Queenstown, New Zealand', *Geojournal*, **76**, 365–81.

9. The super-rich, horses and the transformation of a rural landscape in Kentucky

Susan M. Roberts and Richard H. Schein

INTRODUCTION

Each May, thousands of people flock to Kentucky to witness what is popularly known as the 'most exciting two minutes in sports'. Most of those attending the Kentucky Derby enjoy the party atmosphere in the 'infield' of the venerable Churchill Downs racecourse in Louisville. A select group enjoys the view of the horses from so-called Millionaires' Row: two levels of luxury seating with full services. Each year on Millionaires' Row, celebrities mingle with the rich, sipping mint juleps (Kentucky Bourbon whisky with some sugar syrup and fresh mint leaves over crushed ice) and wearing fashionable sundresses and extravagant hats or beautifully tailored suits. In Britain, the annual race meeting known as Royal Ascot brings with it a similar parade of the well-dressed and the rich, while in Australia, the famous Melbourne Cup is on the social calendar of the well-to-do and fashionable. However, many of the world's super-rich do not just attend the occasional race. They are involved deeply in breeding, training, and racing thoroughbreds (see McManus, this volume). Indeed, the super-rich and thoroughbred horses have long been intimately connected (Cassidy 2002, 2007; O'Connor 2011). In this chapter, we discuss how the investments and involvements of the super-rich in thoroughbred breeding and racing created a particular regional landscape. The super-rich, as Hay and Muller (2012) argue, have extraordinary power to transform places (see also Beaverstock et al. 2004). We focus on how super-rich horse enthusiasts have had a major impact on the rural landscape of central Kentucky.

Kentucky is a small, relatively rural, and relatively poor state in the upper south-eastern United States. It has a population of just over four million, with close to two million living in rural areas (Davis 2009), and a mean household income of about US$40 000, which is US$10 000 lower than the US average (US Census 2010). Louisville, home to the Kentucky Derby, together with Bluegrass Region, centred on the small city of Lexington, enjoy relatively healthy economies compared to some regions of the state. Our focus in this chapter is upon the Bluegrass Region, a place that is today marketed by its boosters as the 'Horse Capital of the World'.

Bluegrass Field is the airport that serves Lexington and its hinterland. It is a minor airport with a single passenger terminal. Every day, travellers arrive and depart on small aircraft for larger airports that serve as airlines' hubs. Twice a year though, one or sometimes two Boeing 747s (jumbo jets) arrive, stay a few days and then leave. The modest airport's runways are not long enough to handle a fully loaded 747 so the planes arrive with the fuel tanks low and take on just enough fuel to get to a larger US airport before they fly on. The planes are owned by the Al Maktoum family, who are the royal family of Dubai, one of the United Arab Emirates. They are configured on the interior as executive jets, and are used for personal travel. The parked jumbos loom over the highway that goes along the perimeter of the airport. Across the highway lies Keeneland Race Track and Sales Pavilion – the reason the jumbo jets' owners come to town. They visit Lexington to do some shopping.

Like many other super-rich, members of the Al Maktoum family are very involved in thoroughbred breeding and racing. It is the Keeneland Yearling Sales that draw the super-rich to Lexington every September. Sheikh Mohammed bin Rashid Al Maktoum and his agent John Ferguson bought 36 horses at the September 2011 Keeneland Yearling Sales (Cooper 2011a). In just a few days they spent almost US$8.9 million. A month before, at the two-day Fasig Tipton Yearling Sales in Saratoga, NY, Ferguson, acting for the sheikh, bought 13 yearlings for a total of US$8.5 million. This included the sales' two most expensive young horses that cost the sheikh US$1.2 million each (Cooper 2011b). Sheikh Mohammed's brother, Sheikh Hamdan bin Rashid Al Maktoum, is also a major buyer at the Keeneland Sales. At the September 2011 Yearling Sales, his Shadwell Racing operations bought six horses and spent nearly US$3 million. At the previous year's Keeneland Yearling Sales, Sheikh Hamdan was the biggest spender – a fact that was greeted as a sign that the sales were possibly recovering from a serious slump in yearling prices over the preceding two years.

The royal brothers do not merely visit Kentucky to buy young horses. They have significant landholdings in the state. Their Bluegrass farms are components in their global thoroughbred operations. Sheikh Mohammed bin Rashid Al Maktoum is Vice President and Prime Minister of the United Arab Emirates. He is also the ruler of one of those emirates:

Dubai. He is reported to have fallen in love with horse racing during his days as an undergraduate at Cambridge University. Since the 1980s he has been building up his thoroughbred breeding business, known as Darley. The highly successful racing arm of his operations is known as Godolphin.

Darley owns and operates some of the most prestigious thoroughbred stud farms in the world. The thoroughbred breeding industry has a geography characterized by regional clusters and Darley is present in each of them (Figure 9.1). Darley is headquartered at Dalham Hall Stud near Newmarket, in England, around which Darley also has pre-training and other facilities. The Irish operations are headquartered at the famous Kildangan Stud in County Kildare but include several other renowned stud farms. In the US, Darley is based at Jonabell and Gainsborough Farms, both outside Lexington, KY, with another facility in Saratoga, NY (Greentree Training Center). In Australia's Upper Hunter Valley, Darley's stallion operations are based at Kelvinside Stud with mare operations centred nearby at The Woodlands Stud and other properties in the region. Darley also has a farm in Victoria. Darley's increasingly global presence is also evidenced in their additional Northern Hemisphere properties in Hokkaido, Japan, and in recently announced partnerships with Chinese breeders (see Darley 2011a). Darley's stallions shuttle across the equator to service mares in both hemispheres' breeding seasons. Sheikh Mohammed's brother Sheikh Hamdan (who is Deputy Ruler of Dubai and the Minister of Finance and Industry of the United Arab Emirates) has his own thoroughbred operations. His Shadwell business group is also global with racing and breeding operations in Australia, Dubai, England, France, Ireland, around Lexington, KY, and with an increasing presence in South America.

Darley and Shadwell are two examples of a small but significant number of globalized thoroughbred operations. Other leading examples would include Coolmore, owned by Irish billionaire John Magnier. Coolmore, like Darley, has a substantial presence in all the major breeding centres of the world and the two are often characterized as arch-competitors in the industry; bidding against each other in the yearling sales, for example. So, in addition to posing the question: why are these super-rich individuals and families drawn to horse breeding and racing? (a question explicitly addressed by Phil McManus in his chapter in this volume), we ask: how do the global circuits of money, labour, and power mobilized by the super-rich shape the rural landscape? And what effects do the investments of the super-rich in these particular rural landscapes have on social relations? We argue that a focus on the transformations of the material landscape can offer a useful window onto these socio-spatial processes.

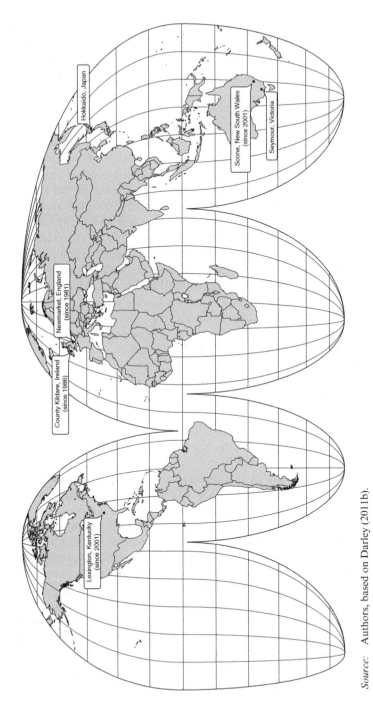

Source: Authors, based on Darley (2011b).

Figure 9.1 Darley's global network of stud farms

County Kildare, Ireland
(since 1986)

Newmarket, England
(since 1981)

Hokkaido, Japan

Scone, New South Wales
(since 2001)

Seymour, Victoria

Lexington, Kentucky
(since 2001)

Source: Authors.

Figure 9.2   Typical Bluegrass horse farm landscape, Old Frankfort Pike, Woodford County, Kentucky

THE BLUEGRASS HORSE FARM LANDSCAPE

There are about 450 horse farms in the Inner Bluegrass Region (Slayman 2007). The grass in the Bluegrass Region itself is not obviously blue, but the apocryphal origins of the regional denomination are traced to the dominance of the grass *poa pratensis*. This grass type, together with the limestone bedrock, and the calcium-rich water that is said to nourish the bones of the horses, are often cited as reasons why bloodstock apparently thrive here (Alvey 1992; Nutt et al. 2011). These 'natural' elements are not arcane facts of biology and geology, for they are central to what Raitz and VanDommelen (1990) call the vocabulary of the prototypical Bluegrass horse farm landscape (Figure 9.2). These touted characteristics of the land are the foundation for the orderly, manicured cultural landscape of the thoroughbred breeding operation. Limestone walls (locally called rock fences), or white or black painted four board fences delineating neat paddocks, well-maintained stables and barns, and stately houses or mansions with imposing brick and stone entrance gates, mark the horse farm landscape as quite different from most rural or agricultural landscapes in the US. Its aesthetic is more pastoral than agricultural. Its appearance reflects a lineage traceable to the landscape ideals of the rural elite of England whose stately homes were set in so-called great parks. The park-like qualities of the Bluegrass landscape reference this cultivated pastoral ideal of a park, distinctly not the public park idea of latter-day urban planners. In short, the Bluegrass horse farm landscape presents a carefully arranged scene that conveys a clear (and accurate) impression of land and wealth. The horse farm landscape of the Bluegrass is a privately-owned and tightly-controlled setting for prized bloodstock, their accommodation, and for the display of the taste and status of the land- and horse-owners (Schatzki 2011). It rests, of course, on the ability of the landowners to mobilize and invest substantial amounts of capital, but also on the perhaps less-obvious labour of vast numbers of workers who attend to the animals and the landscape. Many of these workers on the horse farms of the Bluegrass are migrants from Mexico and Central America. Moreover, it should be stressed that the idealized thoroughbred farm landscape does not envelope the entire Bluegrass Region. There is diversity within the rural Bluegrass, with many ordinary farms focusing on raising cattle and growing hay, for example. There are also decidedly un-pastoral elements such as small towns and cities, power plants, interstate highways, and a modest number of manufacturing facilities; and beyond the Bluegrass Region the state of Kentucky contains diverse landscapes including vast swathes of national forest and 'strip' or 'open cast' coal mines. Nevertheless, the Bluegrass horse farm landscape is heralded as an idealized and idyllic icon of regional identity that is often used to represent the entire state. Meanwhile, unchecked suburban and ex-urban expansion, especially in the counties surrounding Lexington, is regarded by many as a significant threat to this iconic landscape.

THE CREATION OF THE BLUEGRASS HORSE FARM LANDSCAPE

The story of the famed Bluegrass landscape has been one of elite creation and control since Euro-American settlers, especially those from Virginia and Maryland, arrived in Kentucky during the late eighteenth century. The rich among them brought their knowledge and interest in animal breeding, so-called blooded stock (or bloodstock) animals, and horse racing, with them as they crossed the Appalachian Mountains and obtained land on the Kentucky frontier. One colonist was Robert Alexander, who purchased 4000 acres (1618 hectares) in Woodford County, just outside present-day

Lexington. Alexander's son studied at Oxford, and then returned to Kentucky and turned that acreage into an estate, called Woodburn, which he based on the English model, complete with deer parks, stone fences, and country lanes. Because of its meticulous (if sometimes controversial) pedigree records as well as the fame of its bloodstock, including the stallion *Lexington*, one of the industry's leading sires to this day, Woodburn is often considered the home of Kentucky's modern breeding industry. But the Alexanders were not alone in their antebellum farming practices and landscape transformations. They had local competition, for example, from neighbouring Bluegrass farms such as Nantura Farm, Bosque Bonita, and Stone Wall Farm. These farms, worked by slave labour, and with an emphasis on bloodstock came to characterize modern elite farming in the region on the eve of the Civil War (Smith and Raitz 1974; Raitz and VanDommelen 1990; Domer 2005; Nutt et al. 2011).

Though it did not happen rapidly, and was not in any way inevitable, the period after the Civil War ended in 1865 saw Kentucky become increasingly incorporated into burgeoning national and international circuits of capital. The already established Bluegrass thoroughbred farms faced a series of major problems after the war. The equine business had been disrupted by the war in many ways, including the conscription of horses by armies from both sides. Then, the end of slavery (or manumission, mandated in 1865 by the 13th Amendment to the US Constitution) meant farms faced a severe labour shortage. These disruptions made Kentucky ripe for investment, but local stocks of investment capital were modest. Meanwhile a series of challenges (such as anti-gambling measures) faced horse breeders and racing interests in the north. Investors who had weathered the financial crises of 1837 and 1857 and were interested in reviving horse racing looked with interest to Kentucky's Bluegrass. Kentucky's national reputation for thoroughbred breeding and racing and the cultural cachet of its cultivated and genteel farms were touted by Kentucky's boosters who promoted the state as safe for investment and counteracted its reputation as a rough and lawless place. The last few decades of the nineteenth century and first few of the twentieth century saw an influx of investment by the country's super-rich; astute businessmen who were seeking opportunities for profit and for social status (Wall 2010). These investors, many of them from the ranks of the infamous 'robber barons', transformed racing itself as they established institutions such as the Jockey Club in 1894, designed to organize and regulate the business (Case 2000; Howland 2003–4; Wall 2010). As breeding and racing became regularized, so the Bluegrass Region became a key node in its developing national and international networks. Still a rural and provincial place in many ways, the Bluegrass was nonetheless marked by its increasing incorporation into circuits of capital, persons, knowledge, and animals, that made up the thoroughbred industry. As a consequence, the social geography of the region was restructured and the landscape transformed.

The influx of investors who bought vast acreages in the Bluegrass included well-known and super-rich men such as: Joseph Widener, who had inherited wealth made by his father in diverse investments, including Philadelphia's tram system and the steel and tobacco industries; James Cox Brady, whose father had diverse business interests and whose companies owned many railroad and tram lines in New York; William M. Wright, owner of the Calumet Baking Powder Company based in Chicago; James R. Keene, Wall Street broker, financial speculator and adviser to the likes of J.P. Morgan; Edward Bradley, a successful bookmaker and racetrack owner with operations in Florida and Louisiana; and Arthur Hancock whose family owned a large stock farm in Virginia. These wealthy men bought farms that had suffered from under-investment during and after the Civil War and they invested heavily in transforming them into state-of-the-art facilities that featured the latest modern equine innovations. They tended to favour landscapes with an overall aesthetic that melded the English ideal, already evident in the established Bluegrass horse farms, with a more distinctly 'Southern' plantation look, perhaps to evoke the privilege and extreme relative wealth of the historically slave-holding planters. This entailed adding columned porticos to extant mansions, as at Woodburn, or constructing new mansions in the ostensible style of the 'Deep South', such as at Elmendorf (Figure 9.3).

At the same time, workers' (formerly slaves') housing was removed from locations close to the big house – and in many places in the Bluegrass separate settlements for the former slaves were set up on marginal land at the edges of the consolidated thoroughbred farms. This removed African-Americans' modest living places from the ordered landscape of the thoroughbred farm and yet secured a nearby labour force for those farms (Smith and Raitz 1974; see also Hoskins 2011; Schneider 2007; Wall 2010; Wright 1982).

In contrast to the horsemen of pre-Civil War Kentucky, many of the new horse farm owners did not have rural roots and many did not live on their Kentucky farms. Much as for the sheikhs today, the Kentucky horse farm at the turn of the twentieth century was often just one element in a diverse and geographically-dispersed set of properties and residences, and just one component of a complex business portfolio that often included other thoroughbred farms. For example, Widener had many equine business interests beyond his Elmendorf Farm in Kentucky, including another horse farm in France. These absentee owners spent only a small portion of the year in residence in the Bluegrass. This led, in part, to the development

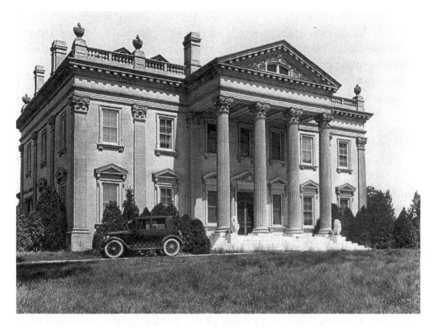

Source: C. Frank Dunn Photographs Collection, Kentucky Historical Society, Special Collections & Archives, Frankfort, Kentucky. Available through Kentuckiana Digital Library, Persistent URL: http://name.kdl.kyvl.org/KNU-1987PH2-1804.

Figure 9.3   Elmendorf Farm mansion, c. 1915

of a professionalized class of horse people in the region, whom the farm owners relied upon to run the daily business of the farms; from horse care, breeding, training, and racing, to managing the labour, the accounts, and the property (Garkovich et al. 2009; Hollingsworth 2004; Nutt et al. 2011; Raitz and VanDommelen 1990; Wall 2010). The turn of the century horse farms also relied on large numbers of relatively less-skilled workers to do the manual labour of animal care and property maintenance. The region's socio-spatial relations today still include absentee landowners whose farms and animals are managed and serviced by an internationally sourced cadre of professionals, and a large pool of low-wage labour, today made up predominantly of migrants from Mexico and Central America.

The super-rich new owners at the turn of the twentieth century spared no expense in transforming the landscape. Widener, for example, hired a nationally prominent architect and reconstructed Elmendorf, moving over 100 000 tons (91 000 tonnes) of earth and rock in the process, planting thousands of trees and shrubs, and building numerous grand structures

(Raitz and VanDommelen 1990). The practice of spending vast sums of money, obtained in other economic sectors and places, to shape a distinct landscape assemblage for thoroughbreds and their owners, continues unabated in the present-day Bluegrass. Two examples make the point.

A.E. Bye was the landscape architect who worked on Gainesway farm, just east of Lexington, between 1974 and 1986. At that time, Gainesway was owned by horseman John Gaines whose family had long been in the horse business and who had made their fortune manufacturing and selling animal feeds. After turning his family farm on the edge of Lexington into a sub-urban housing subdivision, Gaines bought land that was formerly owned by C.V. Whitney, wealthy scion of the Vanderbilt and Whitney families. Gaines hired Bye to re-make his new property. Bye was an internationally-known landscape architect based in Connecticut. His design for the farm was praised by *Landscape Architecture* magazine as one of the most notable design achievements of the 1970s (Rodriguez 1996; Chambers 2002). Perhaps the most famous aspect of that design was the use of a ha-ha, a trench incorporated into the landscape. Ha-has were favoured by eight-eenth century landscape architects such as William Kent and Capability Brown in their designs for English estates. They served to maintain, unin-terrupted, the broad sweeping vistas of the English landscape tradition as well as to hide from the owner's view the details and mundane reminders of the labour necessary to maintain the 'naturalness' of that vista (see Mitchell 1996). Gainesway was sold by Gaines to South African Graham Beck, who had made his money in mining and in wine-making. The farm's landscape continued to be developed under Beck, and now by his son, Anthony. Their ongoing landscape transformations are so extensive as to require a full time director of horticulture (Gainesway 2012).

The Farish family owns Lane's End Farm. William S. Farish III is an heir to the Standard Oil fortune and one-time ambassador to the Court of St James appointed by President George W. Bush. The farm has consist-ently been a top consignor at the Keeneland sales, and is often claimed to be one of the jewels of the Bluegrass landscape. Lane's End reflects the careful and meticulous design interventions of Morgan Wheelock, a landscape architect whose firm has offices in Boston and Palm Beach, and whose projects include several US and Canadian horse farms as well as four or five stud farms for the Aga Khan in Ireland and France. Beginning in 1980, Wheelock helped to take what had been a cattle farm of several hundred acres and, through acquisitions, design, and the labour of many unskilled, semi-skilled and skilled workers, turned it into a world-class equine facility of more than 2000 acres (810 hectares) with all the requisite landscape features (for examples see Morgan Wheelock Incorporated, no date). His designs incorporated Kentucky traditions and English architectural details, but were also attuned to function and the enormous value of the horses. He incorporated several design innovations (for example, in fencing and in barn ventilation) aimed at protecting the valuable livestock as, after all and in Wheelock's own words: 'the concept of the farm is to breed and *sell* horses' (Gillette 1998: emphasis in original). Wheelock emphasized what he called 'topographic eroticism', which likens the humanly designed topography to a sensual human body and is meant to transform the business of sexual reproduction into romance in the landscape. When Mrs Wheelock, the designer's wife, saw the finished product, she is reported to have proclaimed: 'My God! This is a painting! I've never been so moved!' An admiring author of an article on Wheelock's work at Lane's End wrote that the resultant landscape 'traced by dark brown curving fences and narrow roads and punctuated by groups of horses, drifts of trees, a pond, and half concealed barns,' does indeed 'evoke a flood of emotion usually elicited by a painting,' and is nothing short of a 'paradise regained' (Gillette 1998).

Both the transformed Bluegrass landscape and the paintings or art genre it invokes are more than simply an aesthetic preference of the super-rich. They also are historically and geographically traceable to European landscape ideas and ideals (particular ways of seeing or knowing the land) that date from the Italian Renaissance. The view of the land itself is equated with domination and ownership, and has come to reinforce a class structure reliant upon distinctions between owner and labourers in a capitalist economy (Cosgrove 1984 [1998]; Mitchell 1996). In the case of the Bluegrass this is achieved in part through referencing a 'Southern' political economy, replete with its aristocratic pretensions to gentility, though of course founded upon slave labour (see *Life Magazine* 1955 for an example). Slaves no longer work the land, but the tidiness of the ha-ha at Gainesway serves as a material reminder of extreme inequalities of still racialized social relations, even as it hides from (the landowners') view the labourers' everyday practices.

Most of the Bluegrass horse farms have been created from land that was formerly used to raise cattle and crops such as tobacco and hay. Those farm landscapes typically included a ramshackle assortment of outbuildings and barns, and hedgerows full of volunteer species and animals such as rabbits and groundhogs whose burrows can be bone shattering, multi-million dollar hazards in a thoroughbred horse pasture. Creating a horse farm typically entails a labour- and capital-intensive process of remaking those old farms: tearing out hedgerows and old fence lines, scraping the earth (and maybe installing tile drainage systems), laying plumbing and heating for year-round watering troughs, building and painting miles and miles of board fences, and maybe restoring rock fences, in addition to building ponds, constructing highly specialized barns (for stallions, for mares, for breeding, and so on), roadways, offices, residences, and other infrastructure. The equine design industry caters to these specialized needs that so radically transform the landscape (see CMW 2006, as one example). Not surprisingly, thoroughbred horse farms are expensive to create and expensive to maintain. They, or at least the land they occupy, are also under pressure from urban sprawl.

THE SUPER-RICH AND THE POLITICS OF THE LANDSCAPE

In spite of over a century of considerable investment, or perhaps even because of it, there is concern about preserving the iconic Bluegrass horse farm landscape. In 2006, the World Monuments Fund designated the Bluegrass Region 'one of America's most distinctive landscapes' and placed it on an 'endangered' watch list (World Monuments Fund 2010), after it was nominated by the Kentucky Heritage Council, the Bluegrass Trust for Historic Preservation, the University of Kentucky College of Design, and the Bluegrass Conservancy. The dean of the College of Design at the time claimed that 'most Lexingtonians get their identity from the Bluegrass landscape' and he noted 'the irony of that is that it's a private landscape, and the sense of public identity comes from the good will and grace of a series of private owners' (quoted in Slayman 2007, p. 18; see also Carey and Karan 2008).

The fact that it is a privately owned landscape, created by and for elites, has not stopped local people from galvanizing behind the effort to protect the Bluegrass horse farm landscape from suburban development, both contiguous sprawl and guerilla-like, piecemeal attack (Dreistadt 2011, especially Chapter 8; Freilich et al. 2010, pp. 326–32). A number of land protection schemes have been put in place to help maintain the image of rural gentility so favoured by the super-rich thoroughbred farm owners. These are public and private schemes, and some are local and some are statewide programmes. They also intersect with other programmes at the national level aimed at farmland protection, such as that of the American Farmland Trust (AFT). These programmes are about preserving farmland generally, and so also incorporate some concern for non-equine agricultural farming operations, including cattle and tobacco. But the dominant preservation narrative is pinned to the thoroughbred horse farm. In fact, the thoroughbred landscape is so central to regional identity that when famed Calumet Farm, whose neat paddocks and barns are one of the first sights visitors to Lexington see if they arrive by air (Calumet is under the major flight path, and has frontage on the main highway from the airport to the city), was threatened by bankruptcy in the early 1990s, the Mayor of Lexington proposed using taxpayer money to maintain the view. He wanted to spend five to six million dollars to buy one third of the 827 acre (334 hectares) farm to create a drive through park and to place conservation easements on the rest of the property (Bean 1991). The mayor did not have to make good on his proposal, in the end, as the farm was purchased by a rich horse breeder who vowed to maintain its traditional appearance (Carfagno 1992).

The state of Kentucky has had a Purchase of Agricultural Conservation Easements (PACE) programme in place since 1994. It was started by then-governor and horseman Brereton Jones. Jones and his wife own Airdrie Stud, a 2700-acre (1090 hectares) thoroughbred operation located across the road from the original Woodburn. The Joneses recently purchased Woodburn (the house and 500 acres [200 hectares]) and are in the process of renovating the property. When they are finished, they plan on donating the easement to the state PACE programme (Weir 2005; Kentucky Department of Agriculture no date). 'Easement' in a US legal sense refers to the transfer of usage rights; in this case the landowner transfers or gives up the right to develop the land in any capacity other than its farm use, and the agreement is legally bound to the land itself in perpetuity. Two Bluegrass counties, Scott and Fayette, have followed suit with similar Purchase of Development Rights (PDR) programmes, in which a government agency is empowered to purchase the development rights (or easement), thus effectively extinguishing them. Fayette County's programme is also supported by funds from a US Department of Agriculture programme. Neighbouring Woodford County has another variation on the practice: an 'Equine Preserve District' as part of its legally required Comprehensive Plan which sets the tone for the legally binding county-wide zoning ordinance. The Bluegrass Conservancy, a private organization with some involvement of thoroughbred breeders and owners, also has a PDR programme.

Each of these programmes differs slightly in their particulars. All are dedicated to preserving farmland, primarily through conservation easements. Some easements are donated. Many are purchased, with private and taxpayer monies. The purchase generally covers the land value lost to the farmer in the difference between maintaining a property at agricultural land values versus what might be gained if the land was sold at suburban residential subdivision land values (Buckloh et al. no date; AFT no date; NRCS 2008).

The various PDR and easement programmes aimed at protecting the Bluegrass landscape are not without controversy. Public (taxpayer) reaction is mixed, as the programmes can be (and often are) seen as a public subsidy of a private landscape; and one that has potentially conservative consequences extending beyond land conservation per se to include the industry's foundational labour practices and the social relations they solidify. Conserved land could be used for other kinds of agriculture, of course, but short of a financial collapse of the horse industry, it is likely that horse farms will remain horse farms. The existence of conservation easements and purchase of development rights programmes might speak to the real political power of the super-rich and their managers in the state and local legislatures, even as it also might draw upon the hegemonic Bluegrass landscape ideal in central Kentuckians' sense of regional identity. Given that the thoroughbred industry employs so many, the arguments made about the economic importance of the horse farms seem to capture the interests of both the super-rich and the many others who work in the industry. In 2005 horse sales alone brought in over US$1 billion into the region and stud fees in the Bluegrass can total as much as US$250 million per year (Slayman 2007). The thoroughbred industry in Kentucky has spawned a network of associated businesses and can most certainly be considered a significant economic cluster (Garkovich et al. 2009). The Kentucky Horse Council estimated the annual economic impact of the equine industry in the region at over US$1.7 billion, and credited the industry with employing over 30 000 people in the Bluegrass with a payroll of over US$630 million (quoted in Garkovich et al. 2009, p. 97). In addition, the landscape's appeal to tourists is often invoked by those seeking to preserve the horse farms. The revenue from tourists coming to see the horse farm landscapes is reckoned to be about US$1 billion per year for Kentucky (Slayman 2007).

A recent series of public hearings and planning commission meetings in Woodford County held around a proposal to eliminate the Equine Preserve Districts from the Comprehensive Plan generated heated debate from various quarters. While it seemed at first as though it might pit 'regular' folks against those depicted as 'rich horse people', the proposal was defeated in this instance by opposition from an alliance of farm owners with the support of many people with no direct connection to the horse industry. Those non-farmers made impassioned arguments about the 'traditional' landscape, regional identity, landscape preservation, and the aesthetic appeal of the unique local scenery in the face of potentially unchecked suburban sprawl that might threaten the distinctive central Kentucky thoroughbred farm landscape (Woodford County 2011a, 2011b).

CONCLUSIONS

The super-rich have played a dominant role in reshaping the landscape and economy of central Kentucky for at least 150 years. While the thoroughbred breeding and racing industries continue to rely on the hard work of many thousands of low paid workers, including, importantly, migrants from Mexico, Central America and elsewhere, there is no doubt that the direction of the industry is driven in large part by the spending and investment habits of a cadre of the world's super-rich. While there have been some changes in the preferred infrastructure and appointments of the prototypical Bluegrass thoroughbred farm, the particular landscape aesthetic established early on in the development of the region as a centre for thoroughbred breeding has endured. Its appeal for many of the super-rich goes beyond the economic and rests on the social meanings of such landscapes and the claims to status and power they actualize (Duncan and Duncan 2004; Wyckoff 1994).

Moreover, the super-rich are not buying Bluegrass horse farms as holiday homes (in contrast to some of the areas discussed by Hay and Muller 2012, for example). These farms, with their distinctive landscapes are at once trophy properties and sites of accumulation. It is perhaps not surprising then, that the local politics of landscape preservation in central Kentucky is a complicated and serious business. The landscape of the Bluegrass is a working landscape that is home to an unusual but productive agricultural economic cluster at the same time as it works to solidify the social positions of the super-rich players in the industry. These farms may also be seen as part of social relations that are simultaneously local, regional, and global (see also Woods 2007). The Bluegrass is caught up in intensely global networks and flows, but at the same time, these networks and flows, mobilized in large part by the world's super-rich continue to shape a distinct regional rural landscape and impact the lives of many thousands who live and work among the storied thoroughbred farms of Kentucky.

ACKNOWLEDGEMENTS

We gratefully acknowledge the influence of Proinnsias Breathnach, National University of Ireland – Maynooth, with whom fieldwork in the horse country of Ireland and in the Hunter Valley of Australia was conducted.

REFERENCES

AFT [American Farmland Trust] (no date), 'Kentucky-Successes', www.farmland. org/programs/states/KY/KentuckySuccesses.asp, accessed 17 January 2012.

Alvey, R.G. (1992), *Kentucky Bluegrass Country*, Jackson, MS: University Press of Mississippi.

Bean, D. (1991), 'Buffer park sought for Calumet; city plan calls for buying third of horse farm', *Lexington Herald-Leader*, 14 December, p. A1.

Beaverstock, J.V., P. Hubbard and J.R. Short (2004), 'Getting away with it? Exposing the geographies of the super-rich', *Geoforum*, **35**, 401–7.

Buckloh, D., G. Cohn, J. Freedgood, R. McCracken, D. Mittasch and G. Unger (no date), 'Kentucky agricultural landowners guide to conservation and profitability', The American Farmland Trust, www.farmlandinfo.org/documents/30009/Kentucky_Landowner_Guide.pdf, accessed 17 January 2012.

Carey, D. and P.P. Karan (2008), 'From horse farms to Wal-Mart', in P.P. Karan and U Saganuma (eds), *Local Environmental Movements*, Lexington, KY: University Press of Kentucky, pp. 145–64.

Carfagno, J. (1992), 'DeKwiatkowski pays price in full, assumes ownership of Calumet', *Lexington Herald Leader*, 28 March 1992, A10.

Case, C. (2000), *The Right Blood: America's Aristocrats in Thoroughbred Racing*, New Brunswick, NJ: Rutgers University Press.

Cassidy, R. (2002), *The Sport of Kings: Kinship, Class and Thoroughbred Breeding in Newmarket*, Cambridge: Cambridge University Press.

Cassidy, R. (2007), *Horse People: Thoroughbred Culture in Lexington and Newmarket*, Baltimore, MD: Johns Hopkins University Press.

Chambers, J. (2002), 'Rip rap', *Landscape Architecture*, May, 22.

CMW Inc. (2006), 'Gainsborough Farm', www.cmwequine.com/portfolio.html, accessed 12 January 2010.

Cooper, R.K. (2011a), 'Saratoga horse crowd spends big at Keeneland Sales', *The Business Review* (online), 26 September, www.bizjournals.com/albany/morning_call/2011/09/locals-spend-big-at-keeneland-sale.html, accessed 1 December 2011.

Cooper, R.K. (2011b), 'No signs of Wall Street gloom at Fasig-Tipton's Saratoga auction', *The Business Review* (online), 12 August, www.bizjournals.com/albany/print-edition/2011/08/12/no-signs-of-wall-street-gloom-at.html, accessed 1 December 2011.

Cosgrove, D.E. (1984 [1998]), *Social Formation and Symbolic Landscape*, Madison, WI: University of Wisconsin Press.

Darley (2011a), 'Press release: Darley to stand two stallions in China in 2012', 17 October, www.darley.co.jp/news/press-release-3, accessed 12 January 2012.

Darley (2011b), 'Darley', www.darleyamerica.com/, accessed 12 January 2012.

Davis, A.F. (2009), 'Kentucky's urban/rural landscape: what is driving the differences in wealth across Kentucky?', University of Kentucky College of Agriculture, www2.ca.uky.edu/CEDIK-files/KYRuralUrbanWealthDifferences. pdf, accessed 17 January 2012.

Domer, D. (2005), 'Inventing the horse farm', *Kentucky Humanities*, October, 3–12.

Dreistadt, R. (2011), *Lost Bluegrass: History of a Vanishing Landscape*, Charleston, SC: The History Press.

Duncan, J.S. and N. Duncan (2004), *Landscapes of Privilege: The Politics of the Aesthetic in an American Suburb*, New York: Routledge.

Freilich, R.H., R.J. Sitkowski and S.D. Mennillo (2010), *From Sprawl to Sustainability*, 2nd edn, Chicago, IL: American Bar Association Publishing.

Gainesway (2012), 'Gainesway', www.gainesway.com/index.html, accessed 12 January 2012.

Garkovich, L., K. Brown and J.N. Zimmerman (2009), 'We're not horsing around: conceptualizing the Kentucky horse industry as an economic cluster', *Community Development*, **39** (3), 93–113.

Gillette, J.B. (1998), 'Kentucky romance', *Landscape Architecture*, September, 58–65, 82–4.

Hay, I. and S. Muller (2012), '"That tiny, stratospheric apex that owns most of the world" – exploring geographies of the super-rich', *Geographical Research*, **50** (1), 75–88.

Hollingsworth, R. (2004), *Lexington: Queen of the Bluegrass*, Charleston, SC: Arcadia.

Hoskins, S. (2011), *The Homeplace*, www.sarahhoskins.com/#/the-homeplace/sarahhoskinsthehomeplace, accessed 12 January 2012.

Howland, J.S. (2003–4), 'Let's not spit the bit in defense of the law of the horse: the historical and legal development of American thoroughbred racing', *Marquette Sports Law Review*, **14** (2), 473–507.

Kentucky Department of Agriculture (no date), 'Farmland preservation program', www.kyagr.com/marketing/farmland/index.htm, accessed 12 January 2012.

Life Magazine (1955), 'The blue grass country: a beautiful part of old Kentucky flourishes as horse farms prosper', 25 April.

Mitchell, D. (1996), *The Lie of the Land: Migrant Workers and the California Landscape*, Minneapolis, MN: University of Minnesota Press.

Morgan Wheelock Incorporated (no date), 'Morgan Wheelock', www.morgan wheelock.com/Webpages/Projects/Equestrian/Equestrian.htm, 12 January 2012.

NRCS [Natural Resources Conservation Service] (2008), 'Farm & ranch land protection program helps entity reach milestone', United States Department of Agriculture Natural Resources Conservation Service, www.ky.nrcs.usda.gov/news/FRPP_LFUCG.html, accessed 17 January 2012.

Nutt, J., M. Clark, R. Graycarek, C.T. Hall and J. Roenker (2011), 'The Kentucky thoroughbred breeding industry and state programs that assist the equine industry', draft, Program Review and Investigations Committee, Legislative Research Commission, Frankfort, KY.

O'Connor, C. (2011), 'Triple crown billionaires: meet horse racing's richest people', *Forbes* (online), 9 June, www.forbes.com/sites/clareoconnor/2011/06/09/triple-crown-billionaires-meet-horse-racings-richest-people/, accessed 12 January 2012.

Raitz, K. and D. VanDommelen (1990), 'Creating the landscape symbol vocabulary for a regional image: the case of the Kentucky Bluegrass', *Landscape Journal*, **9**, 109–21.

Rodriguez, A. (1996), 'A subtle hand', *Landscape Architecture*, May, 83–7, 102–4.

Schatzki, T.R. (2011), 'Landscapes as temporalspatial phenomena', in J. Malpas (ed.), *The Place of Landscape: Concepts, Contexts, Studies*, Boston, MA: The MIT Press, pp. 65–89.

Schneider, K.L. (2007), 'Negotiating the image of the Inner Bluegrass', *Landscape Journal*, **26** (1), 134–50.

Slayman, A. (2007), 'A race against time for Kentucky's Bluegrass Country', www.wmf.org/sites/default/files/wmf_article/pg_14-19_bluegrass.pdf, accessed 17 January 2012.

Smith, P.C. and K.B. Raitz (1974), 'Negro hamlets and agricultural estates in Kentucky's Inner Bluegrass', *Geographical Review*, **64**, 217–34.

United States Census (2010), *State and County Quick Facts: Kentucky*, http://quickfacts.census.gov/qfd/states/21000.html, accessed 12 January 2012.

Wall, M. (2010), *How Kentucky Became Southern*, Lexington, KY: University Press of Kentucky.

Weir, T. (2005), 'The Bluegrass battle: horse farms vs. developers', *USA Today* (online), 2 November, www.usatoday.com/sports/horses/2005-11-02-kentucky-horse-country-cover_x.htm, accessed 17 January 2012.

Woodford County (2011a), minutes of the Versailles-Woodford County Planning and Zoning Commission, public hearing, 3 November.

Woodford County (2011b), minutes of the Versailles-Woodford County Planning and Zoning Commission, meeting, 10 November.

Woods, M. (2007), 'Engaging the global countryside: globalization, hybridity and the reconstitution of rural place', *Progress in Human Geography*, **31**, 485–507.

World Monuments Fund (2010), 'Bluegrass cultural landscape', www.wmf.org/project/bluegrass-cultural-landscape-kentucky, accessed 7 April 2012.

Wright, J.D. (1982), *Lexington: Heart of the Bluegrass*, Lexington, KY: Lexington Fayette County Historical Commission.

Wyckoff, W.K. (1994), 'Landscapes of private power and wealth', in M.P. Conzen (ed.), *The Making of the American Landscape*, New York: Routledge, pp. 335–54.

10. The sport of kings, queens, sheikhs and the super-rich: thoroughbred breeding and racing as leisure for the super-rich

Phil McManus

Breeding racehorses for a living is not something that a sane, intelligent, mature person experienced in American capitalism would ever attempt to do.
Squires 2002, p. xi.

Horse ownership is the only currency that distinguishes the truly wealthy from the rest of us.
Ken England quoted in Sugar 2003, p. 48.

If geographies of the super-rich is an area of study that appears to have been largely ignored (Hay and Muller 2012), then the work that has been done within this field of study has generally overlooked the important activity of leisure as an area of critical inquiry. This is particularly note-worthy given the potential time and financial resources that the super-rich have at their disposal to engage in leisure activities, and the significance of their involvement in changing the character of the leisure activities in which they choose to engage. One of the few studies of super-rich leisure appeared in *Forbes Magazine* (Hesseldahl and Dubow 2000), where the purchase of private jets, yachts, artworks and sports teams was noted among the Forbes 400 rich list. These included American football and basketball teams (Microsoft cofounder Paul Allen owned the Seattle Seahawks and the Portland Trailblazers) while in 1999 Texan billionaire Robert McNair spent US$700 million building a new team, the Houston Texans, to bring football back to Houston after the departure in the late 1990s of the Houston Oilers to Nashville to eventually become the Tennessee Titans. Involvement of the super-rich in club ownership also includes transnational ownership of football/soccer teams, particularly in the English Premier League, where there is foreign ownership of Chelsea (Russian billionaire Roman Abramovich – the 68th richest person in the

world in 2012 with a fortune exceeding US$12 billion), Manchester City
(Sheikh Mansour bin Zayed bin Sultan Al Nahyan, a member of ruling
family of Abu Dhabi), and Fulham (owned by Mohamed Al-Fayed, an
Egyptian-born businessman who formerly owned Harrods) (based on
Beckett 2010).

Academic studies about the super-rich have focused on their wealth relative to the rest of the population, their spatial distribution, the source(s)
of their wealth, changes over time, and questions about the justice of this
dynamic wealth distribution pattern (Beaverstock et al. 2004; Haseler
1999; Irvin 2008; Neumayer 2004). This research has generally revealed
that despite an overall rise in income and wealth over time, inequality
between the very wealthy and the remainder of society has been increasing. This has fuelled concerns about the political values underpinning the
widening gap, particularly the emphasis on neoliberalism and the erasure
of equity-based discourses from the political landscape (Irvin 2008). Such
concerns permeate popular representations of the super-rich, as seen
in Tritch (2006), particularly in the George W. Bush era of US politics
when inequality increased and the will to address the consequences of this
inequality through the taxation system was noticeably absent.

This chapter does not engage directly with issues of inequity and
inequality, although they are inevitably present in any discussion of the
super-rich. Instead, it focuses on the overlooked activity of leisure, and
particularly on the activities of thoroughbred breeding and racing. The
unique world of thoroughbred breeding and racing, popularly known as
'the sport of kings', has appeal to some among the super-rich because of
their past personal links to these activities. For others it offers opportunities to display wealth and the ability to engage socially with people of a
particular cultural standing. This is not a new trend, given the importance
of patronage by Charles II in establishing the English horseracing centre
of Newmarket in the seventeenth century, but it is particularly important for the nouveau riche, where economic worth does not immediately
translate into cultural capital. That said, it is important to remember
that thoroughbred racing, while serving no necessary purpose in an age
dominated by internal combustion engines, is important geographically,
socially, economically and environmentally (see McManus et al. 2013).
While the super-rich typically engage in thoroughbred breeding and
racing for reasons other than the maximization of economic gain, they
become involved with the intention of being successful and being seen to
be successful.

The chapter begins with an introduction to the work of the economist
and sociologist Thorstein Veblen in the late nineteenth century, including recent engagement with his writings by scholars from a variety of

academic disciplines. The next section of the chapter introduces the unique world of thoroughbred breeding and racing. This is followed by an examination of how the super-rich have participated in this world, which leads to an analysis of the impacts of their participation. The chapter concludes by highlighting the main insights derived from applying concepts drawn from Veblen's analysis of the leisure class approximately 110 years ago to the contemporary super-rich, and particularly their involvement in the 'elaborate futility' that is more popularly known as 'the sport of kings'.

THORSTEIN VEBLEN AND THE LEISURE CLASS

Thorstein Veblen (1857–1929) was an American of Norwegian ancestry who introduced the notions of conspicuous leisure and conspicuous consumption. Veblen argued in his 1899 book *The Theory of the Leisure Class* that simply being wealthy was insufficient to achieve status in society. It was necessary to have time to devote to leisure activities while other people were working. It was also necessary to be seen to consume, to share the consumption with others as a way of increasing (or at least maintaining) social standing. In short, it was necessary to display wealth. It was also important to be seen with the 'right people', and to distance oneself from those people who could diminish one's social standing. This process, which Veblen called 'emulation' is important in attaining social standing as it necessitates a degree of engagement with, and conformation to, those people who are considered respectable. The leisure class is, in effect, Veblen's equivalent of the modern-day super-rich.

Veblen's book was a scathing attack on this class of people in America in the late nineteenth century (Jorgensen and Jorgensen 1999), although as Scott (2010, p. 289) acknowledges, Veblen recognized that emulation was a practice that occurred 'across all socio-economic levels'. In fact, he had a more global outlook, examining the rise of industrial Germany and imperial Britain. This analysis included a sweeping dismissal of the British colonization of India as being to 'keep occupied the scions of its leisure class who otherwise would have nothing to do' (Jorgensen and Jorgensen 1999, p. 150). Veblen focused not simply on the use of financial resources, but on the use of a particularly finite resource, time. He considered conspicuous leisure to be the non-productive use of time but recognized that this escape from everyday work was productive for the leisure class in that it elevated or maintained their position in society, so much so that it eventually grew into a 'laborious drill in deportment and an education in taste and discrimination' that had to be maintained (Veblen 1899, p. 31). He also recognized that only the very wealthy could avoid the need to work, so for other people of wealth conspicuous leisure was often replaced by conspicuous consumption, which did not necessitate an effort to learn the customs and social mores of the established leisure class required to engage in desired leisure pursuits. This learning of customs and social mores is similar to Bourdieu's notion of cultural capital, which is acquired almost unknowingly through immersion in a particular *habitus* (Bourdieu 1984). For the purposes of this chapter, I focus on Veblen's contribution to the concepts of conspicuous leisure and conspicuous consumption.

Veblen's work has been advanced by scholars in a number of fields, most notably Institutional Economics (see Jorgensen and Jorgensen 1999; Knoedler et al. 2007). While many aspects of his work are considered dated, there has been some resurgence in the use of his insights, particularly since the decline of Marxism and as Western economies have become less production-oriented and more consumer- and service-oriented. It is the insights of Veblen into the processes of capitalism, particularly the importance of culture in consumption, that are relevant for a post-industrial economy. Some readers may question what insights Veblen may offer to an analysis of horseracing, particularly given his view of sport as a leisure class value that permeates all levels of society and which he saw 'as emulation of the predatory prowess' that was present in the leisure class approach to business and political dealings in the world (Lambert 1999, p. 975). While this perception resonates with modern sporting competitions it is, I believe, overly simplistic. Veblen saw football, particularly, as an activity that encouraged intense competition. Horse racing was mentioned once in *The Theory of the Leisure Class*, and that being in a negative comment about the leisure class of the southern US in the late nineteenth century: 'Among this population offenses of an archaic character also are and have been relatively more prevalent and less deprecated than they are elsewhere; as, for example, duels, brawls, feuds, drunkenness, horseracing, cock-fighting, gambling' (Veblen 1899, pp. 199–200).

In his book *Imperial Germany and the Industrial Revolution*, Veblen (1915, p. 142) highlighted the importance of tradition in influencing culture. He wrote that 'it is quite beyond the reach of imagination that any male adult citizen would, of his own motion, go in for the elaborate futilities of British shooting or horse-racing, for example, or for such a tour de force of inanity as polo, or mountain climbing, or expeditions after big game'. According to Veblen, the explanation of why people did engage in such activities was based on each of these activities requiring 'all the authenticity that tradition can give it, and then its inculcation in the incoming generation must be begun in infancy and followed up throughout the educational system' (Veblen 1915, pp. 142–3).

This view of the sporting activities of the leisure class is consistent with

Veblen's view of expenditure and activities as only being useful if they serve directly to enhance human life generally, which meant to Veblen that they must pass 'the test of impersonal usefulness – usefulness as seen from the point of view of the generically human' (Veblen 1899, p. 60). By 'generically human', Veblen was referring to 'the life process taken impersonally' (Tilman 2004, p. 130). The horse-racing industry would fail this test for a number of reasons, including its reliance on gambling, vital to the economic base of the thoroughbred breeding and racing industry, but regarded by Veblen as a waste of resources (see Tilman 2004).

While it is impossible to state categorically what Veblen would make of the contemporary global thoroughbred breeding and racing industry, one suspects that beneath the glamour and hype of racing carnivals, he would detect intense competition between the super-rich, permeating other strata of society. Further, given that in 1915 horses were used in agriculture, mining, for the movement of freight and for personal transport, it is likely that Veblen would concur with Cassidy (2007, p. 117) who, drawing on Veblen's idea of conspicuous consumption, suggested that today 'racing itself is pointless. It has no product . . . What could better express the separation of men of this world from that of the masses?' Rather than simply dismiss horseracing as an 'elaborate futility' to keep the super-rich occupied, this chapter draws on Veblen's concepts of conspicuous leisure and conspicuous consumption to identify why and highlight how the super-rich engage in this activity, and the impacts of their participation.

THOROUGHBRED BREEDING AND RACING

Thoroughbred breeding and racing combines both conspicuous leisure and conspicuous consumption and, through gambling and the disposal of unwanted thoroughbreds, Veblen's notions of waste. Veblen saw waste as inevitable in people's efforts to keep up appearances and engage in conspicuous leisure and consumption that benefited a privileged few, rather than the 'generically human'. The horse racing industry is a globalized industry that has constructed networks across much of the world, linked by electronic communications, long-distance air travel and the movement of animals between places for the purposes of racing and breeding (McManus et al. 2013). Thoroughbred breeding has been transformed 'from a gentleman's hobby to a global agricultural industry now worth nearly $1 billion annually' (Cain 2004, p. 12). As the Global Financial Crisis demonstrated, such estimations of value can fluctuate markedly, as shown by an average drop in auction value of racing stock of about 25 to 30 per cent between 2008 and 2009 (Wincze 2009a; 2009b).

Thoroughbred breeding and racing is an industry that invokes tradition and discourses that prioritize being 'natural' within breeding, despite reproductive practices that bear little resemblance to what has occurred in the animal world for thousands of years. Innovation is permitted in areas such as the manipulation of time for breeding seasons, but not for the actual transfer of semen. The breeding seasons in different hemispheres do not correspond with natural breeding times based on sunlight hours and mares' ovulation, which means technological aid is employed to bring the mares to ovulation in time for the designated breeding season. The introduction of other forms of reproductive technologies, however, is not permitted because of the regulations of each country's Stud Book and the International Stud Book. A thoroughbred cannot be registered unless the birth is by the mare in which the natural conception occurred. And without registration it cannot race and cannot breed, according to the rules of the Stud Book. The multi-scalar aspect of the industry is apparent when no single country will challenge this requirement lest they be excluded from the International Stud Book, thereby ruining the ability of that country to export thoroughbreds, or for thoroughbreds that may be racing in that country to travel overseas and compete internationally.

While thoroughbreds are registered in the stud books of particular countries, rather than the legislation of individual countries, it is primarily the wealth of the super-rich that shapes the sport of thoroughbred breeding and racing at the global level and through the political economy of regional markets (Sugar 2003; Beaverstock et al. 2004; Cummings 2009; Squires 2009). This is despite the different taxation rates and incentives operating in different jurisdictions. In effect, these incentives tend to relocate activity, rather than increase it, although they can be very effective in building a thoroughbred industry in particular locations as exemplified by the Stallion Tax Exemption in Ireland, which was introduced in 1969 and ceased in 2008 having attracted many top stallions to Ireland (McManus et al. 2013).

The transnational focus of the 'truly wealthy' (in Sugar 2003, p. 48) or super-rich reinforces the existing relations around thoroughbred breeding, because it is these people who control the semen and have the ability to move it to where they choose, to increase or limit its use, and to charge for its dissemination. These practices are currently the subject of legal action in Australia, initiated by Bruce McHugh, a former bookmaker and chairman of the Sydney Turf Club (which since February 2011 is part of the Australian Turf Club), acting as an individual businessperson. McHugh is challenging existing breeding practices as being a restriction on trade under the Trade Practices Act (Murphy 2011). It is a move that may have widespread implications.

The international dimension is crucial, because the thoroughbred breeding and racing industry is reliant on attracting new investors on a regular basis. This raises the question posed in the Squires' (2002, p. xi) quotation presented above as to why people invest in thoroughbred racing, particularly when it is widely known that many people do not make money by doing so, and many lose money. In this sense, following Thorstein Veblen, thoroughbred breeding is an activity that embodies both conspicuous leisure and conspicuous consumption.

As an industry, the various scales of operation of thoroughbred breeding and racing articulate, sometimes awkwardly, so that no single country will unilaterally breach the existing laws of breeding and racing. If they do so, the stud book of that particular country will no longer be recognized internationally, meaning that the horses cannot compete internationally nor be part of the international breeding market. This means that in order to become part of this industry, newcomers have to buy their way into the industry on the industry's terms. Despite the sentiments of Squires (2002) about the economic (ir)rationality of this sports business, wealthy people who have excelled in other industries (including Squires, who was a former newspaper editor), do enter willingly into thoroughbred breeding and racing, regardless of the rational arguments that demonstrate it makes little economic sense as an investment. Once inside, they are accepted, but not always readily, because they may lack the traditions of thoroughbred breeding and the pedigree (Fox 2005; Cassidy 2007).

THE SUPER-RICH PARTICIPATING IN THOROUGHBRED BREEDING

Since the initial research was undertaken for this chapter, Forbes released a 'list' of the richest people involved in thoroughbred breeding and racing around the world (O'Connor 2011). O'Connor (2011) wrote that 'some of the power players on the Forbes Billionaires list own and breed thoroughbreds, attending bloodstock auctions to select future winners and becoming familiar figures behind the scenes at both stud farms and race tracks'. Among the super-rich identified were the ruler of Dubai, Sheikh Mohammed bin Rashid Al Maktoum (owner of the linked Darley breeding and Godolphin racing operations), Excel Communications founder Kenny Troutt who owns Winstar Farm in Versailles, KY, and Gerald Harvey of Harvey Norman fame in Australia who now wholly owns the Magic Millions thoroughbred auction company and some 1000 horses at the Vinery, Baramul and Broombee stud farms in New South Wales, plus two New Zealand stables that are recent purchases (O'Connor 2011).

One notable omission from this list of 14 individuals (counting related co-owners as one entity) was Queen Elizabeth II, whose personal net worth is in the hundreds of millions of dollars and who is responsible for the billions of dollars of crown estate. The Queen is reputed to be very knowledgeable about thoroughbred breeding and attends the major racing events at Royal Ascot and other venues (Smith 2001). The Queen's horses have won four of England's five classic flat races – the 2000 Guineas, the 1000 Guineas, the Oaks and the St Leger (Smith 2011). They have yet to win the Epsom Derby. In 2011 her horse, Carlton House, started favorite but finished third. This high-profile involvement in the thoroughbred racing industry is almost certain to generate what Veblen called 'emulation', as other people perceive the industry in a positive way due to the Queen's involvement. This explicit participation is important for the industry as it faces competition from other activities – notably yachting but also the ownership of sports teams – that lure the super-rich and their wealth.

Interviews with thoroughbred breeders, in both the dominant regions of Australia and the US (the Upper Hunter and Kentucky respectively) highlighted the importance of competing against other industries such as luxury yachts, investing in stock markets and other financial instruments, or in owning sports teams. This competition appears to be mostly socio-cultural, because while the primary source of the wealth of the super-rich is economically-oriented, their leisure activities are, as Veblen noted in relation to the leisure class, about attaining and maintaining status. This is most clearly demonstrated in the US by the decision of Robert and Janice McNair, in late 2008, to sell Stonerside Stable in the Bluegrass Region of Kentucky so that they could concentrate on their ownership of the Houston Texans, a National Football League team. While financial resources may be available, time is still somewhat limited and being popular owners of a football team that replaced the city's former team that departed to Nashville, TN, carries widespread cultural cachet when compared with the ownership of racehorses.

Thoroughbred breeding is both an economic proposition, albeit one that is not directly financially rewarding for many participants, and an 'emotional economy' that involves landscaping, the construction of networks of desirable people, and the performance of experiences, to attract new money into the industry (McManus et al. 2011). Landscaping provides the branding, the experience economy, for the super-rich to participate in this industry. Landscaping must meet functional needs related to animal husbandry, but this can be done at a lower cost than what is incurred by many of the larger thoroughbred farms. Landscaping provides more than functionality for the care of horses, it provides the setting for the super-rich to engage in an activity that, from a purely economic perspective, is not likely to be a good investment. The importance of landscaping was highlighted by one thoroughbred breeder who noted:

> This is painting the picture, this is reassuring them. Again, it's the emotive thing and to a degree it's part of the way we survive. We offer a damn good service but again it's perception because a lot of these people, not all of them, but a lot of them, are not agriculturally based or minded or educated. This is that one horse, . . . and if they're comfortable that it's been looked after and that it's safe and they're comfortable with the people looking after it that's really what they want. That's all they want to know. There's a lot more to it than that, but that appeal, that presentation, is all important.

Another thoroughbred breeder emphasized the importance of this land-scaping and, as shown in the quote below, the role of advertising in attracting participants who may have little knowledge of the industry:

> You really are launching a share market deal, aren't you? Each stud seems to put out its own prospectus each year saying these are the stallions we've got and this is what they did, and all that sort of thing. I guess there's an air of competi-tion but it's an air of doing something that will catch an eye. Its advertising and promotion, and they use the big boys in the advertising industry to do it, and yes I think it plays a role because you're getting a lot of people who own a horse who don't own property. A lot of people who own a horse really don't know which end of a horse you start at now, which is good for the industry!

In order to project this image of status, and perhaps to show off their new wealth and to attract clientele with similar expectations of what a thor-oughbred stud should look like, thoroughbred studs are landscaped so as to attract investment. In Kentucky this landscaping ranges from Calumet Farm's white fences through to the lake, mansion and the stars on the gate of WinStar Farm. In the Upper Hunter region of Australia, it includes the lawns and statue at Arrowfield, the green grass and the steep roof lines at Darley and the ornate, solid gates of Patinack Farm that exude connota-tions of wealth and power (see also Roberts and Schein, this volume). The need to relate to clients has an impact on landscaping. This was recognized by a thoroughbred breeder in the Upper Hunter who said: 'We could do this without the black fences for a lot less money, but that's the emotive image people are looking for.'

Of course, the thoroughbred breeding and racing industry offers many opportunities to engage in conspicuous consumption – apart from the landscaping of breeding farms and hosting visitors on farms where poten-tial participants can emulate the customs of people within the industry and the hosts can interest the guest in racehorse ownership. Two notable opportunities are: the auction ring when horses, and particularly year-lings, are sold; and, the racetrack for major events.

Thoroughbred auctions, according to Cassidy (2007, p.99), are 'tre-mendous entertainment', but they require a knowledge of the nuances of words and phrases. The 'uneven distribution of knowledge' (Cassidy 2007, p.100) is an important aspect of the competitive activity of purchasing thoroughbreds because it helps create 'distinctions between people who would otherwise be similar'. The auction is a duel, which accords with Veblen's notion of sport promoting institutional conservatism and com-petitive values. At the top end of the market, where major studs such as Coolmore and Darley are competing against each other and where novice participants can achieve fame through their high-profile purchase, the acquisition of a potential champion is perceived as a victory or defeat, depending on who made the successful bid (Squires 2009). Whether the horse will actually win races, or have a successful breeding career, is still unknown at this stage, but the thoroughbred breeder and the auction house have likely made money by exploiting the ego and/or lack of knowledge of a super-rich person who is accustomed to winning in other industries. This was demonstrated in the US with the so-called 'Righteous Brothers' – the Indian computer whiz Satish Sanan and the Californian billionaire Jess Jackson who made his fortune in the wine industry – when they challenged the horse racing establishment. They suspected that they had over-paid for purchases at auctions due to agents' behind-the-scenes 'deals' (Squires 2009). What was unusual was that these two men chal-lenged the establishment, whereas others are likely to have kept silent due to embarrassment.

In Australia, the importance of attracting new super-rich participants to the industry has been shown through the recent example of Nathan Tinkler, whose net worth is estimated to be $1.1 billion Australian dollars (about US$1.16 billion). Analysis by Reilly (2011) suggests that Tinkler's spending of about A$300 million on horses and horse properties since 2007 has resulted in a return of A$32.5 million from racing and breeding, calculated as:

> at least $140 million buying horses, $70 million on acquiring and developing farms and studs, and $90 million more in running costs . . . but his returns have been minimal: about $14 million in prize money from racing, $4.5 million in receipts from horses sold and a further $14 million in income from the stallions he keeps on his studs. (Reilly 2011, p.9)

It is too early to tell whether this investment by Nathan Tinkler will ulti-mately be successful or not, but despite the involvement of knowledgeable buyers and advisers (including Anthony Cummings, a successful racehorse trainer and son of Australia's most successful trainer, Bart Cummings), the scale of expenditure highlights the costs of becoming involved in the upper echelons of this industry and aiming for immediate success.

The racetrack itself also affords an opportunity for the super-rich to be successful. Wealthy owners can appear in the Winner's Circle, collect the trophy, be photographed, appear in the sporting pages of newspapers, make televised speeches – while rich spectators have to watch and applaud. And when a horse wins, unlike a football team captain or a race car driver, there is no risk of the horse grabbing the microphone and claiming the glory! While speeches are made to acknowledge the role of the trainer, the jockey and so on (see Fox 2005), the owner keeps the trophy and gets to mingle with other wealthy people they may be attempting to emulate. For those people not wealthy enough to own racehorses in their own right, or not able to pay the high price for young horses considered likely to be successful, the expansion of syndication has enabled existing owners to spread their risks across a number of horses, and has attracted new participants to the industry such that the demographics of ownership are not limited to the wealthier portions of society (Fox 2005). There may be many members of a syndicate. While there is a maximum of about twenty members per syndicate in some jurisdictions, this figure varies. For example, in New Zealand the minimum number of owners is five, but there is no maximum (New Zealand Racing 2012). Syndicate members can collect the trophy, be in the photograph, and experience all the excitement enjoyed by the super-rich, with less financial risk and, of course, fewer financial rewards given that the returns have to be divided among all syndicate members. Nonetheless, they are emulating the behaviour of the super-rich.

IMPLICATIONS OF SUPER-RICH PARTICIPATION IN THOROUGHBRED BREEDING AND RACING

The involvement of the super-rich in thoroughbred breeding and racing brings an increase in the price of horses (given the limitations of supply and demand created primarily by the control of the most desired semen), an increase in land values in breeding regions, improved facilities, the changing nature of the activity (through practices such as shuttle-stallions moving between hemispheres, or the internationalization of racing) and an increase in prize money as the super-rich sponsor races.

The entry of new super-rich people in to the thoroughbred breeding and racing industry generally means that prices of horses (particularly yearlings) rise at the top-end of the market, dragging other prices upwards too.

This is positive for established breeders, particularly in the short-term. In less favourable economic circumstances the entry of new super-rich can support the industry in significant ways. For example, the post-2007 Global Financial Crisis would have caused major economic problems for the thoroughbred breeding industry in Australia and New Zealand (as it did in other locations such as Kentucky where yearling prices declined by about 30 per cent, and stallion service fees followed this downward path), except for the arrival of Nathan Tinkler into the industry. Tinkler was Australia's richest man under the age of 40, a result of investing indirectly in Macarthur Coal and later selling his stake. Tinkler was establishing Patinack Farm in 2007, and was an active buyer at the major yearling sales in early 2008 in Karaka (New Zealand, where he bought 24 yearlings at the top end of the market), Melbourne (20 lots) and at the Magic Million sales on the Gold Coast (where he signed for 59 yearlings) (*The Courier Mail* 2008). The arrival of Nathan Tinkler and his Patinack Farm operation was most significant for the industry because of the extent of his buying and the contrast with the prevailing pattern of activity at the time.

The impact of the super-rich in re-shaping places is immense. They 'can transform places substantially' (Hay and Muller 2012, p. 79) as shown in Midway, KY (see Roberts and Schein, this volume). One impact is the increase in land values, particularly in prime thoroughbred breeding regions such as the Inner Bluegrass of Kentucky and the Upper Hunter. This is an ongoing process that has overspill impacts, including the development of secondary breeding regions (for example, Florida and California in the US, as well as in New South Wales' Southern Highlands, parts of south-east Queensland and north-east Victoria in Australia). These breeding regions may benefit from the establishment of new facilities, being relatively unfettered by the constraints of the prime region. The development of impressive new facilities at Northwood Park in Seymour, northeast Victoria, for Darley Australia (owned by Sheikh Mohammed bin Rashid Al Maktoum) highlights this scenario. Darley does not operate as state-based units, which is the focus of racing clubs and administrations in Australia, but are working on a global regional basis (Australia, Europe, Japan and the United States) and then within Australia (Upper Hunter and Seymour) to enable the movement of animals between various nodes in its operation if desired. The movement of animals, such as the transport between hemispheres of 'shuttle stallions', is possible when the super-rich own facilities in both hemispheres and can use their stallions for breeding in two seasons rather than a single season in one hemisphere. Darley, and the giant Coolmore operation, are leaders in this activity. In 2011 Coolmore had 12 stallions shuttling between Australia and the Northern Hemisphere, ten from Ireland and two from the US.

The involvement of the super-rich in this sport necessitates many people working for them, including stud managers, horse handlers, transport workers and people to clean stables. Conspicuous leisure creates work for other people, which could be interpreted positively but, if Veblen were alive, would likely be interpreted by him as wasteful because the sport of thoroughbred breeding and racing is about perpetuating competitive values and would not be seen as useful to the generic human.

CONCLUSION – THOROUGHBRED BREEDING AND RACING AS AN ELABORATE FUTILITY OF THE SUPER-RICH?

Veblen's critique of British horse-racing in the early twentieth century, or the inanity of activities such as polo, mountain climbing, and big game hunting, would not endear him to the likes of the late Kerry Packer, once Australia's richest man. Veblen's dismissal of these activities on the basis that they would not be considered useful to a generic human (presumably as determined by Veblen) is somewhat less sweeping than to see the colonization of India as important for keeping the British leisure class in that country occupied. Importantly, Veblen was primarily critiquing the people of the leisure class and their values, perpetuated through their expenditure and activities. While Veblen's critique was referring to the leisure class of the late nineteenth and early twentieth centuries, the similarities with the contemporary super-rich are striking.

For Veblen, the wealth gap between the very rich (call them the leisure class or the super-rich, it does not matter) and the rest of society was not simply something to be calculated by identifying assets. Veblen understood that this gap was not just an economic gap, but was reinforced in a socio-cultural context by the very wealthy with time to spend on their leisure activities, and the financial resources to engage in conspicuous consumption around these leisure activities.

Thoroughbred breeding has, for many years, offered super-rich people the opportunity to participate in an activity that makes little functional sense. Horses are no longer needed as a form of transport. Artificial insemination and other breeding practices are permitted in various animal industries, ranging from dairy cattle farming to the standard-bred (harness racing, that is, pacers and trotters) industry, whereas in thoroughbred breeding and racing only 'natural' processes are permitted. Thoroughbreds are raced for human pleasure, including the thrill of gambling. The thoroughbred breeding operations (where the big money is made by knowledgeable breeders who can charge high service fees if they own the most sought-after stallions, or sell the offspring of these stallions at auction), are sometimes critiqued from within the thoroughbred industry as being too separate from thoroughbred racing, as if the breeding of horses to be sold at auction and to perpetuate breeding is an end in itself.

Yet, contrary to Veblen (1915, p. 142) and to Squires' (2002, p. xi) idea that no 'sane, intelligent' person would engage willingly in thoroughbred breeding and racing, it is apparent that the super-rich (and others, including through the process of syndication) do enter the world of thoroughbred breeding and racing of their own accord. The explanations for this willingness to enter this domain are partly their personal tastes, partly that this particular sport allows participation but requires no athletic achievement or effort on their part, and partly that the activity enables them to engage in conspicuous leisure and conspicuous consumption as a way of emulating people they consider respectable and with whom they wish to be associated.

This participation invariably changes the activity of thoroughbred breeding and racing, whether it is through the construction of new facilities, changing breeding practices, or raising prices. Rather than dismiss these changes as merely an elaborate futility of the super-rich, the argument in this chapter is that the super-rich engage in such activities given the myriad of choices available to them because of an interest in horses, because they love competition but perhaps cannot compete with their own bodies, and because the emulation of traditional wealth and prestige includes participation in leisure activities such as horse-racing to convert economic wealth into cultural cachet. And it is vital for the thoroughbred breeding and racing industries that the super-rich continue to be involved, a point not lost on this industries' current participants.

ACKNOWLEDGEMENTS

This research was supported by the Australian Research Council under ARC DP 0773790 Constructing Nature, Tradition and Thoroughbreds.

REFERENCES

Beaverstock, J., P. Hubbard and J.R. Short, (2004), 'Getting away with it? Exposing the geographies of the super-rich', *Geoforum*, **35** (4), 401–7.
Beckett, J. (2010), 'Owners of the 20 Premier League clubs, 2010–11 season', posted 24 November, www.epltalk.com/owners-of-the-20-premier-league-clubs-2010-11-season-26898, accessed 16 March 2012.

Bourdieu, P. (1984), *Distinction: A Social Critique of the Judgement of Taste*, translated by Richard Nice, Cambridge, MA: Harvard University Press.

Cain, G. (2004), *The Home-Run Horse: Inside America's Billion-Dollar Racehorse Industry and the High-Stakes Dreams that Fuel It*, New York: Daily Racing Form Press.

Cassidy, R. (2007), *The Sport of Kings: Kinship, Class and Thoroughbred Breeding in Newmarket*, Cambridge: Cambridge University Press.

Cummings, J.B. (2009), *Bart, My Life*, Sydney, NSW: Macmillan.

Fox, K. (2005), *The Racing Tribe: Watching the Horsewatchers*, London: Metro Publishing.

Haseler, S. (1999), *The Super-Rich: The Unjust New World of Global Capitalism*, New York: St Martin's Press.

Hesseldahl, A. and C. Dubow (2000), 'Toys of the super-rich', *Forbes.com*, 28 September, www.forbes.com/2000/09/28/0930forbes400.html, accessed 6 October 2011.

Hay, I. and S. Muller (2012), '"That tiny, stratospheric apex that owns most of the world" – exploring geographies of the super-rich', *Geographical Research*, **50** (1), 75–88.

Irvin, G. (2008), *Super Rich: The Rise of Inequality in Britain and the United States*, Cambridge: Polity Press.

Jorgensen, E.W. and H.I. Jorgensen (1999), *Thorstein Veblen: Victorian Firebrand*, New York: M.E. Sharpe.

Knoedler, J.T., R.E. Prasch and D.P. Champlin (eds) (2007), *Thorstein Veblen and the Revival of Free Market Capitalism*, Cheltenham, UK and Northampton, MA, USA: Edward Elgar.

Lambert, T. (1999), 'Thorstein Veblen and the higher learning of sports management education', *Journal of Economic Issues*, **33** (4), 973–84.

McManus, P., G. Albrecht and R. Graham (2011), 'Constructing thoroughbred breeding landscapes: manufactured idylls in the Upper Hunter region of Australia', in Stanley D. Brunn (ed.), *Engineering Earth: The Impacts of Megaengineering Projects*, Dordrecht, the Netherlands: Springer Science + Business Media, pp. 1323–9.

McManus, P., G. Albrecht and R. Graham (2013), *The Global Horseracing Industry: Social, Economic, Environmental and Ethical Perspectives*, London: Routledge.

Murphy, D. (2011), 'Dark horse sows seed of doubt over breeding', *The Sydney Morning Herald*, (Weekend Edition), 3–4 September, p. 10.

Neumayer, E. (2004), 'The super-rich in global perspective: a quantitative analysis of the Forbes list of billionaires', *Applied Economics Letters*, **11**, 793–6.

New Zealand Racing (2012), 'NZ Racing: the official site for NZ thoroughbred racing', www.nzracing.co.nz/Ownership/OwnershipTypes.aspx, accessed 18 March, 2012.

O'Connor, C. (2011), 'Triple Crown billionaires: meet horse racing's richest people', www.forbes.com/sites/clareoconnor/2011/06/09/triple-crown-billionaires-meet-horse-racings-richest-people/, accessed 8 October 2011.

Reilly, T. (2011), 'Big bills, few winners for Tinkler the breeding tyro', *The Sydney Morning Herald*, 29–30 October, p. 9.

Scott, D. (2010), 'What would Veblen say?', *Leisure Sciences*, **32** (3), 288–94.

Smith, S. (2001), *Royal Racing: The Queen and Queen Mother's Sporting Life*, London: BBC Worldwide Limited.

Smith, S. (2011), 'Will she finally be Elizabeth the first? The Queen is on the brink of fulfilling her life-long ambition of winning the Derby', *Mail Online*, 16 May, www.dailymail.co.uk/femail/article-1387761/Queen-brink-fulfilling-lifelong-ambition-winning-Derby.html, accessed 8 October 2011.

Squires, J.D. (2002), *Horse of a Different Color: A Tale of Breeding Geniuses, Dominant Females, and the Fastest Derby Winner since Secretariat*, New York: Public Affairs.

Squires, J.D. (2009), *Headless Horsemen: A Tale of Chemical Colts, Subprime Sales Agents, and the Last Kentucky Derby on Steroids*, New York: Times Books, Henry Holt and Company.

Sugar, B., (with C. Richardson) (2003), *Horse Sense: An Inside Look at the Sport of Kings*, Hoboken, NJ: Wiley.

The Courier Mail (2008), 'Nathan Tinkler the new force in Australian racing', *The Courier Mail* (online), 4 April, www.couriermail.com.au/sport-old/turf/tinkler-the-new-force/story-e6frepmx-1111115976589, accessed 14 May 2008.

Tilman, R. (2004), *Thorstein Veblen, John Dewey, C. Wright Mills and the Generic Ends of Life*, Lanham, MD: Rowman and Littlefield Publishers.

Tritch, T. (2006), 'The rise of the super-rich', *The New York Times* (online), 19 July, www.nytimes.com/2006/07/19/opinion/19talkingpoints.html?pagewanted=all, accessed 26 September 2011.

Veblen, T. (1899), *The Theory of the Leisure Class*, reprinted as Veblen, T. (1965), *The Theory of the Leisure Class*, New York: Forgotten Books.

Veblen, T. (1915), *Imperial Germany and the Industrial Revolution*, reprinted as Veblen, T. (2006), *Imperial Germany and the Industrial Revolution*, New York: Cosimo.

Wincze, A. (2009a), 'Market takes "terrible" hit', *Lexington Herald-Leader*, 15 September, p. C1.

Wincze, A. (2009b), 'Buyer's market reigns at Keeneland yearling sale: top horses proving to be affordable', *Lexington Herald-Leader*, 18 September, p. C7.

11. Making art history – wealthy private collectors and contemporary visual art

Melanie Fasche

> Maybe as a collector I have the chance . . . to make a serious contribution to the next page of this book about art history.
>
> Victor Pinchuk, Kiev, quoted in Ruiz 2011a.

INTRODUCTION

Investments in the next generation of canonical artists are made now. In the Western-rooted art world reputation and legitimation of artists and their artworks traditionally come with exhibitions, reviews and sales – especially acquisitions for public museum collections. This process of making art historical and commercial value for artists and their artworks is driven by the interrelated dynamics of status, demand and price. Growing global demand for contemporary visual art, the enormous sums private collectors are willing to spend, and shifting philanthropic practices have been changing the geography and organization of making art history.

Rising prices and growing competition for artworks make acquisitions by cash-strapped public museums for their public collections more difficult. Furthermore worldwide the conventional philanthropic practices of donating artworks and eventually entrusting private collections to public museums are being abandoned by a growing number of wealthy private collectors. Instead these private collectors pursue more comprehensive philanthropic missions by moving into what has traditionally been the domain of public museums, curators, critics and historians. They create private museums showcasing their private collections thereby emulating more-or-less the scholarly and social role of public museums. These private museums have become central in places where public museums are weak or unfamiliar institutions and public access to contemporary visual art limited.

Thus, changes in the geography and organization of making art history are driven by two interrelated dynamics: growing demand worldwide has expanded the Western centred art world to new places outside the West, and display and preservation of contemporary visual art are no longer only facilitated by public but increasingly also by private museums. A new generation of wealthy private collectors seems to have a growing influence on what is purchased on the art market and preserved and thus what might pass the test of time to eventually be integrated into the canon of great artists and artworks. The rising power of these wealthy private collectors in the process of making art history raises questions among art world stakeholders about scholarly expertise and the preservation of artistic heritage, and causes unease that money may eventually trump art historical scholarship.

MAKING ART HISTORY

Contemporary visual art is contemporary by its very nature since neither the artists nor their artworks have passed the test of time to eventually be integrated into the art historical canon (McCarthy et al. 2005; Roelstrate 2009). Artists and their œuvre only stand the test of time if they successfully go through a highly competitive process of making value. For both their art historical and commercial value artists and their artworks have to be appreciated and compared relative to each other over time and space by the intersubjective community of the art world (Becker 2008 [1982]).

The process of making art historical and commercial value of artists and their artworks is driven by the enduring success of the Western invention of art as status good (Shiner 2001) and its dynamic of price and demand (Veblen 1934 [1899]). Art as status good emerged in the eighteenth century in Western European societies when art was released from any utilitarian purpose and distinguished from craft (Shiner 2001). The desire for status continues to attract private collectors who increasingly come from countries outside the Western-rooted art world. Their will and ability to pay large sums for valuable artworks (Bourdieu 1984) gives rise to an upwardly pressured race for value and status (Frank and Cook 1995).

Art world events such as exhibitions, reviews and sales position artists and their artworks within a status hierarchy and build up reputations that translate into art historical value (McCarthy et al. 2005). Traditionally, art historical value is reflected by the price level of artworks at galleries and auctions. Thus, rising prices are commonly associated with rising art historical value and a promising art career stimulating demand and increasing competition, whereas falling prices signal a declining art career and lower demand (Plattner 1998). More recently the function of high price as an indicator for high value seems increasingly inflated. In this sense, rising prices are primarily an expression of growing competition due to higher demand and purchasers' aims to keep-up-with-the-Joneses (Veblen 1934 [1899]). Therefore, high prices may be misleading about the art historical value of particular artists and their artworks if they are not sufficiently supported by a substantial reputation build-up that comes with reviews, exhibitions and acquisitions for public and increasingly private collections.

These positioning and status-conferring events are facilitated by art world stakeholders such as artists, gallerists, curators and private collectors who, while making art historical and commercial value for artists and their artworks, build up their own reputation as well as that of their respective venues. In fact conferring status is a reciprocal affair among all stakeholders involved in a particular event at a particular venue at a particular location. These events take place in art world venues such as galleries, project spaces, public museums, art fairs, auction houses, art magazines and websites and lately also in private museums run by private collectors. These different art world venues are predominantly located in established Western art world centres such as New York City, London and Paris, up-and-coming centres such as Berlin and Los Angeles and increasingly in new places previously not connected to the Western art world particularly in the former USSR, the Gulf region and Asia.

Thus, investing large amounts of money into contemporary visual art does not automatically ascribe a high status to new private collectors and their private museums. For their reputation and position in the art world hierarchy both private collectors and their venues have to be viewed and compared relative to each other and in relation to other art world stakeholders over time and space. In other words, the organization and geography of making art history entangle a territorial with a relational perspective (Pike 2009).

The Rising Power of Private Collectors

The art world appears as an international network of five main stakeholder groups: artists, gallerists, art historical establishment, private collectors and auction houses (Becker 2008 [1982]; Kallir 2007; McCarthy et al. 2005; Rosler 1997). These stakeholders collectively decide through their cooperative and competitive activities – and informed by their general knowledge of rules and practices of making value (Becker 2008 [1982]) – how artworks are distributed, exhibited and reviewed and how art careers are built.

The *artists* supply the artworks. Once taken up into a gallery programme the *gallerists* actively promote the artists and their artworks and support the development of artists' careers (White and White 1993 [1965]). The gallerists put on gallery shows, participate in art fairs and market online to introduce the artists and their artworks to a broader audience. Furthermore they try to get reviews, promote the artists and their artworks for inclusion into biennales and museum shows, and place artworks in public and increasingly in private collections.

The *auction houses* facilitate the speculative resale of artworks which are returned to the market by private collectors, or entire private collections that have not been entrusted to a public museum. In comparison to gallerists who conduct sales discretely by 'gentleman's agreement', the auctions are more transparent, liquid and democratic (McCarthy et al. 2005). The artwork under auction goes to the highest bidder who does not have to prove their reputation and taste to a gallerist for potential placement of an artwork. Sales at both galleries and auctions usually capitalize the art historical value of artists and their artworks. However, prices at auctions are driven by competitive bidding, often resulting in record prices, whereas the gallerists raise price levels slowly and consistently with reputational build-up. In line with the dynamic of price and value outlined above, high prices at auctions raise the price level for the artist's œuvre whilst a lower price could signal the decline of an art career. But success at auction is no guarantee for passing the test of time if the price level is not sufficiently supported by reviews, exhibitions and integration into public and private collections.

The *art historical establishment* of public museums, curators, critics and historians maintains the historicizing project of contemporary visual art (Kallir 2007). Public museums are expected to pursue both a social and a scholarly mission in exchange for their tax-exempt status (Weil 1999). Curators, critics and historians facilitate the critical dialogue about artists and their artworks, publish reviews and studies, curate exhibitions and build public collections. Reviews and repeated displays in curated public exhibitions position the artworks, expand the audience and increase the reputation of artists and their œuvres, and thus guide what is bought and sold at galleries and auctions (McCarthy et al. 2005). Traditionally, only the integration into the collection of a public museum legitimizes the art historical value of artists and their artworks. Once accepted for integration into the public collection the artworks become part of the canon since the de-accessioning of artworks is rather the exception than the rule (International Council of Museums 2006).

However, more recently the public museums have begun to lose their power to give legitimacy to contemporary visual artists and their artworks and thus their influence in the process of making art history (Pes 2011). Public museums are increasingly challenged by external and internal pressures. These pressures are resulting from higher acquisitions costs due to rising prices of artworks, but also from growing operations costs, often because of a recent museum extension (designed by a brand-name architect), stable or declining revenues and support from governments and private collectors, and increasing competition for visitors, donations and bequests due to a worldwide museum boom (McCarthy et al. 2005). To cope with these pressures public museums cooperate more closely with gallerists and private collectors by loaning artworks from private collections and galleries for public museum exhibitions. This practice is contested in the art world because private collectors and gallerists may use the public museum show as a value booster for their artists and artworks, eventually translating into higher prices at galleries and quicker sales at auctions (Lind 2010).

The *private collectors* buy artworks from gallerists and auction houses for their private collections and they also support public museums. If collectors return artworks to the market too quickly they may diminish their reputation and damage their relations with gallerists. Private collectors loan artworks from their holdings for public exhibitions, donate artworks and money, and may eventually bequeath their collection to a public museum (McCarthy et al. 2005). In addition, in the US, private collectors serve as trustees on the boards of public museums and shape museum operations including decisions about new acquisitions (McCarthy et al. 2005) – a level of influence that is still unthinkable in European public museums that are largely government funded.

More recently private collectors have increasingly abandoned the conventional practices of donating artworks and entrusting their collection to a public museum (Kallir 2007; Pollock and Adam 2008). Instead they pursue more comprehensive philanthropic missions by building their own museums which perform more-or-less the scholarly and social role of public museums. These private museums, such as Palazzo Grassi and Punta della Dogana in Venice displaying artworks from the collection of French luxury goods magnate François Pinault, or Crystal Bridges in Bentonville, AR, US housing the collection of Wal-Mart heiress Alice Walton, are often iconic buildings designed or rebuilt by high profile architects. Besides putting on shows for the public, private museums also employ curators, publish catalogues, offer educational programmes and engage with the local community. These activities are central in places where public museums are weak and public access to contemporary visual art is limited (Adam 2011). Thus, the collectors have a growing influence on what is shown to the public, and they gain power in the process of making art historical and commercial value of artists and their artworks by reducing their support for public museums and instead performing the legitimating and historicizing role of public museums themselves.

The growing influence of the new generation of international wealthy private collectors in the process of making history is seen as critical among a certain group of art world stakeholders. These pessimistic voices suspect that private collectors are not as knowledgeable as public museum curators and are guided by personal taste and vanity rather than art historical scholarship (Kallir 2007). It is feared that wealthy private collectors and their social networks will shape tomorrow's canon of great artists and artworks by creating a parallel historicizing system that bypasses public museums (Maak 2011, p. 50). These critics claim that artistic heritage should not be dominated by private tastes and interests but rather be determined by art historical scholarship and curatorial consideration focusing on artworks that have value for society and cultural identity (Beckstette et al. 2011).

In fact, wealthy private collectors have been influential on the art historical canon ever since the Renaissance (Lind 2010). Today's leading public museums once started their life as private, feudal or Church collections with much of today's canon of great artists and artworks only made possible by wealthy private collectors' purchases and commissions back then. Thus, today's prestigious public collections could have been built with donations, bequests and access to supporting audiences in central art world locations such as New York City, London and Paris from early on (Quemin 2006). These public superstar museums enjoy the historic advantage of the reputation of their world-famous collections over smaller and younger public and private museums. Therefore, integration into the collection of a public superstar museum such as The Museum of Modern Art (MoMA) or the Salomon R. Guggenheim Museum in New York, Tate Modern in London, or Centre Pompidou in Paris has still more legitimation power than integration into a private collection of one of the emerging international collectors performing the legitimating and historicizing role of public museums themselves (Ruiz 2011b) – for now.

THE NEW GENERATION OF WEALTHY PRIVATE COLLECTORS

During past decades the numbers of collectors, their geographical diversity and the wealth they are willing to devote to contemporary visual art have been growing (McCarthy et al. 2005). According to the latest *World Wealth Report* (Capgemini and Merrill Lynch 2011) art is the second most popular so-called investment of passion amongst the super-rich. Art has a share of 22 per cent of all investments of passion just behind the leading category 'luxury collectibles such as cars, yachts and jets' accounting for a share of 29 per cent (Capgemini and Merrill Lynch 2011). Demand for contemporary art is generated by a mix of aesthetic, decorative, intellectual and historical reasons, lifestyle appeal, status aspirations and philanthropic mission (TEFAF 2010; Capgemini and Merrill Lynch 2011). A recent survey of private collectors revealed that the majority of collectors buy out of passion 'whenever something of interest appeared on the market' (quoted in TEFAF 2010, p. 128). Thus, the decision to commit large sums to collecting art seems to follow emotions and feelings rather than monetary reasons, despite a growing belief that contemporary visual art can be a good long-term monetary investment (TEFAF 2010, p. 128) – if the artists and their artworks pass the test of time.

In fact most of the growing demand for contemporary visual art worldwide is still rather local and thus not yet influential at the global level. New collectors usually start collecting art of their compatriots before they broaden their focus to international art (Adam 2011). China has become the largest market in terms of annual auction turnovers but collectors there still focus predominantly on Chinese art (Artprice 2011). India also has a huge potential group of collectors but its market remains rather closed (Adam 2011). In contrast, most Latin American collectors and the handful of collectors from the Gulf buy internationally (Adam 2011). The ruling family of Qatar has recently been revealed as the most active buyer of contemporary art worldwide (Adam and Burns 2011). The growing volumes of sales in Asia and in the Gulf region are reflected by a geographical shift from West to East on the annual list of 'Top Ten Art Capitals' by Artprice (2011). According to the ranking New York is still the most important art capital, but London and Paris have dropped to positions four and six. Now Beijing and Hong Kong rank second and third, Shanghai fifth, followed by Hangzhou, Stockholm, Singapore and Dubai at positions seven to ten.

The growing influence of wealthy private collectors is reflected by the amount of investable assets they are able to spend for contemporary art at galleries and auctions, and for creating and running a private museum. As set out by Iain Hay earlier in this book, the super-rich have investable assets worth US$1 million or more, and while 1 per cent of this population have investable assets of US$30 million or more, these 103 000 Ultra-High Net Worth Individuals (UHNWI) hold over 35 per cent of the overall wealth possessed by the super-rich (Capgemini and Merrill Lynch 2011, p. 4). Most international art collectors surveyed by The European Fine Art Foundation (TEFAF 2010) revealed that they make their artwork purchases within a limited price range, while for a few collectors the price does not matter at all when they want to buy a particular artwork. Thus, the influence of the super-rich is felt at lower price levels while the enormous spending power of the ultra-rich is felt at higher price levels (Burns 2010; Fraser 2011). Wealthy private collectors who pursue more comprehensive philanthropic missions by creating private museums to showcase their art collections increase their influence as tastemakers even further.

Worldwide, founding new museums for contemporary visual art has become a largely private endeavour, with the exception of India and China, where new publicly funded museums are created too (Ruyters 2012). These new private museums perform the scholarly and social role of public museums but each in its individual educational, curatorial and public way. The Miami collectors Rosa and Carlos de la Cruz, Martin Z. Margulies, Ella Fontanals-Cisneros, the Rubell family and London collector Charles Saatchi were among the first of their generation who built private museums for the public, and they set the trend (Kastner 2010, p. 317). Recently opened private museums can be found in places ranging from central rural Brazil (where mining tycoon Bernardo Paz built his Inhotim) (Ruiz 2010), to Mexico City (where the richest man in the world, Carlos Slim Helú, re-opened his Museo Soumaya in a new building) to just outside Delhi (where Lekha and Anupam Poddar's Devi Art Foundation is located) to Beijing's Today Art Museum and Shanghai's Zendai Museum of Modern Art (both founded by real estate developers) (Kastner 2010, p. 317). Building is underway for a not-yet-named museum in Shanghai (where new super-collector Budi Tek hopes to be the first Chinese-Indonesian to turn his collection into an institution) (Kolesnikow-Jessop 2012).

Wealthy private collectors and their private museums play a central role especially in places where public museums are weak or unfamiliar institutions, and public access to contemporary visual art limited. They foster exposure and appreciation of contemporary visual art for local audiences and help to connect these places to the art world geography by building up a reputation. The following section portrays two wealthy private collectors from such places; the now-established collector Eli Broad from up-and-coming Los Angeles and the emerging collector Victor Pinchuk from peripheral Kiev.

Eli Broad and Victor Pinchuk

Eli Broad, 79 and Victor Pinchuk, 53, both ultra-rich entrepreneurs and philanthropists, are selected as cases because they represent two different generations of wealthy private collectors whose practices provide a more detailed picture of recent changes in the organization and geography of making art history. Here, their activities are illustrated along six dimensions: financial power and status, approaches to collecting, organizational stage, philanthropic mission, and organizational form.

The enormous *financial power and status* of Broad and Pinchuk are reflected by their appearances in respective rankings such as the Forbes' World's Billionaires list, *ARTnews'* 200 top collectors, and *ArtReview*'s Power 100. On the Forbes' World's Billionaires list Broad ranks 157th with an estimated net worth of US$6.3 billion whereas Pinchuk ranks 255th with an estimated net worth of US$4.2 billion, among a current total of 1153 billionaires worldwide (*Forbes* 2012). Although both are among the richest people worldwide, their status and reputation in the art world are different from one another. On the list of 200 top collectors by *ARTnews* Broad has been among the top ten international collectors every year since the list started in 1998 (Ng and Finkel 2010) whereas Pinchuk has only appeared on the list since 2008 (*ARTnews* 2011). The Power 100 list by *ArtReview* ranks all art world stakeholders according to their influence on the global production of art, their financial power and activities in the past year (*ArtReview* 2011). Broad has been positioned among the top 25 of the Power 100 since the list started in 2002 while Pinchuk made his first appearance, ranked 67th, in 2008, and has climbed to 35th position since then (*ArtReview* 2011).

Broad and his wife Edythe, and Pinchuk, have similar *approaches to collecting* contemporary visual art. Both started their collection with artworks from their compatriots before they broadened their focus to collecting internationally. Furthermore both aim to collect artists in-depth and purchase several artworks by the same artist over time in order to provide a comprehensive understanding of the development of an individual art career (The Broad Foundations 2010; Victor Pinchuk Foundation 2011). Today, the holdings of the Broads consist of more than 2000 artworks by nearly 200 artists, including now canonical artists Ed Ruscha and Mike Kelly from their hometown Los Angeles, and US pop artists Andy Warhol and Roy Lichtenstein (The Broad Foundations 2010). Pinchuk predominantly collects brand new contemporary visual art produced in the twenty-first century in his home country Ukraine, already internationally recognized Western artists such as Damien Hirst, Jeff Koons and Takashi Murakami, and lately also Chinese artists (Ruiz 2011a). Critics say that Pinchuk has been buying a lot of lower quality art for high prices pretty quickly, since he is said to have neither substantial knowledge of contemporary visual art nor yet a refined taste (Ruiz 2011a).

The private collections of Broad and Pinchuk are at different *organizational stages*. The Broads are established collectors and aim at manifesting the legacy of their collection, whereas Pinchuk is in the process of building a reputable collection. The Broads have bought contemporary visual art from gallerists and at auctions for more than four decades and claim to have one of the most prominent contemporary visual art collections worldwide (The Broad Foundations 2010, p. 55). To manifest their legacy for future generations they decided to create a private museum (Ng and Finkel 2010). In contrast, Pinchuk has been a serious collector for only a few years but opened a private museum in a former hotel soon after having started. Pinchuk is said to be in a hurry to build a reputable collection by spending hundreds of millions on artworks at galleries and auctions (Ruiz 2011a). In 2007 he temporarily set an auction record for a living artist (*Hanging Heart (Magenta/Gold)* by Jeff Koons) for a hammer price of US$ 23.6 million (Ruiz 2011a).

The Broads and Victor Pinchuk pursue similar *philanthropic missions*. Both are driven by their intellectual passion and belief in contemporary visual art's power of giving new insight (The Broad Foundations 2010, Victor Pinchuk Foundation 2011). Their central mission of sharing artworks from their collections with the public to foster exposure and appreciation of international contemporary art is reinforced by their successes. Since its creation in 1984 The Broad Art Foundation has facilitated more than 8000 artwork loans from the private collection to nearly 500 museums worldwide (The Broad Foundations 2010). The new private museum in downtown Los Angeles, The Broad, will house both the foundation and their private collection and display 300 artworks for the public at any given time (Ng and Finkel 2010). Since its inauguration in 2006 more than a million predominantly young visitors have seen displays from Pinchuk's private collection at PinchukArtCentre (PAC) in Kiev (Ruiz 2011a). But rumours suggest buying contemporary visual art and making it accessible to the public may have been recommended by a public relations company to improve Pinchuk's damaged family reputation (Ruiz 2011a). His father-in-law, Ukraine's former president Leonid Kuchma, had been accused of being involved in the killing of an investigative journalist in 2000 but in late 2011 the charge was finally dismissed because of illegitimate evidence (Ruiz 2011a).

Furthermore both the Broads and Pinchuk pursue a more civic mission of reshaping the built environment in their cities (Hay and Muller 2012) by selecting iconic architectural designs for their new private museums. The Broad will be the first building of the long-planned Grand Avenue project in downtown Los Angeles which is intended to jumpstart the stalled redevelopment project to revitalize downtown Los Angeles as a vibrant cultural centre (Ng and Finkel 2010). Last year Pinchuk revealed that he aims to build a new home for PAC which he hopes to become an iconic building of Kiev and the Ukraine (Ruiz 2011a). However, urban regeneration fostered by these new museums may eventually promote gentrification and thus change the social structure of surrounding neighbourhoods.

The philanthropic activities of Broad and Pinchuk have different *organizational forms.* Broad's activities have largely been shaped by the conventional philanthropic practices of supporting public museums. Only lately have he and his wife decided to build a private museum instead of entrusting their collection to a public museum because none would have sufficient space for display (Storm 2008). In contrast Pinchuk has created a private museum straight away and seeks advice from powerful art world stakeholders by inviting them to get involved in activities at his museum – and to confer their status upon it.

Broad has long been a powerful patron for public museums in his hometown, Los Angeles (Steinhauer 2010). He serves as life trustee on the museum board of The Museum of Contemporary Art (MOCA) in Los Angeles, Los Angeles County Museum of Art (LACMA) and The Museum of Modern Art (MoMA) in New York City. Broad was founding member of MOCA in 1979 and recently bailed out the museum with a US$30 million grant. He has been one of the biggest donors and fund-raisers in the history of LACMA and donated US$60 million for a much needed museum extension, the Broad Contemporary Art Museum (BCAM) which opened in 2008 and shows rotating loans from the Broads' private collection. The new private museum will be inaugurated in downtown Los Angeles in 2013 (Ng and Finkel 2010). Even Broad's critics admit that his philanthropy and patronage have been overwhelmingly positive for the region as an art world location (Steinhauer 2010).

In 2009 Pinchuk created two biannual prizes; one for international and one for Ukrainian emerging artists (Victor Pinchuk Foundation 2011). Each winner receives US$100 000, currently the highest prize money for an artistic competition worldwide (Maak 2011). Four artists who have artworks in Pinchuk's collection, Andreas Gursky, Damien Hirst, Jeff Koons and Takashi Murakami, serve as mentors to the prizewinners. The prize board includes Eli Broad and the directors of public superstar museums MoMA, Tate, Centre Pompidou and Guggenheim. All these stakeholders are currently or previously listed in the Power 100 list of art world stakeholders mentioned above (*ArtReview* 2011).

To sum up, both Broad and Pinchuk are key stakeholders in creating an infrastructure for display and appreciation of contemporary visual art in their cities. Broad represents the conventional wealthy private collector type who supports public museums and who has only recently adopted the new practice of creating a private museum to historicize their private collection rather than entrusting the collection to a public museum. During the past decades Broad's philanthropic activities have been crucial for the development of the public museums in Los Angeles, and have helped to build up the reputation of once peripheral Los Angeles as an art world location (Steinhauer 2010). Pinchuk represents the new generation of wealthy private collectors. The new generation comes increasingly from places not previously connected to the Western art world and where public museums are weak or unfamiliar institutions – similar to the position of Los Angeles when Broad started collecting contemporary visual art and supporting public museums more than 40 years ago. This new wealthy private collector type invests large amounts of money at an incredible pace and builds new private museums that emulate more-or-less the scholarly and social role of public museums. It remains to be seen whether Victor Pinchuk will turn out to be Kiev's Eli Broad.

A NEW GEOGRAPHY OF MAKING ART HISTORY

The chapter reveals changes in the geography and organization of making art history. These changes are driven by two interrelated dynamics. Demand from wealthy private collectors for contemporary visual art is growing, especially in new places previously not connected to the Western art world, pushing up price levels and increasingly pricing out cash-strapped public museums. A growing number of private wealthy collectors are abandoning the conventional philanthropic practices of supporting public museums and instead are creating private museums and performing the legitimating and historicizing roles of public museums themselves. However, the growing influence of wealthy private collectors and their private museums in making art history has to be viewed in perspective. Enormous wealth should not be mistaken as high status since the territorial art world geography is cross-cut by a status hierarchy (Plattner 1996, p.9) that carries the histories of reputation of all art world stakeholders and their venues – and reputations are only built up relative to each other and in relation to the other art world stakeholders over time and space.

The growing influence of wealthy private collectors in making art history causes unease that money may trump art historical scholarship. The worst fears are that the art historical canon could be shaped by a few super-collectors lacking refined taste and substantial art historical knowledge, and perhaps being more interested in signature architectural designs than curatorial programmes of their private museums. These fears reflect enduring Western ideals of art being autonomous and public museums being pristine institutions. In fact, making art history has never been autonomous but dependent on both activities and power relations among art world stakeholders and general conditions. Furthermore in an expanding art world it remains to be seen whether Western ideals, institutions and practices will be adopted or rather recombined, blurred and possibly abandoned in new places such as Russia, the Gulf region and

Asia previously not connected to the Western art world. In this sense both art historical canon and artistic heritage are prisms of society at large at a particular time.

History seems to repeat itself. In the late nineteenth century the European-centred art world expanded to America, and by the mid-twentieth century New York had become its new centre. Wealthy American industrialists built private collections that became the foundations of public museums in the early twentieth century. Throughout the twentieth century a few of these public museums developed into public superstar museums now preserving the most prestigious art collections worldwide. Today, one only needs to follow the money of wealthy private collectors to map the expansion of the art world beyond the West. Although New York is sustaining its central position, Beijing, Hong Kong and Dubai have ascended well into the list of the top ten art world capitals. It is likely that the Western public museum as a pristine institution may turn out to be a short historical parenthesis (Adam 2011) and that the prestigious art collections of the twenty-first century will no longer be built by public museums in the West but by wealthy private collectors in the East – and one of them may be Victor Pinchuk.

ACKNOWLEDGEMENTS

For conversations and critical comments on an earlier draft I would like to thank Iain Hay and Josephine Rekers, and the two anonymous reviewers.

REFERENCES

Adam, G. (2011), 'Art market analysis: are domestic collectors ready to take the world?', *The Art Newspaper* (online), **225**, 8 June, www.theartnewspaper. com/articles/Art-market-analysis-Are-domestic-collectors-ready-to-take-on-the-world?/23913, accessed 20 April 2012.

Adam, G. and C. Burns (2011), 'Qatar revealed as the world's biggest contemporary art buyer', *The Art Newspaper* (online), **226**, 7 July, www. theartnewspaper.com/articles/Qatar-revealed-as-the-world-s-biggest-contemp orary-art-buyer/24185, accessed 18 April 2012.

ARTnews (2011), *The ARTnews 200 Top Collectors*, www.artnews.com/2011/08/15/ the-artnews-200-top-collectors-2011/, accessed 15 October 2011.

Artprice (2011), *Contemporary Art Market. The Artprice Annual Report* (online), www.artmarketinsight.com, accessed 15 October 2011.

ArtReview (2011), *Power 100*, www.artreview100.com, accessed 15 October 2011.

Becker, H.S. (2008 [1982]), *Art World. Updates and Expanded 25th Anniversary Edition*, Los Angeles, CA: University of California Press.

Beckstette, S., B. von Bismark and I. Graw (2011), 'Preface', *Texte zur Kunst*, **83**, 6–7.

Bourdieu, P. (1984), *Distinction*, Cambridge, MA: Harvard University Press.

Burns, C. (2010), 'Millionaires buy more art than ever', *The Art Newspaper* (online), 6 July, www.theartnewspaper.com/articles/millionaires-buy-more-art-than-ever/21117, accessed 18 April 2012.

Capgemini and Merrill Lynch (2011), *The World Wealth Report 2011*, www.capgemini.com/services-and-solutions/by-industry/financial-services/solutions/wealth/worldwealthreport/, accessed 15 October 2011.

Forbes (2012), *The World's Billionaires*, www.forbes.com/billionaires/, accessed 10 April 2012

Frank, R.H. and P.J. Cook (1995), *The Winner-Take-All Society*, New York: The Free Press.

Fraser, A. (2011), 'L'1%, C'est moi', *Texte zur Kunst*, **83**, 114–27.

Hay, I. and S. Muller (2012), '"That tiny, stratospheric apex that owns most of the world" – exploring geographies of the super-rich', *Geographical Research*, **50** (1), 75–88.

International Council of Museums (2006), *Code of Ethics for Museums*, Paris: International Council of Museums.

Kallir, J. (2007), 'The problem with a collector-driven market', *The Art Newspaper*, **182**, 1 July.

Kastner, J. (2010), 'New foundations', *Artforum*, Summer, 314–19.

Kolesnikow-Jessop, S. (2012), 'Chinese-Indonesian collector makes up for lost time', *The New York Times* (online), 15 March, www.nytimes.com/2012/03/16/arts/16iht-rartjessop16.html, accessed 15 March 2012.

Lind, M. (2010), 'Laissez faire: Maria Lind on carte blanche', *Artforum*, Summer, 147.

Maak, N. (2011), 'Between Pinault and Pinchuk', *Texte zur Kunst*, **83**, 38–55.

McCarthy, K.F., E.H. Ondaatje, A. Brooks and A. Szántó (2005), *A Portrait of the Visual Arts. Meeting the Challenges of a New Era*, Los Angeles, CA: RAND Corporation.

Ng, D. and J. Finkel (2010), 'Eli Broad says Grand Avenue will be site of new contemporary art museum', *Los Angeles Times* (online), 24 August, http://articles.latimes.com/2010/aug/24/entertainment/la-et--broad-museum-20100823, accessed 18 April 2012.

Pes, J. (2011), 'To have and have not', *The Art Newspaper*, Art Basel daily edition (online), 16 June, www.theartnewspaper.com/articles/To+have+and+have+not/24007, accessed 18 April 2012.

Pike, A. (2009), 'Geographies of brands and branding', *Progress in Human Geography*, **33** (5), 619–45.

Plattner, S. (1998), 'A most ingenious paradox: the market for contemporary fine art', *American Anthropologist*, **100** (2), 482–93.

Plattner, S. (1996), *High Art Down Home*, Chicago, IL: The University of Chicago Press.

Pollock, L. and G. Adam (2008), 'Why the rise of the private museum is rewriting the rules of the market', *The Art Newspaper*, Art Basel daily edition, 5 June, 1.

Quemin, A. (2006), 'Globalization and mixing in the visual arts. An empirical survey of "high culture" and globalization', *International Sociology*, **21** (4), 522–50.

Roelstrate, D. (2009), 'What is not contemporary art?: The view from Jena', *e-flux journal*, **11**, www.e-flux.com/journal/what-is-not-contemporary-art-the-view-from-jena/ www.e-flux.com, accessed 15 October 2011.

Rosler, M. (1997), 'Money, power, contemporary art – money, power, and the history of art', *Art Bulletin*, **LXXIX**, 20–24.

Ruiz, C. (2011a), 'A "landmark" museum for Ukraine', *The Art Newspaper* (online), 10 October, www.theartnewspaper.com/articles/A+%E2%80%9Clandmark%E2%80%9D+museum+for+Ukraine/24752, accessed 18 April 2012.

Ruiz, C. (2011b), 'The tastemakers are here', *The Art Newspaper*, Art Basel daily edition (online), 16 June, www.theartnewspaper.com/articles/The+tastemakers+are+here/24013, accessed 18 April 2012.

Ruiz, C. (2010), 'Where dreams come true', *The Art Newspaper* (online), 22 November www.theartnewspaper.com/articles/Where-dreams-come-true/21858, accessed 18 April 2012.

Ruyters, D. (2012), 'Future museum: Public or private?', *Metropolis M* (online), February–March, http://metropolism.com/archive/searchEnglish?author=64, accessed 18 April 2012.

Shiner, L. (2001), *The Invention of Art: A Cultural History*, Chicago, IL: The University of Chicago Press.

Steinhauer, J. (2010), 'Wielding iron checkbook to shape cultural Los Angeles', *The New York Times* (online), 7 February, www.nytimes.com/2010/02/08/arts/design/08broad.html?pagewanted=all, accessed 18 April 2012.

Storm, S. (2008), 'To keep or to donate: foundations wrestle with the question', *The New York Times* (online), 12 March, www.nytimes.com/2008/03/12/arts/artsspecial/12donors.html?pagewanted=all, accessed 18 April 2012.

TEFAF [The European Fine Art Foundation] (2010), *The International Art Market 2007–2009*, Helvoirt, the Netherlands: The European Fine Art Foundation.

The Broad Foundations (2010), *The Broad Foundations 2009/10 Report*, Los Angeles, CA: The Broad Foundations.

Veblen, T. (1934 [1899]), *The Theory of the Leisure Class*, New York: Random House.

Victor Pinchuk Foundation (2011), *Annual Report 2010*, Kiev: Victor Pinchuk Foundation.

Weil, S.E. (1999), 'From being about something to being for somebody', *Daedalus*, Summer, 229–58.

White, H.C. and C.A. White (1993 [1965]), *Canvases and Careers. Institutional Change in the French Painting World*, Chicago, IL: The University of Chicago Press.

12. Islanders, immigrants and millionaires: the dynamics of upper-class segregation in St Barts, French West Indies

Bruno Cousin and Sébastien Chauvin

Gordon Gekko: "That's great, pal, it's really great . . . So what's up next?"
Bud Fox: "You're looking at it: golf, winters in St Barts, philanthropy".
Oliver Stone, *Wall Street: Money Never Sleeps*, 2010.

A French island of 21 km² located in the northern part of the Lesser Antilles, Saint-Barthélemy (St Barts) is one of the world's most exclusive vacationing localities. In 2007, this municipality, which used to belong to the département of Guadeloupe, acquired the more autonomous status of Overseas Collectivity (COM, for *Collectivité d'Outre-Mer*). Most of its 8600 permanent inhabitants act as a local service class to the international economic elites patronizing the island as seasonal residents, amateur sailors or vacationers (IEDOM 2009). St Barts' specialization as a resort for the super-rich and the upper class began as early as in the 1950s. It has resulted in a distinctive set of relations between the three main groups – predominantly white – cohabitating on the island: (1) the Saint-Barths, descendants of the French settlers who populated the island from the 17th century on; (2) the immigrants, who for the most part come from Metropolitan France (and Europe) to work there; finally (3) a well-to-do clientele shared with other seaside localities such as the Hamptons, Cape Cod and its islands (Higley 1995), Saint-Tropez and the French Riviera, Portofino, and the Costa Smeralda.

This chapter describes how the three populations combine to maintain the existing class exclusivity of the site, which is its explicit model of development, and one of its main sources of attractiveness to the super-rich (Cousin and Chauvin 2012). The first section provides some historical background to the socio-economic genesis of St Barts. The second describes local upper-class sociability on the island, insisting on the importance of ostentation practices. The third shows how interactions between vacationers and service professionals fabricate the island's socially distinctive exoticism in ways that minimize its Caribbean heritage. Finally, the fourth section examines the strategies implemented today by the Saint-Barths to orient the island's development in ways that preserve their control of numerous political and economic levers.

Our research draws on ethnographic fieldwork[1] carried out in December and January 2003–4 and 2004–5, July and August 2010; on formal and informal interviews carried out during those same periods;[2] and archival study of the local press.

FROM SHORTAGES TO ROCKEFELLER

A mountainous island, St Barts was discovered in 1493 by Christopher Columbus.[3] The French occupied it in 1648, resulting in the permanent settlement of peasants after 1659. While the island was regularly assailed by pirates and visited by privateers, its economy gradually developed around subsistence agriculture and cotton growing. Poor whites worked often side by side with black slaves. In 1785, Louis XVI handed the island to the Swedish Crown. A first period of prosperity ensued, during which the free port of Gustavia benefited from strong commercial and demographic growth. But the end of the Napoleonic naval wars, along with competition from the neighbouring islands of Sint Eustatius and St Thomas, which were better positioned to serve as hubs for transatlantic trade, caused the gradual decline of the Swedish colony from the 1820s onwards. Commercial activities disappeared almost completely, and in 1878 the island was retroceded to France with the agreement of the Saint-Barths. Even as Europe and the United States were going through the Industrial Revolution, St Barts reverted to a shortage economy supported by a closed and endogamous community structure. The decline of port activities and the abolition of slavery in 1847 gave way to the departure from the island of almost all of its black population, for lack of sufficient land to exploit. Much later, this exodus allowed numerous promoters of local tourism to recurrently use as a selling point the fact that the population is not *métissée* (miscegenated) in St Barts – even if it wrongly implied slavery had never existed on the island.[4]

The development of luxury vacationing in the Caribbean gradually put an end to over a century (circa 1840–1950) of insular destitution: during that period, the difficulties of daily life, along with isolation from the French mainland, had led many Saint-Barths to emigrate to neighbouring islands or to the American continent. Fishing, farming, and small domestic craftsmanship were about the only local activities available (Leiris

1955; Benoist 1966; Morrill 1977). But, in 1957, David Rockefeller Sr, who had just discovered St Barts during amateur sailing trips, bought a promontory of 27 hectares overhanging the Anse de Colombier, one of the island's most beautiful coves, and built a villa on it. He also bought two other plots of land located on Mont Jean and in the Anse du Gouverneur. The first one was sold the following year to another investment banker also fond of sailing, the French–Swiss Edmond de Rothschild (1926–97). The second was bought by the American Francis Goelet (1926–98), heir to a Francophile high-society family of Manhattan real estate developers. During the 1960s and the beginning of the 1970s, many other friends and partners of the Rockefellers[5] – primarily middle-aged Americans – began patronizing St Barts and established secondary residences there, leading their neighbours from Park Avenue and elsewhere to do the same (Pinçon and Pinçon-Charlot 2007, p. 151–2). Those arrivals inaugurated the island's mutation into an 'exceptional site, ensuring a family-oriented and confidential ambiance to tourists during the high season, and a high degree of security, distinguishing this destination from the other Caribbean islands' (Baverez 2000, p. 30, translated by us). Real estate and temporary accommodation became very expensive in the 1980s. Access to St Barts has also remained difficult: landing is only possible for small planes, liners cannot dock in the harbour, and there is no public transportation on the island. As a result, St Barts 'captured the high-end clientele, intent on preserving the destination's confidentiality' and 'the market segment of super-yachts, rapidly expanding in the Caribbean' (Baverez 2000, p. 26). On the island's streets, very dense retail activity developed, centred on French luxury products. Indeed, processes of mutual symbolic legitimization between the place, its residents and commodities that are sold in Saint-Barthélemy, have led to the reinforcement of the local spatial brand (Pinçon and Pinçon-Charlot 1992). Its prestige is all the more easily appropriated as the brand presents a rich distinctive polysemy: today 'St Barts' simultaneously connotes insular exclusiveness, tropical exoticism, French refinement and Euro-American cosmopolitanism, while evoking the transatlantic mobility inherent to luxury yachting.

Thus, our research has strong links to the sociology of bourgeois seaside resorts and to the analysis of upper-class multi-territoriality, initiated in France in the last 20 years by Michel Pinçon and Monique Pinçon-Charlot. But several aspects also distinguish this case study. Past research by Pinçon and Pinçon-Charlot mostly focused on the first generation of resorts (Deauville, Biarritz, Arcachon), whose rise during the nineteenth century was connected to the aristocratic sociability of the Second French Empire and to railway development. Today those localities have lost part of their prestige and their attractiveness to economic elites, notably in favour of the French Riviera. They are now mostly patronized on weekends, and less socially selective than in their early days. By contrast, St Barts was 'discovered' by the high bourgeoisie and became one of its retreats at a time when tourism was already a mass phenomenon. It developed primarily by attracting rich Americans, taking advantage of the growth of air traffic in the Caribbean. Today, it continues to receive the world's wealthiest families for seasonal stays, and to maintain a high level of exclusivity. It is therefore a better adapted site for the contemporary study of the spatial segregation of the super-rich.

A SEASIDE HAUNT FOR GLOBAL BOURGEOISIES

While the island hosted only a few hundred visitors in 1963, there were 47000 in 1980, and 323850 in 2007 (INSEE 2009). Those figures signal obvious but moderate touristic development compared with most of the Lesser Antilles (McElroy and De Albuquerque 1998), especially the neighbouring island of St Martin (Chardon and Hartog 1995a; Redon 2006). St Barts has primarily remained a socializing site for the upper classes, both the old bourgeoisie and the newcomers. Even in times of global economic crisis or during the boreal summer, when most of their wealthiest customers prefer the shores of the Mediterranean or the Northern Atlantic, the island's 635 rental villas[6] and almost all its 520 hotel rooms are offered at a price making them unaffordable to middle-class vacationers (IEDOM 2009, pp. 39–40). Their owners prefer to take the risk of keeping their properties temporarily vacant and thus miss monetary profit opportunities rather than to adopt a strategy of partial democratization that could lead to the symbolic devaluation of the destination.

A second concern for the island's regular patrons is to avoid co-presence with a mass of less wealthy 'spectators' personifying for them the spectre of social promiscuity associated with Saint-Tropez. Acting on those fears, shop owners and inhabitants of St Barts' main town and capital, Gustavia, staged a protest in January 1996 against cruise liner tourists brought on the island for a one-day visit. Three years later, the number and size of ships authorized to land their passengers in St Barts were officially restrained by local authorities. Cruise passenger visits have been cut by 60 per cent since then, plummeting from 106 656 in 1998 to 42 477 in 2008 (IEDOM 2009, p.40).

In contrast with this drop in middle-class and upper-middle-class tourists, the old United States' East Coast families which originally patronized the island were joined by many of their European friends and counterparts in the 1970s, and later by the new tycoons of the global economy. During

New Year celebrations in January 2005, the cove of Gustavia accommodated Bill Gates, Paul Allen (Microsoft founders), Larry Ellison (Oracle founder) and Roman Abramovich[7] among others. Their respective yachts, all registered in British offshore centres – George Town (Cayman Islands) or Hamilton (Bermuda) – can be described as floating palaces. They are simultaneously symbols and vessels of their residential multi-territoriality. Old patrimonial families and new industrial elites intermingled with entertainment moguls such as David Letterman, Steven Spielberg, Jerry Bruckheimer and Sean Combs, as well as with many fashion, music and Hollywood stars such as George Michael, Uma Thurman, John Travolta and Brad Pitt, who would walk the streets and patronize the beaches eliciting no visible sign of local excitement.

However, socializing by business and show business celebrities on the island is often confined to private spaces (boats and houses). This is true both during the 'landlord month' (August) when villa owners enjoy their houses in the calm of the low season and visit each other. But it is even more salient during the very high season around Christmas and New Year celebrations. For instance, on 31 December 2009, Roman Abramovich invited (and in some cases privately flew in) 250 noted guests to his new property, where he offered them a pop music concert by Prince, Gwen Stefani and Beyoncé, along with a party intended to mark his establishment in St Barts by expressing unequalled magnificence, for a total cost of US$5 million.

Festive commercial venues such as beach bars, restaurants and nightclubs generate a higher degree of social mixing: they are also patronized by less wealthy vacationers, as well as by immigrants and Saint-Barths. Thus, the Yacht Club, the island's most prized discotheque, is not primarily frequented by yacht owners. True, one night in January 2005, one could see Colonel Qaddafi's sons seated nearby members of the British and French branches of the Rothschild family, sharing the dance floor with them along with American actor Zach Braff. However, most of the customers around them were less rich or less prominent in the media. The Yacht Club and the Nikki Beach – another popular local venue – have numerous attributes in common with some of Paris' Right Bank nightclubs. Both offer a dramatization of success appealing to the economic upper class and those aspiring to it (Réau 2006), and provide the possibility of 'meeting' multi-millionaires without having to know them personally. Wealth is performed without always being really possessed. Fame seems to be acquirable by mere contact with famous people, or with the places they have patronized, which are regularly mentioned in the international press in the case of St Barts. Finally, they are places where mainstream canons of contemporary feminine beauty are exhibited, legitimized and embodied

– all the more so, as supermodels and other professional mannequins often figure among the clientele of the winter high season.

Those are favourable venues for practices of ostentatious spending, occasioning for a few hours an apparent narrowing of economic gaps between customers, whether the €2215 magnum of Cristal Roederer represents an exceptional collective effort or an insignificant individual expense.[8] The consumption of such bottles cannot go unnoticed. First, it qualifies the ordering party for a table and seats, allowing them to take an exclusive although publicly visible place within the venue. Second, each bottle is brought in with a clamour. The ice buckets are endowed with sparkle cannons whose pyrotechnics attract looks from all corners of the room. Such manufactured visibility promotes competitive consumption between tables, often triggered by the venue's owner and his or her friends. This competition can sometimes lead to the purchase of entire champagne cases. Although most bottles are consumed, others are occasionally showered upon the party, or shared with neighbouring tables.

Among other St Barts places combining characteristics of a bar, a restaurant, a beach and/or a nightclub, the Yacht Club and the Nikki Beach contribute to a global space of entertainment and partying, which is simultaneously worldwide in its reach and limited in its clientele. From 25 December 2009 to 9 January 2010 – and every year since – the Yacht Club hosted the VIP Room's team and events. The association with this prestigious and flashy Paris nightclub, which relocates to Cannes during the Film Festival, to Monaco during the F1 Grand Prix, and to Saint-Tropez during the summer, strengthened the island's position within the jet-set calendar. Along with the Nikki Beach brand, whose few establishments are present in Miami and Saint-Tropez as well as Marrakech and Ko Samui (in Thailand), it contributes to reinforcing and expanding the geographical repertoire of luxury seaside leisure (Corbin 1994; Pinçon and Pinçon-Charlot 1994, 1998, 2000).

In contrast with the latter destinations, however, St Barts is more often chosen for family-oriented vacations. During summer afternoons around the swimming pool of the Hotel Guanahani, an establishment on the island's north-eastern shore, adults of all ages danced to house music mixed by a guest DJ (Claude Challe and his own family in August 2010), as children played in the water, and nannies swung a little while cradling the younger ones. At Le Ti St-Barth (a lounge-restaurant in Pointe Milou), late teenagers dined, drank and danced[9] side by side with their parents and grandparents,[10] until the latter paid the evening bill using their AmEx Centurion Card, recognizable by its characteristic black colour. Such inter-generational co-presence results in a certain level of restraint, limiting exaltation, intense dancing or the overt sexualization of interactions. This restraint distinguishes St Barts from other elite resorts where the festive supply is more differentiated or more geared towards amorous encounters.

Caribbean ethnology and the sociology of tourism have studied extensively the successive migration and acculturation processes that led to the archipelago's contemporary diversity, including those processes related to the development of tourism in the most popular destinations. By contrast, however, social scientists have rather overlooked the often smaller and less populated islands – in the West Indies and elsewhere – that turned into specifically upmarket vacation spots: for instance St Barts, Mustique, Saba (in the Caribbean) and the Out Islands of the Bahamas, but also the Île de Ré (in France), Capri (in Italy), Formentera (in Spain), Martha's Vineyard, Nantucket and Mount Desert Island (in New England). Yet, the study of St Barts shows how heuristic the understanding of these territories can be for the sociology and social geography of the super-rich. First, they interrogate the articulation between geographical insularity, spatial isolation, social self-segregation, and the imaginary of remoteness (Bernardie-Tahir 2005), thus allowing comparisons with the more 'urban' Fisher Island in Florida (Hay and Muller 2012) or Sentosa Island in Singapore (Pow 2011). Second, these resort localities are even more segregated and socially exclusive than the most high-end neighbourhoods of the global cities, where so many of the super-rich have their main residences. Third, as holiday escapes, they enable us to observe specific forms of upper-class sociability and inter-class relations: the rich may no longer be the only leisure class, but their forms of leisure still function as marks of distinction (Réau 2011). In addition, and in a more methodological perspective, our fieldwork pinpoints the fact that – if individually owned, and entirely or almost entirely privatized islands do obviously exist – many other luxury islands are, like St Barts, largely made of public spaces where numerous interactions are directly available for social scientific observation.

IMPORTING GENERIC EXOTICISM

In St Barts, as elsewhere, facilities and services offered to rich vacationers come with discourses celebrating authenticity and personal regeneration (Rauch 1988; MacCannell 1999; Cousin and Réau 2009) for which local business managers present themselves as inspired mediators. Here, however, this offer to rediscover oneself entails no change of cultural landscape, nor any emphasis on an exoticized local culture. Secondary residences on the island do not come from the rehabilitation of traditional

Saint-Barth houses, aside from a few cases. Among the 50 or so touristic restaurants, only one specializes in Caribbean cuisine (the owner comes from the island of Marie-Galante): most of them – even when advertised as 'world cuisine' – offer no Creole dish. The music played in bars and nightclubs is imported from Europe and the US. That which is composed on the island fashions itself as emancipated from the local legacy.[11] Finally, statistical data (INSEE 2010) complemented by direct observation indicate that the service staff in contact with hotel and restaurant clients come mainly from Metropolitan France, rarely from St Barts and almost never from the rest of the West Indies.

Employees in those establishments bring with them high-end international standards, as much by their schooling as by their accumulated professional experience in the luxury world (from palatial hotels to haute couture boutiques), and by the type of service they offer [corporal hexis (Bourdieu 1990), interactional scripts with the clientele (Goffman 1967), products presentation]. Indeed, the comfort standards, practices and expectations of continental luxury, which surfaced in St Barts during the 1980s, have gained ground since and became hegemonic in the 2000s. Today for example, vacation houses conceived by Saint-Barth builders compete with an increasing number of creations by international architects. In all domains, former production styles are becoming stigmatized. Thus, one establishment run by Saint-Barths was signalled disapprovingly as a 'local restaurant' by vacationers ('they still haven't understood what a restaurant is', proclaimed a villa owner to us in August 2010, warning against patronizing it).

Exoticism is nonetheless ubiquitous in St Barts, but it is almost always imported from elsewhere. 'I remember thinking how strange it was that elements of the original house, like the support beams from Bali, or the stone paths or certain views, reminded me of my grandfather's farm in Indonesia. It felt oddly familiar and comforting', recalled Miki Singh, evoking the purchase of his estate in Gouverneur (*VIP Guide St-Barth* 2004, pp. 51–4).[12] The valorization of cultural otherness, with its investments in symbolic universes reputedly old and sophisticated such as Bali, Polynesia, Brazil or Sub-Saharan Africa, functions mainly by importing and adapting to St Barts the geocultural references of global exoticism. More precisely, it brings to the island a version of exoticism that Western upper classes concur in finding distinctive, by contrast with places typical of the middle-class touristic imaginary, such as Hawaii or the Dominican Republic for example. The entire Antillean heritage remains very marginal within it.

Objects, practices and styles with diverse origins, all valorized by the tastes of the high bourgeoisie, are thus transplanted locally. As for the island itself, it is perceived as a virgin natural terrain rather than as a pre-existing cultural substrate to incorporate. Thus architect Patrick Benaben, simultaneously invoking his scholarly training at the Beaux-Arts in Paris, new international comfort standards, and his Brazilian and Congolese experiences, claimed to 'build smart tropical houses, real tropical houses, and not just "new" Saint-Barth cabins'[13] (*VIP Guide St-Barth* 2007 pp. 102–6).

However, such exoticism differs from the orientalist and 'polynesian-ist' fantasies analysed by Jean-Didier Urbain's study of the seaside resort utopia (Urbain 1994). Rather than marking a rupture with ordinary life in a deliberately derealizing gesture, this exoticism displays familiarity with the 'great' cultures of the world. Such relative familiarity may have been acquired by direct contact while travelling and vacationing. But it also rests on the labour of highly qualified specialists established in St Barts: these local professionals and managers (Dehoorne 2002) act as artistic and cultural directors of the island. They are the artisans of its reinvention. Most of their personal histories combine three features: (1) an official certification from prestigious training institutions, (2) empathy for the ethos of their clients, and (3) an almost obligatory passage through one or several peripheral places, from which they draw their charismatic originality.[14] Those can vary from India for the yoga teacher to Africa for hotel managers expected to ensure comfort in difficult natural conditions, to East and South-east Asia for antique dealers and decorators having to assist in the elaboration of refined interiors, and to Polynesia for the night-clubs owner (or the chefs) intent on offering the rediscovery of authentic pleasures.

By contrast, St Barts' vacationers tend to associate the Antilles, especially in their Afro-Caribbean dimension, with negative traits such as slackness or lack of safety. Numbers of Guadeloupians figure among the immigrants who have had a successful career in St Barts, often as business owners. But they are almost always white (Béké or Blanc-Pays ethnicity), even though whites only count for a small minority of Guadeloupe's population. Thus, while their particular descent disconnects white Guadeloupians from negative Antilles associations, it also keeps them from acting as local promoters of an inclusive Caribbean heritage.

Such downplaying of Antillean creolized identity in favour of an ideal-ized elsewhere sometimes takes unexpected forms, as in the case of Marius Stakelborough. This descendant of slaves, born in 1923 and owner of the oldest bar-restaurant of St Barts, has been the only black Saint-Barth to hold a prominent public position on the island in the last several decades. Marked by the racism of the white majority during his childhood (*VIP Guide St-Barth* 2004, pp. 22–4), he became a sailor after World War II, and then an increasingly respected business owner in Gustavia (Wall and Wall 2008). However he only obtained the recognition he enjoys today in the 1970s by becoming an advocate – and later the very icon – of the rediscovery of the island's forgotten identity as . . . Swedish. After having learned from Scandinavian amateur sailors and vacationers that he certainly owed his last name to a Swedish ancestor from the era when the island belonged to the Crown, Stakelborough founded several associations with them dedicated to strengthening the links between Sweden and its former colony. Those initiatives led him to travel to Sweden several times and to welcome King Carl Gustaf on the island. The King then received him in Stockholm, decorated him and appointed him as honorary consul in St Barts. Hence, although Stakelborough's originality as both Black and Swedish made him an exceptional character, his ethno-cultural creolity (along with that of St Barts) remained euphemized, and was substituted for by the celebration of the island's white international past in light of its cosmopolitan present.

Processes of exoticization and constructions of ethnicity in St Barts are thus tightly connected with the embeddedness of the entire island within the global luxury world and the symbolics of upper-class cosmopolitanism.

BEYOND THE RESORT ECONOMY?

From its beginnings, the development of tourism in St Barts resulted from a combination of the arrival of immigrants and external investments, as the biography of Rémy de Haenen (1916–2008) testifies. A French–Dutch venturer and occasional smuggler born in London, de Haenen initiated the island's first regular air connections, owned its first hotel (the Eden Rock) starting in 1953, and was its mayor from 1962 to 1977. Water and power supply as well as phone lines were installed during his terms, thus establishing him as a local figure of adventure capitalism (Weber 2008) while also ensuring his reputation as master builder concerned with long-term development. Today, St Barts' hotels and luxury real estate figure within the portfolios of many international investors, such as Laurence Parisot (the current head of the French national business organization), who also owns a villa on the island, or André Balazs (the American owner of several high-end hotels, including the Chateau Marmont in Los Angeles).

However, the Saint-Barths – particularly the large historic families like the Magras, the Lédées and the Gréaux – have maintained control over entire sectors of the island's economy and over local politics. They hold a quasi-monopoly over available land, construction companies,[15] hardware stores, food retailing, and transportation. Many of them have become multi-millionaires (Chardon and Hartog, 1995b). Even though they now only make up half the permanent population of St Barts, they still dominate the legislative and executive bodies of the Collectivity, and represent it in the French Parliament: Michel Magras, the Senator for the island, is the younger brother of Bruno Magras, President of the COM. Indeed, the local ruling class has been using its political influence to secure its long-term perpetuation. For the last decades of the twentieth century and the beginning of the new one, they have held the power to recognize or deny official residency status (and thus potential voting rights, in the case of French citizens) to immigrants established on the island. More recently, they organized St Barts' transition to the status of Overseas Country/Territory (OCT) of the European Union. The new status, approved in October 2010 by the European Council, became effective on 1 January 2012. It allows St Barts – no longer directly subject to EU law – to exert local control over the permanent and temporary immigration of foreign workers (including non-French European citizens).

Such demographic restrictions have officially been justified by concerns for preserving the island's natural environment, and for ensuring the total safety of people and property (routinely presented as a decades-old characteristic of St Barts). In the last few years, those restrictions have also involved a stricter control of the local planning scheme and a quasi-total freeze on building permits. Those delivered today are for the most part authorizations to demolish in order to rebuild something more luxurious on the same plot.[16] Restrictions resulted in an increase in the socio-economic status of buyers (two local real estate agencies have now partnered with Sotheby's and Christie's respectively), thus reinforcing the island's collective bourgeois cultural inwardness. In addition, among other situational boons, local selectivity has benefited St Barts' permanent inhabitants through the generous euergetism of the billionaire seasonal residents, from the island's first asphalted roads offered by David Rockefeller half a century ago to the Collectivity's new sports facility funded by Roman Abramovich in 2010.

However, land restrictions and prohibitive real estate prices have made it impossible for working- and middle-class immigrants to become homeowners on the island, discouraging them from settling there in the long run. And sometimes, the tightness of the market even hurts the interests of hotels and restaurants in need of affordable housing for their workers.

Yet, several recent developments could presage St Barts' diversification beyond the resort mono-economy characterizing it today. The generalization on the island of high-speed Internet, whose capacity will increase even more upon completion of the fibre optic cabling that began in 2008, already allows numerous residents and vacationers to work from there. Some multinationals have moved part of their staff to the island: in the luxury sector, for instance, the Hermès International group's regional head for Latin America and the Caribbean is based in St Barts. Also, more and more local consulting professionals (lawyers, tax specialists) offer to assist companies in taking advantage of the new legal context: the COM status conferring autonomy to St Barts in fiscal matters. Householders who have been residing there for more than five years are exonerated from almost all national taxes. Local companies only have to pay the Collectivity an annual flat tax of €300, plus €100 per worker, up to a cap of €5000. According to several analysts (see Chavagneux and Palan 2007, pp. 13–14), such generalized tax exemption could trigger the gradual constitution of an offshore financial centre in the increasingly autonomous elite residential haven that St Barts is today.

CONCLUSION

Exploring an area overlooked by the social scientific literature of the last decades, this chapter described the features and transformations that have made the island of Saint-Barthélemy a beacon of social exclusivity and upper-class inwardness. We have shown how Atlantic insularity, small size, and white ethnic identity combined to make it a privileged meeting spot for and between US and French elites, while keeping mass tourism at a distance. 'St Barts' is thus now well settled in the global territorial space of the high bourgeoisie.

The particular type of social mixing that was gradually established between vacationers, immigrant professionals of the luxury sector, and the Saint-Barths, allowed for the importation of high-end generic exoticism on the island: a brand of exoticism which owes much more to the international upper class' strategies of cultural distinction than to Caribbean heritage.

In addition, local complementarity between these three groups ensured that the rewards of concerted development benefited them all. In particular, it allowed historic Saint-Barth families to preserve their local political power, and their control over many economic sectors. By insisting on the multi-class co-production of elite seaside spaces, which up to now had only been done exceptionally (Dolgon 2005), we bring attention to the roles of service relations and upper-class dynamics of distinction in the reconfiguration of local cultures within the places patronized by the super-rich.

NOTES

1. We thank Carole Cousin and Tabatha Lyn, without whose help the fieldwork would not have been possible. We also thank Niko Besnier, Luc Boltanski, Julien Bonhomme, Guy Numa, Monique Pinçon-Charlot, Anne Raulin, Monique de Saint Martin, Martine Segalen and Tommaso Vitale for their comments on previous versions of this text.
2. The first two rounds of fieldwork were conducted by Bruno Cousin (who was housed in Saint-Jean in 2003–4, and in Vitet in 2004–5), and the third one by both of us in 2010 (we were housed in Grand Fond). Each time, we have benefited from material facilities (accomodation and a car) made available to us by Carole Cousin, Bruno's sister, who lived and worked in St Barts for 15 years, and who was our initial local contact. Most notes and quotes were gathered through participant observation.
3. At the end of the fifteenth century, the island – named *Ouanalao* – was between the territories of the Taínos and the Caribs, an expansionist people often at war with their neighbours, and mounting raids against them (Allaire 1980).
4. These advertising practices almost disappeared after 2006, when the newly-born website *Mémoire St Barth* (www.memoirestbarth.com) started a public campaign of memory work against them. This site also offers the most complete bibliographical compilation on the history of the island.
5. A prestigious figure (among the super-rich themselves), acting both as symbolic promoter and property developer, has often played a crucial role in the rise of new luxury resorts. Notable historical examples are the part played by the Duke of Morny in the development of Deauville, Normandy (during the 1860s); by John D. Rockefeller Jr and his descendants in Mount Desert Island, Maine (since the 1910s); by Noémie de Rothschild and her son Edmond in Megève, French Alps (from the 1920s on); by Giovanni Agnelli in Sestriere, Italian Alps (during the 1930s); and by the Aga Khan in Costa Smeralda, Sardinia (since the 1960s).
6. In 2006, there were 3350 main residences and 561 secondary residences on the island (INSEE, 2010). The latter are generally rented out when their owners are absent, making up the bulk of the rental housing stock. During the Christmas break, they are rented for a price that can vary from about €10 000 to several hundred thousand euros per week, depending on their locations, sizes, and levels of luxury. Like big yachts, they are thus sources of both profit and use value for their owners.
7. First, 2nd, 5th and 25th world's richest people according to the 2004 *Forbes* ranking. In 2009, Abramovich, the Russian oligarch who already owned three super-yachts, including the longest ever built (*Eclipse*, 163 m), bought for US$90 million from the Indian-Indonesian-American Miki Singh the 28-hectare estate which until 1998 had belonged to Francis Goelet, and 40 years earlier to David Rockefeller.
8. The three-litre jeroboam of Dom Pérignon costs more than €5000. As for those of Cristal Roederer – which St Barts' establishments order in advance for New Year's Eve – they are sold €12 000 per unit. Prices rise exponentially with bottle sizes.
9. Drinking is illegal in the US for those under 21, making the island all the more attractive to young Americans.
10. According to an estimate by the Tourism Office of St Barts, in 2007 vacationers paying for a villa rental (for their family and/or their friends) were 55 years old on average (IEDOM 2009, p. 39).
11. US singer-songwriter Jimmy Buffett, a eulogist of 'island escapism' and a regular of St Barts, is considered to be the main musical figure from the island.
12. Similarly, one of the properties of the late Edmond de Rothschild in the *Anse Maréchal* was built by shipping traditional houses from Indonesia. More recently, during the 2000s, several houses were built in Bali to be reassembled in St Barts.
13. The word 'new' was already in English in the original French quote.
14. Each annual issue of the *VIP Guide St-Barth* contains 10 to 18 short interviews retracing the personal biographies of notable permanent residents of the island. Supplemental life histories were collected through fieldwork.

15. However, several construction companies employ Portuguese immigrants and some have been founded by them. The Portuguese community counts for about half of the (non-French) foreigners residing in St Barts, thus 6 per cent of the permanent population of the island (INSEE 2010).
16. However, some new large-scale projects are currently being discussed (Ward 2011).

REFERENCES

Allaire, L. (1980), 'On the historicity of Carib migrations in the Lesser Antilles', *American Antiquity*, **45** (2), 238–45.

Baverez, N. (2000), *Evolutions statutaires de Saint Barthélemy en territoire d'outre-mer*, Gustavia: Commune de Saint-Barthélemy.

Benoist, J. (1966), 'Du social au biologique: étude de quelques interactions', *L'Homme*, **6** (1), 5–26.

Bernardie-Tahir, N. (2005), 'Des "bouts du monde" à quelques heures: l'illusion de l'isolement dans les petites îles touristiques', *Annales de géographie*, **644**, 362–82.

Bourdieu, P. (1990; 1st French edition 1980), *The Logic of Practice*, Cambridge: Polity Press.

Chardon, J.-P. and T. Hartog (1995a), 'Saint-Martin ou l'implacable logique touristique', *Les Cahiers d'Outre-mer*, **189**, 21–34.

Chardon, J.-P. and T. Hartog (1995b), 'Saint-Barthélemy: un choix et ses limites', *Les Cahiers d'Outre-mer*, **191**, 261–76.

Chavagneux, C. and R. Palan (2007), *Les paradis fiscaux*, Paris: La Découverte.

Corbin, A. (1994, 1988 for the French version), *The Lure of the Sea*, Cambridge: Polity Press.

Cousin, B. and S. Chauvin (2012), 'L'entre-soi élitaire à Saint-Barthélemy', *Ethnologie française*, **42** (2), 335–45.

Cousin, S. and B. Réau (2009), *Sociologie du tourisme*, Paris: La Découverte.

Dehoorne, O. (2002), 'Tourisme, travail, migration', *Revue Européenne des Migrations Internationales*, **18** (1), 7–36.

Dolgon, C. (2005), *The End of the Hamptons*, New York: NYU Press.

Goffman, E. (1967), *Interaction Ritual*, New York: Anchor Books.

Hay, I. and S. Muller (2012), '"That tiny, stratospheric apex that owns most of the world" – exploring geographies of the super-rich', *Geographical Research*, **50** (1), 75–88.

Higley, S.R. (1995), *The Geography of the American Upper Class*, Lanham, MD: Rowman & Littlefield.

IEDOM [Institut d'Émission des Départements d'Outre-mer – French Central Bank's Institution for the Overseas Departments] (2009), *Saint-Barthélemy – Rapport annuel 2008*, Paris.

INSEE [Institut National de la Statistique et des Études Économiques – National Institute of Statistics and Economic Studies, France] (2009), '2008, An 1 de la collectivité de Saint-Barthélemy', *Antiane Éco*, **71**, 7.

INSEE [Institut National de la Statistique et des Études Économiques – National Institute of Statistics and Economic Studies, France] (2010), 'Saint-Barthélemy. Une île qui se démarque', *Antiane Éco*, **72**, 40–43.

Leiris, M. (1955), *Contacts de civilisations en Martinique et en Guadeloupe*, Paris: UNESCO/Gallimard.

MacCannell, D. (1999), *The Tourist*, 3rd edn, Berkeley, CA: University of California Press.

McElroy, J.L. and K. De Albuquerque (1998), 'Tourism penetration index in small Caribbean islands', *Annals of Tourism Research*, **25** (1), 145–68.

Morrill, W.T. (1977), 'French peasants in the Caribbean: St. Barthélemy', in G.L. Hicks and P. E. Leis (eds), *Ethnic Encounters*, Pacific Grove, CA: Duxbury Press, pp. 137–51.

Pinçon, M. and M. Pinçon-Charlot (1992), *Quartiers bourgeois, quartiers d'affaires*, Paris: Payot.

Pinçon, M. and M. Pinçon-Charlot (1994), 'L'aristocratie et la bourgeoisie au bord de la mer', *Genèses*, **16**, 69–93.

Pinçon, M. and M. Pinçon-Charlot (1998; 1st French edition 1996), *Grand Fortunes. Dynasties of Wealth in France*, New York: Algora.

Pinçon, M. and M. Pinçon-Charlot (2000), *Sociologie de la bourgeoisie*, Paris: La Découverte.

Pinçon, M. and M. Pinçon-Charlot (2007), *Les Ghettos du Gotha*, Paris: Seuil.

Pow, C.-P. (2011), 'Living it up: super-rich enclave and transnational elite urbanism in Singapore', *Geoforum*, **42** (3), 382–93.

Rauch, A. (1988), *Vacances et pratiques corporelles*, Paris: PUF.

Réau, B. (2006), 'Enchantements nocturnes: ethnographie de deux discothèques parisiennes', *Ethnologie française*, **37** (2), 333–9.

Réau, B. (2011), *Les Français et les vacances*, Paris: CNRS Éditions.

Redon, M. (2006), 'Saint-Martin/Sint-Maarten, une petite île divisée pour de grands enjeux', *Les Cahiers d'Outre-mer*, **234**, 233–66.

Urbain, J.-D. (1994), *Sur la plage*, Paris: Payot.

Wall, I. and J. Wall (2008), *A Man, An Island, A Life. The Story of Marius Stakelborough, Le Select and Saint-Barthélemy*, Trelleborg, Sweden: The Marius Foundation.

Ward, V. (2011), 'The storming of St. Barth's', *Vanity Fair*, **605** (January issue).

Weber, M. (2008; 1st German edition: 1904–05), *The Protestant Ethic and the Spirit of Capitalism*, Oxford: Oxford University Press.

Index